ACCESS TO SHAKESPEARE

The Tragedy of

Hamlet

Prince of Denmark

A Facing-pages Translation into Contemporary English

Edited by

Jonnie Patricia Mobley, Ph.D.
Drama Department
Cuesta College
San Luis Obispo, California

Lorenz Educational Press
P.O. Box 802 • Dayton, OH 45401-0802
www.LorenzEducationalPress.com

Cover border taken from the First Folio (1623)

Denmark's coat of arms (c. 1115)

Cover design by Tamada Brown Design, Chicago

Interior design and typesetting by David Corona Design, Dubuque

ISBN: 978-1-8855-6408-5

Library of Congress Card Catalog Card Number: 96-76069
Manufactured in the United States of America.

6 7 8 9 0 6 5 4 3 2 1

The Tragedy of

Hamlet

Prince of Denmark

Contents

Introduction

This volume of William Shakespeare's *The Tragedy of Hamlet, Prince of Denmark* consists of two versions of the play. The first is the original, based on the *Globe* edition of 1860, which was in turn based on the Folio of 1623. The second is a translation of that version into contemporary English. In both versions spelling and punctuation have been updated, and the names of the characters have been spelled out in full for easier reading. Insights from modern scholars have been included in both versions.

The translation of *Hamlet* is not meant to take the place of the original. Instead, it is an alternative to the notes usually found in current editions. In many cases these notes interfere with the reading of the play. Whether alongside or below the original text, the notes break the rhythm of reading and frequently force you to turn back to an earlier page or jump ahead to a later one. Having a translation that runs parallel to the original, line for line, allows you to move easily from Elizabethan to contemporary English and back again. It's simply a better way to introduce Shakespeare.

Also, this translation is suitable for performance, where notes are not available to the audience. Admittedly, a well-directed and well-acted production of the original can do much to clarify Shakespeare's language. And yet, there will be numerous references and lines whose meanings are not clear on a first hearing. What, for instance, does Claudius mean when he says, "And in the cup an union shall he throw"?

Shakespeare's Language

Shakespeare's language does present problems for modern readers. After all, more than four centuries separate us from him. During this time words have acquired new meanings or have dropped from the language altogether, and sentence structures have become less fluid. But these are solvable problems.

First of all, most of the words that Shakespeare used are still current. For those words whose meanings have changed and for those words no longer in the language, modern equivalents are found in this translation. For a small number of words—chiefly names of places, biblical and mythological characters, and formal titles—a glossary can be found on page 262.

The meaning of words is one problem. The position of words is another. Today, the order of words in declarative sentences is almost fixed. The subject comes first, then the verb, and finally, if there is one, the object. In Shakespeare's time, the order of words, particularly in poetic drama, was more fluid. Shakespeare has Claudius say,

Madness in great ones must not unwatched go.
Whereas we would usually arrange the words in this order,
Madness must not go unwatched in great ones.

Earlier in the play, Francisco says,
For this relief much thanks.
We would probably say,
Much thanks for this relief.

This does not mean that Shakespeare never uses words in what we consider normal order. As often as not, he does. Here, for instance, are Guildenstern and Hamlet in conversation,

Introduction

GUILDENSTERN My lord, we were sent for.
HAMLET I will tell you why.

When Shakespeare does invert the order of words, he does so for a reason or for a variety of reasons—to create a rhythm, to emphasize a word, to achieve a rhyme. Whether a play is in verse, as most of this play is, or in prose, it is still written in sentences. And this means that, despite the order, all the words needed to make complete sentences are there. If you are puzzled by a sentence, first look for the subject and then try rearranging the words in the order that you would normally use. It takes a little practice, but you will be surprised how quickly you acquire the skill.

Shakespeare sometimes separates sentence parts—subject and verb, for example — that would normally be run together. Here are some lines in which Horatio describes the background politics of Denmark,

> ... Our last king,
> Whose image even but now appeared to us,
> Was, as you know, by Fortinbras of Norway,
> Thereto pricked on by a most emulate pride,
> Dared to the combat....

Between the subject, king, and the verb, was dared, come clauses and phrases that interrupt the normal sequence. Again, look for the subject and then the verb and put the two together. You'll find, however, that your rearranged sentence, while clear, is not as rhythmical as Shakespeare's.

Stage Directions

In drama written for the modern stage, the playwright usually provides detailed directions for the actors—how to move and speak, what emotions to convey to an audience. In the plays of Shakespeare, stage directions are sparse. One reason for this could be that Shakespeare was a member and an owner of the company for which he wrote these plays. He was on hand to tell the other actors how to say a line or what gesture to use. Even so, the dialogue itself offers clues to actions or gestures. For example, Horatio, in Act One, tells Hamlet that he has seen his father's ghost. He says,

> I knew your father,
> These hands are not more like.

And he probably extends his hands, meaning that one hand is as like the other as the ghost was to Hamlet's father. Again, in Act Two, Polonius says,

> Take this from this, if this be otherwise.

One critic thought that Polonius first pointed to his head, then his shoulders, suggesting that he be beheaded if he were wrong about Hamlet's problem. Another critic has suggested that Polonius raised his hand holding the baton of his office. In either case the line must be accompanied by a gesture, but, lacking a stage direction, one can't be sure exactly what it is.

Reading the printed play, you must be alert to whom a line of dialogue is addressed. For example, Hamlet is talking to Rosencrantz and

Guildenstern when a trumpet blast announces the arrival of the players. Guildenstern says,

> There are the players.
>   Hamlet continues,
>   Gentlemen, you are welcome to Elsinore.

Hamlet is still talking to Rosencrantz and Guildenstern, not to the players, who have yet to come on stage. But there is no stage direction to show this. You have to try to picture the characters in your mind.

Solo Speeches

There is another difference between the plays of Shakespeare and most modern ones—the solo speeches. These are the asides and the soliloquies in which a character reveals what is on his or her mind.

Modern dramatists seem to feel that the solo speech is artificial and unrealistic. Oddly enough, modern novelists frequently use a variety of the solo speech, and some critics feel that this convention has given the novel extra power and depth, allowing it to probe deeply into the motives of its characters. One thing is certain—Shakespeare's plays without the solo speeches would not be as powerful as they are.

Characters

HAMLET, Prince of Denmark, son of the late King Hamlet
and Queen Gertrude

HORATIO, friend of Hamlet

CLAUDIUS, King of Denmark, Hamlet's uncle

GERTRUDE, Queen of Denmark, mother of Hamlet

POLONIUS, councillor to King Claudius, father of Ophelia and Laertes

LAERTES, son of Polonius

OPHELIA, daughter of Polonius

VOLTEMAND	}	Danish courtiers
CORNELIUS	}	
OSRIC	}	
GENTLEMAN	}	
ROSENCRANTZ	}	former fellow students of Hamlet
GUILDENSTERN	}	

PRIEST

MARCELLUS	}	officers
BARNARDO	}	

FRANCISCO, Danish soldier

REYNALDO, servant of Polonius

PLAYERS, members of a touring acting company

GRAVEDIGGERS (two clowns)

FORTINBRAS, Prince of Norway

CAPTAIN in the army of Fortinbras

ENGLISH AMBASSADORS

GHOST of Hamlet's father

Lords, Ladies, Soldiers, Sailors, Messengers, and
other Attendants

1

Act One

Scene 1 [*Royal castle of Elsinore, Denmark*]

     Enter BARNARDO *and* FRANCISCO, *two sentinels*

BARNARDO Who's there?

FRANCISCO Nay, answer me. Stand and unfold yourself.

BARNARDO Long live the king!

FRANSCICO Barnardo?

BARNARDO He.   5

FRANCISCO You come most carefully upon your hour.

BARNARDO 'Tis now struck twelve; get thee to bed, Francisco.

FRANCISCO For this relief much thanks. 'Tis bitter cold,
  And I am sick at heart.

BARNARDO Have you had quiet guard?   10

FRANCISCO Not a mouse stirring.

BARNARDO Well, good night.
  If you do meet Horatio and Marcellus,
  The rivals of my watch, bid them make haste.

FRANCISCO I think I hear them.   15

     Enter HORATIO *and* MARCELLUS

  Stand, ho! Who is there?

HORATIO Friends to this ground.

MARCELLUS And liegemen to the Dane.

FRANCISCO Give you good night.

MARCELLUS O, farewell, honest soldier.   20
  Who hath relieved you?

FRANCISCO Barnardo hath my place.
  Give you good night.

         Exit FRANCISCO

MARCELLUS Holla, Barnardo!

BARNARDO Say—   25
  What, is Horatio there?

HORATIO A piece of him.

Act One

Scene 1 [*Royal castle of Elsinore, Denmark*]

                Enter BARNARDO *and* FRANCISCO, *two sentinels*

BARNARDO Who's there?

FRANCISCO No, you answer me. Stand and identify yourself!

BARNARDO Long live the king!

FRANCISCO Barnardo?

BARNARDO Yes.   5

FRANCISCO You're right on time.

BARNARDO It just struck twelve. Get off to bed, Francisco.

FRANCISCO For this relief, much thanks. It's bitter cold,

    And I have had enough.

BARNARDO Have you had a quiet watch?   10

FRANCISCO Not a mouse stirring.

BARNARDO Well, good night.

    Should you meet Horatio and Marcellus,

    The others on the watch, tell them to hurry.

FRANCISCO I think I hear them.   15

                  Enter HORATIO *and* MARCELLUS

    Halt! Who goes there?

HORATIO Friends to this land.

MARCELLUS And loyal subjects of the king.

FRANCISCO Good night to you.

MARCELLUS Oh, farewell, good soldier.   20

    Who has relieved you?

FRANCISCO Barnardo took my place.

    Good night to you.

                          Exit FRANCISCO

MARCELLUS Hello, Barnardo!

BARNARDO Say,   25

    What, is Horatio there?

HORATIO A part of him.

BARNARDO Welcome, Horatio. Welcome, good Marcellus.

MARCELLUS What, has this thing appeared again tonight?

BARNARDO I have seen nothing.   30

MARCELLUS Horatio says 'tis but our fantasy,
          And will not let belief take hold of him
          Touching this dreaded sight, twice seen of us.
          Therefore I have entreated him along
          With us to watch the minutes of this night,   35
          That, if again this apparition come,
          He may approve our eyes, and speak to it.

HORATIO Tush, tush, 'twill not appear.

BARNARDO Sit down awhile,
          And let us once again assail your ears,   40
          That are so fortified against our story,
          What we two nights have seen.

HORATIO Well, sit we down,
          And let us hear Barnardo speak of this.

BARNARDO Last night of all,   45
          When yond same star that's westward from the pole
          Had made his course t' illume that part of heaven
          Where now it burns, Marcellus and myself,
          The bell then beating one—

                          Enter GHOST

MARCELLUS Peace, break thee off. Look where it comes again.   50

BARNARDO In the same figure, like the king that's dead.

MARCELLUS Thou art a scholar. Speak to it, Horatio.

BARNARDO Looks a not like the king? Mark it, Horatio.

HORATIO Most like. It harrows me with fear and wonder.

BARNARDO It would be spoke to.   55

MARCELLUS Question it, Horatio.

HORATIO What are thou that usurp'st this time of night,
          Together with that fair and warlike form
          In which the majesty of buried Denmark

BARNARDO Welcome, Horatio. Welcome, my good Marcellus.
MARCELLUS Well, has this thing appeared again tonight?
BARNARDO I have seen nothing.   30
MARCELLUS Horatio says it's just imagination
    And will not let himself believe
    In this fearsome sight we have seen twice.
    That's why I begged him to join us
    And keep watch for a period of this night,   35
    So that if this apparition comes again,
    He may confirm what we saw and speak to it.
HORATIO Come, come, it will not appear.
BARNARDO Sit down awhile,
    And let us tell you once again,   40
    Although you're skeptical of our story,
    What we have seen these last two nights.
HORATIO Well, let's sit down,
    And let's hear what Barnardo has to say.
BARNARDO Only last night,   45
    When that same star that's to the west of the North Star
    Had made its path to light that part of heaven
    Where now it burns, Marcellus and myself,
    The bell having struck one—
Enter GHOST
MARCELLUS Wait, say no more. Look, here it comes again.   50
BARNARDO In the same form, like the king who's dead.
MARCELLUS You're a scholar. Speak to it, Horatio.
BARNARDO Doesn't it look like the king? Look at it, Horatio.
HORATIO Very like him. I shake with fear and wonder.
BARNARDO It wishes to be spoken to.   55
MARCELLUS Question it, Horatio.
HORATIO What are you that intrudes this time of night,
    Dressed in the fair and warlike armor
    Which his majesty the dead king

Did sometimes march? By heaven, I charge thee, speak.   60
MARCELLUS It is offended.
BARNARDO See, it stalks away.
HORATIO Stay! Speak, speak, I charge thee, speak!

Exit GHOST

MARCELLUS 'Tis gone and will not answer.
BARNARDO How now, Horatio? You tremble and look pale.   65
   Is not this something more than fantasy?
   What think you on 't?
HORATIO Before my God, I might not this believe
   Without the sensible and true avouch
   Of mine own eyes.   70
MARCELLUS Is it not like the king?
HORATIO As thou art to thyself.
   Such was the very armor he had on
   When he the ambitious Norway combated;
   So frowned he once when, in an angry parle,   75
   He smote the sledded Polacks on the ice.
   'Tis strange.
MARCELLUS Thus twice before, and jump at this dead hour,
   With martial stalk hath he gone by our watch.
HORATIO In what particular thought to work I know not,   80
   But in the gross and scope of mine opinion
   This bodes some strange eruption to our state.
MARCELLUS Good now, sit down, and tell me, he that knows,
   Why this same strict and most observant watch
   So nightly toils the subject of the land,   85
   And why such daily cast of brazen cannon,
   And foreign mart for implements of war,
   Why such impress of shipwrights, whose sore task
   Does not divide the Sunday from the week.
   What might be toward, that this sweaty haste   90
   Doth make the night joint-laborer with the day?

Often used to wear. In the name of heaven, speak!   60
MARCELLUS It has taken offense.
BARNARDO See, it stalks away.
HORATIO Stop! Speak! Speak! I demand you speak!
                                        Exit GHOST
MARCELLUS It's gone and will not answer.
BARNARDO Well now, Horatio, you tremble and look pale.   65
    Is this not something more than a fantasy?
    What do you think of it?
HORATIO Before God, I wouldn't have believed this
    Unless I had clearly and actually seen it
    With my own eyes.   70
MARCELLUS Isn't it like the king?
HORATIO As you are to yourself.
    This was the very armor he wore
    When he fought the King of Norway;
    He frowned exactly like that, when in an angry dispute,   75
    He attacked the Poles on their sledges crossing the ice.
    It's strange.
MARCELLUS Twice before, exactly at this dead hour,
    Walking with a military stride, he has passed on our watch.
HORATIO I don't know how in particular this applies,   80
    But in general, so far as I can judge,
    This points to some strange disruption in our country.
MARCELLUS Please, sit down, and he who knows tell me
    Why we have this strict and careful watch that
    Nightly wearies the subjects of our land?   85
    And why so many brass cannons are daily made
    And there is foreign trade in implements of war?
    Tell me why shipwrights are drafted into service
    That has them work all seven days a week?
    What's going on, with all this sweaty haste,   90
    That calls for labor day and night?

Who is 't that can inform me?

HORATIO That can I—

At least the whisper goes so. Our last king,

Whose image even but now appeared to us,   95

Was, as you know, by Fortinbras of Norway,

Thereto pricked on by a most emulate pride,

Dared to the combat; in which our valiant Hamlet—

For so this side of our known world esteemed him—

Did slay this Fortinbras; who by a sealed compact,   100

Well ratified by law and heraldry,

Did forfeit (with his life) all those his lands

Which he stood seized of, to the conqueror.

Against the which a moiety competent

Was gaged by our king, which had returned   105

To the inheritance of Fortinbras

Had he been the vanquisher, as, by the same comart

And carriage of the article designed,

His fell to Hamlet. Now sir, young Fortinbras,

Of unimproved mettle hot and full,   110

Hath in the skirts of Norway here and there

Sharked up a list of landless resolutes

For food and diet to some enterprise

That hath a stomach in 't; which is no other,

As it doth well appear unto our state,   115

But to recover of us, by strong hand

And terms compulsatory, those foresaid lands

So by his father lost. And this, I take it,

Is the main motive of our preparations,

The source of this our watch, and the chief head   120

Of this posthaste and rummage in the land.

BARNADO I think it be no other but e'en so.

Well may it sort that this portentous figure

Who can explain it to me?

HORATIO That I can—

    Or at least what the rumor is. Our late king,

    Whose ghost has just appeared to us,   95

    Was, as you know, dared by King Fortinbras,

    Prompted by a most envious pride,

    To single combat; in which our valiant Hamlet—

    For so he was regarded in our part of the world—

    Killed this Fortinbras, who, according to a formal contract,   100

    Sanctioned by law and the code of chivalry,

    Forfeited then (with his life) all those lands

    He owned personally, to the conqueror.

    Against this, a similar portion of land

    Was pledged by our king, which would have gone   105

    To the estate of Fortinbras

    Had he been the conqueror, as, by that same bargain,

    And the purpose of the contract drawn up,

    His fell to Hamlet. Now, sir, young Fortinbras,

    Hot and full of uncontrolled spirit,   110

    Has from around Norway, here and there,

    Gathered up a band of landless gentry,

    Paying their food and expenses, for an enterprise

    That has some guts in it, which is no other,

    As it appears clearly to our government,   115

    Than to recover by armed force

    And terms compulsory, those aforesaid lands

    Lost by his father. And this, I take it,

    Is the main reason for our preparations,

    The explanation for our watch, and the chief source   120

    Of this hasty commotion in the land.

BARNADO I think it could not be otherwise.

    It agrees with the appearance of this specter

Comes armed through our watch so like the king
That was and is the question of these wars. 125
HORATIO A mote it is to trouble the mind's eye.
In the most high and palmy state of Rome,
A little ere the mightiest Julius fell,
The graves stood tenantless, and the sheeted dead
Did squeak and gibber in the Roman streets; 130
As stars with trains of fire, and dews of blood,
Disasters in the sun; and the moist star,
Upon whose influence Neptune's empire stands,
Was sick almost to doomsday with eclipse.
And even the like precurse of feared events, 135
As harbingers preceding still the fates
And prologue to the omen coming on,
Have heaven and earth together demonstrated
Unto our climatures and countrymen.
Enter GHOST
But soft, behold, lo where it comes again! 140
I'll cross it though it blast me. Stay, illusion.
Spreads his arms
If thou hast any sound or use of voice,
Speak to me.
If there be any good thing to be done
That may to thee do ease and grace to me, 145
Speak to me.
If thou art privy to thy country's fate,
Which happily foreknowing may avoid,
O, speak!
Or if thou hast uphoarded in thy life 150
Extorted treasure in the womb of earth,
For which, they say, you spirits oft walk in death,
The cock crows.
Speak of it. Stay and speak! Stop it, Marcellus.

Dressed in armor and visiting our watch, looking
Like the late king who is the center of this dispute. 125
HORATIO A speck of dust to irritate the mind's eye.
When Rome was at its greatest,
Just before the mighty Caesar was slain,
The graves opened, and the shrouded dead
Were seen to squeak and gibber in the Roman streets; 130
Stars trailed fiery paths, dew of blood fell,
Portents of disaster in the sun; and the moon,
Whose influence governs the sea,
Was almost totally eclipsed.
As even the advanced warning of feared events, 135
Like messengers always preceding the fates
And the prologue to coming calamity,
Have heaven and earth here together demonstrated
Their warnings to our country and our countrymen.
Enter GHOST
Enough! Behold, see where it comes again! 140
I'll cross its path though it destroy me. Stop, ghost!
GHOST *spreads his arms*
If you can make a sound or use a voice,
Speak to me.
If there is any good deed that can be done
That may bring peace to you and grace to me, 145
Speak to me.
If you know something that may befall our country,
Which perhaps knowing beforehand, we may avoid,
Oh, speak.
Or, if you have horded ill-gotten treasure in your life, 150
And buried it in the womb of earth,
The reason, so they say, spirits often walk in death,
The cock crows.
Speak of it. Stay and speak. Stop it, Marcellus!

MARCELLUS Shall I strike at it with my partisan?
HORATIO Do, if it will not stand.   155
BARNARDO 'Tis here.
HORATIO 'Tis here.
MARCELLUS 'Tis gone.

Exit GHOST

We do it wrong, being so majestical,
To offer it the show of violence,   160
For it is as the air, invulnerable,
And our vain blows malicious mockery.
BARNARDO It was about to speak when the cock crew.
HORATIO And then it started like a guilty thing
Upon a fearful summons. I have heard,   165
The cock, that is the trumpet to the morn,
Doth with his lofty and shrill-sounding throat
Awake the god of day; and at his warning,
Whether in sea or fire, in earth or air,
Th' extravagant and erring spirit hies   170
To his confine. And of the truth herein
This present object made probation.
MARCELLUS It faded on the crowing of the cock.
Some say that ever 'gainst that season comes
Wherein our Savior's birth is celebrated,   175
This bird of dawning singeth all night long;
And then, they say, no spirit dare stir abroad,
The nights are wholesome; then no planets strike,
No fairy takes, nor witch hath power to charm,
So hallowed and so gracious is that time.   180
HORATIO So I have heard and do in part believe it.
But look, the morn in russet mantle clad
Walks o'er the dew of yon high eastward hill.
Break we our watch up, and by my advice
Let us impart what we have seen tonight   185

MARCELLUS Shall I strike out at it with my spear?
HORATIO Do so, if it won't stop.   155
BARNARDO It's here.
HORATIO No, here.
MARCELLUS It's gone.

                                                     Exit GHOST

    We do it wrong to be so overbearing
    And make this show of violence,   160
    For it is like the air, invulnerable,
    And our vain blows mock our malice.
BARNARDO It was about to speak when the cock crowed.
HORATIO And then startled, it was like a guilty thing
    Being challenged. I have heard that   165
    The cock, that trumpet of the dawn,
    With his lofty and shrill-sounding voice,
    Wakes the god of day; and at this warning,
    Whether in sea or fire, in earth or air,
    The spirit wandering beyond bonds hastens   170
    To its place. And the truth of this
    The present spirit has confirmed.
MARCELLUS It faded with the crowing of the cock.
    Some say that just before that season
    In which our Savior's birth is celebrated,   175
    This bird of dawn sings all night long,
    And then, they say, no spirit dares to roam,
    The nights are wholesome, the stars friendly,
    No fairy will attack, no, nor witch cast spells,
    So holy and so full of grace is that time.   180
HORATIO So I have heard and am inclined to believe it.
    But look, the morning clad in rosy garments
    Walks over the dew on the far, high eastern hill.
    Let's end our watch, and my advice is
    That we should tell what we have seen tonight   185

Unto young Hamlet, for upon my life,
This spirit, dumb to us, will speak to him.
Do you consent we shall acquaint him with it,
As needful in our loves, fitting in our duty?
MARCELLUS Let's do 't, I pray, and I this morning know   190
　　Where we shall find him most conveniently.

Exeunt

Scene 2 [*An audience chamber in the palace*]
Flourish. Enter CLAUDIUS, *King of Denmark;* GERTRUDE, *the Queen;*
　　HAMLET, POLONIUS, LAERTES, OPHELIA, VOLTEMAND,
　　CORNELIUS, LORDS *attendant*
CLAUDIUS Though yet of Hamlet our dear brother's death
　　The memory be green, and that it us befitted
　　To bear our hearts in grief, and our whole kingdom
　　To be contracted in one brow of woe,
　　Yet so far hath discretion fought with nature   5
　　That we with wisest sorrow think on him,
　　Together with remembrance of ourselves.
　　Therefore our sometime sister, now our queen,
　　Th' imperial jointress to this warlike state,
　　Have we, as 'twere with a defeated joy   10
　　With one auspicious and one dropping eye,
　　With mirth in funeral and with dirge in marriage,
　　In equal scale weighing delight and dole,
　　Taken to wife. Nor have we herein barred
　　Your better wisdoms, which have freely gone   15
　　With this affair along—for all, our thanks.
　　Now follows that you know: Young Fortinbras,
　　Holding a weak supposal of our worth,
　　Or thinking by our late dear brother's death
　　Our state to be disjoint and out of frame,   20
　　Colleagued with this dream of his advantage,

To young Hamlet. I'll bet my life that
This spirit will talk to him, though not to us.
Do you agree that we should tell him of it,
As befits our friendship and our duty?
MARCELLUS Let's do that, please, and I know   190
    Where we can easily find him this morning.

They exit

Scene 2 [*An audience chamber in the palace*]
  Trumpet fanfare. Enter CLAUDIUS, *King of Denmark;* GERTRUDE,
    the Queen; HAMLET, POLONIUS, LAERTES, OPHELIA,
    VOLTEMAND, CORNELIUS, *and various* LORDS
CLAUDIUS Though the death of Hamlet, our dear brother,
    Is fresh in our memory, and though it was proper
    That we mourned him, and our whole country
    Was drawn into one face of woe,
    Yet common sense fights with natural feeling,   5
    So that while we with sorrow think of him,
    We also remember our responsibilities.
    Therefore, our former sister-in-law is now our queen,
    And the joint ruler of our warlike state.
    We have, as it were, with subdued joy,   10
    With one bright and one tearful eye,
    With joy in the funeral and sorrow in the marriage,
    Delight and sorrow equally balanced,
    Taken a wife. Nor have we disregarded
    Your wise counsel, which has freely supported   15
    These decisions. To all, our thanks.
    What follows, you already know. Young Fortinbras,
    Holding a low opinion of our ability,
    Or believing that our late dear brother's death
    Has caused our state to be disordered and disorganized,   20
    Saw these illusions as a favorable opportunity.

He hath not failed to pester us with message
Importing the surrender of those lands
Lost by his father, with all bands of law,
To our most valiant brother. So much for him.   25
Now for ourself and for this time of meeting.
Thus much the business is: we have here writ
To Norway, uncle of young Fortinbras,
Who, impotent and bed-rid, scarcely hears
Of this his nephew's purpose, to suppress   30
His further gait herein, in that the levies,
The lists, and full proportions are all made
Out of his subject; and we here dispatch
You, good Cornelius, and you, Voltemand,
For bearers of this greeting to old Norway,   35
Giving to you no further personal power
To business with the king, more than the scope
Of these dilated articles allow.
Farewell, and let your haste commend your duty.
CORNELIUS   }   In that and all things will we show our duty.   40
VOLTEMAND   }
CLAUDIUS We doubt it nothing, heartily farewell.
                              Exeunt VOLTEMAND *and* CORNELIUS
And now, Laertes, what's the news with you?
You told us of some suit, what is 't, Laertes?
You cannot speak of reason to the Dane
And lose your voice. What wouldst thou beg, Laertes,   45
That shall not be my offer, not thy asking?
The head is not more native to the heart,
The hand more instrumental to the mouth,
Than is the throne of Denmark to thy father.
What wouldst thou have, Laertes?   50
LAERTES My dread lord,
Your leave and favor to return to France,

He has not failed to pester us with messages
Demanding the surrender of those lands
Lost by his father, all legally binding,
To our most valiant brother. So much for him.   25
As for our own response and the reason for this meeting,
Here's how things stand. We have written
To Norway's king, young Fortinbras' uncle—
Who, helpless and bedridden, scarcely knows
Of his nephew's intentions—to suppress   30
His further course of action, since the conscripts,
The troops, and the supplies all come
From his subjects. We here dispatch
You, good Cornelius, and you, Voltemand,
To carry this greeting to the old king,   35
Giving you no further personal powers
To negotiate with the king, beyond the scope
Allowed by these amply detailed instructions.
Farewell, and let haste accompany your duty.
CORNELIUS } In this, as in all things, we will perform our duty.   40
VOLTEMAND }
CLAUDIUS We do not doubt it. A hearty farewell.

                    Exit VOLTEMAND *and* CORNELIUS

And now, Laertes, what's your news?
You mentioned a request. What is it, Laertes?
You cannot ask anything reasonable of the king
And waste your words. What would you have, Laertes,   45
That I would not offer without your asking?
The head is not closer to the heart,
The hand more useful to the mouth,
Than is your father to the throne of Denmark.
What would you have, Laertes?   50
LAERTES My mighty lord,
Your leave and permission to return to France,

17

From whence though willingly I came to Denmark
To show my duty in your coronation,
Yet now I must confess, that duty done,   55
My thoughts and wishes bend again toward France,
And bow them to your gracious leave and pardon.
CLAUDIUS Have you your father's leave? What says Polonius?
POLONIUS He hath, my lord, wrung from me my slow leave
By laborsome petition, and at last   60
Upon his will I sealed my hard consent.
I do beseech you give him leave to go.
CLAUDIUS Take thy fair hour, Laertes, time be thine,
And thy best graces spend it at thy will.
But now, my cousin Hamlet, and my son—   65
HAMLET [*Aside*] A little more than kin, and less than kind.
CLAUDIUS How is it that the clouds still hang on you?
HAMLET Not so, my lord; I am too much i' th' sun.
GERTRUDE Good Hamlet, cast thy nighted color off,
And let thine eye look like a friend on Denmark.   70
Do not forever with thy vailed lids
Seek for thy noble father in the dust.
Thou know'st 'tis common, all that lives must die,
Passing through nature to eternity.
HAMLET Ay, madam, it is common.   75
GERTRUDE If it be,
Why seems it so particular with thee?
HAMLET Seems madam? Nay, it is. I know not seems.
'Tis not alone my inky cloak, good mother,
Nor customary suits of solemn black,   80
Nor windy suspiration of forced breath,
No, nor the fruitful river in the eye,
Nor the dejected havior of the visage,
Together with all forms, moods, shapes of grief,
That can denote me truly. These indeed seem,   85

From where I willingly came to Denmark
To show my loyalty at your coronation.
Yet now, I must confess, my duty done,   55
My thoughts and wishes incline toward France again,
Subject to the favor of your permission.
CLAUDIUS Have you your father's permission? What does Polonius say?
POLONIUS He has, my lord, wrung from me grudging permission
    By constant pleading. In the end,   60
    I endorsed his wishes with reluctant consent.
    I ask you to give him leave to go.
CLAUDIUS Take these youthful days, Laertes, the time is yours,
    And spend them as you think best.
    But now, my kinsman Hamlet, and my son—   65
HAMLET [*Aside*] A little more than kin, but less than kind.
CLAUDIUS How is it that you're still under a cloud?
HAMLET Not so, my lord, I am too much in the sun.
GERTRUDE Dear Hamlet, throw off your dark colors,
    And let your gaze look like a friend upon the king.   70
    Do not always with lowered eyes
    Seek for your noble father in the dust.
    You know it's common: all that lives must die,
    Passing through life to eternity.
HAMLET Yes, madam, it is common.   75
GERTRUDE If that's so,
    Why does this case seem so special to you?
HAMLET "Seems," madam? No, "is." What do you mean "seems"?
    It's not only my dark clothes, good mother,
    Nor the customary garb of solemn black,   80
    Nor the windy sighing of forced breath,
    No, nor the rivers of tears from the eyes,
    Nor is it my dejected expression,
    Together with these forms, moods, shapes of grief,
    That can truly show what I feel. These things "seem."   85

For they are actions that a man might play,
But I have that within which passes show—
These are but the trappings and the suits of woe.
CLAUDIUS 'Tis sweet and commendable in your nature, Hamlet,
To give these mourning duties to your father. 90
But you must know, your father lost a father,
That father lost, lost his, and the survivor bound
In filial obligation for some term
To do obsequious sorrow; but to persevere
In obstinate condolement is a course 95
Of impious stubbornness. 'Tis unmanly grief.
It shows a will most incorrect to heaven,
A heart unfortified, a mind impatient,
An understanding simple and unschooled.
For what we know must be, and is as common 100
As any the most vulgar thing to sense,
Why should we in our peevish opposition
Take it to heart? Fie, 'tis a fault to heaven,
A fault against the dead, a fault to nature,
To reason most absurd, whose common theme 105
Is death of fathers, and who still hath cried,
From the first corse till he that died today,
"This must be so." We pray you, throw to earth
This unprevailing woe and think of us
As of a father, for let the world take note 110
You are the most immediate to our throne,
And with no less nobility of love
Than that which dearest father bears his son,
Do I impart toward you. For your intent
In going back to school in Wittenberg, 115
It is most retrograde to our desire,
And we beseech you, bend you to remain
Here in the cheer and comfort of our eye,

These are actions that anyone might play,
But I have within me something beyond show—
These are only the outward signs and dress of woe.
CLAUDIUS It's sweet-natured and commendable of you, Hamlet,
To mourn your father in this dutiful way.   90
But you must know that your father lost a father,
And that lost father lost his, and the survivor was bound
By a son's obligations for a certain period
To go into deep mourning. But to persist
In obstinate grieving is to steer a course   95
Of wicked stubbornness. It's unmanly grief.
It shows a willful disrespect to heaven,
A heart unfortified, a mind impatient,
An ignorant and unschooled intellect.
For we know what must be, and it's as common   100
As the most obvious thing to the senses.
Why, then, in foolish perversity
Take it to heart? Rubbish, it's an offense to heaven,
An offense to the dead, an offense against nature,
An absurd kind of reason, whose norm   105
Is the death of fathers and who has cried,
From the very first corpse to the one that died today,
"This must be so." We beg you, bury
This purposeless grief and think of us
As a father. Let the world take note: 110
You are the most immediate in line to our throne,
And with a love no less profound
Than that which a dear father bears for his son,
I express myself to you. As for your intention
To return to the University of Wittenberg,   115
That's the opposite of our wishes,
And we entreat you to dispose yourself to remain
Here in the warmth and comfort of our court,

Our chiefest courtier, cousin, and our son.
GERTRUDE Let not thy mother lose her prayers, Hamlet.   120
    I pray thee, stay with us. Go not to Wittenberg.
HAMLET I shall in all my best obey you, madam.
CLAUDIUS Why, 'tis a loving and a fair reply.
    Be as ourself in Denmark. Madam, come.
    This gentle and unforced accord of Hamlet   125
    Sits smiling to my heart, in grace whereof,
    No jocund health that Denmark drinks today
    But the great cannon to the clouds shall tell,
    And the king's rouse the heaven shall bruit again,
    Respeaking earthly thunder. Come away.   130
                Flourish. Exeunt all but HAMLET
HAMLET O that this too too solid flesh would melt,
    Thaw and resolve itself into a dew,
    Or that the Everlasting had not fixed
    His canon 'gainst self-slaughter. O God, God,
    How weary, stale, flat, and unprofitable   135
    Seem to me all the uses of this world!
    Fie on 't, ah fie, 'tis an unweeded garden
    That grows to seed. Things rank and gross in nature
    Possess it merely. That it should come to this!
    But two months dead—nay not so much, not two—   140
    So excellent a king, that was to this
    Hyperion to a satyr, so loving to my mother
    That he might not beteem the winds of heaven
    Visit her face too roughly. Heaven and earth,
    Must I remember? Why, she would hang on him   145
    As if increase of appetite had grown
    By what it fed on, and yet within a month—
    Let me not think on 't; frailty, thy name is woman—
    A little month, or ere those shoes were old
    With which she followed my poor father's body,   150

Our highest courtier, our kinsman, and our son.
GERTRUDE Don't let your mother waste her prayers, Hamlet.   120
    I beg you, stay with us. Don't go to Wittenberg.
HAMLET I shall, to the best of my ability, obey you, madam.
CLAUDIUS Why, that's a loving and courteous reply.
    Act like a king in Denmark. Madam, come.
    This gentle and free consent of Hamlet's   125
    Sits smiling in my heart. To celebrate,
    The king shall drink no toast today
    Without firing the great cannon to inform the clouds,
    And the king's toast shall be proclaimed again,
    Reechoing the thunder from the earth. Come, let's go.   130
             Trumpets sound. Exit all but HAMLET
HAMLET Oh, that this all too solid flesh would melt,
    Thaw, and turn itself into a dew.
    Or that the Almighty had not fixed
    His decree against self-slaughter. Oh, God, God,
    How weary, stale, flat, and purposeless   135
    Seem to me all the things of this world!
    A blight on it, all's filth, an untended garden
    That's gone to seed. Things rank and gross in nature
    Possess it entirely. That it should come to this!
    Just two months dead—no, not so much, not two!   140
    So excellent a king! He was to this king
    As the sun god is to a goatish beast; so loving to my mother,
    He would not allow the winds of heaven
    To blow too roughly on her face. Heaven and earth,
    Must I remember? Why, she would cling to him,   145
    As if an insatiable appetite had grown
    By what it fed on. And yet within a month—
    I mustn't think about it; frailty, your name is woman.
    A mere month, before those shoes were old
    In which she followed my poor father's body,   150

Like Niobe, all tears—why she, even she—
O God, a beast that wants discourse of reason
Would have mourned longer—married with my uncle,
My father's brother—but no more like my father
Than I to Hercules. Within a month, 155
Ere yet the salt of most unrighteous tears
Had left the flushing in her galled eyes,
She married. O most wicked speed! To post
With such dexterity to incestuous sheets!
It is not, nor it cannot come to good. 160
But break, my heart, for I must hold my tongue.
       Enter HORATIO, MARCELLUS, *and* BARNARDO
HORATIO Hail to your lordship.
HAMLET I am glad to see you well.
    Horatio, or do I forget myself.
HORATIO The same, my lord, and your poor servant ever. 165
HAMLET Sir, my good friend. I'll change that name with you.
    And what make you from Wittenberg, Horatio?
    Marcellus?
MARCELLUS My good lord.
HAMLET I am very glad to see you. [*To* BARNARDO] Good even, sir. 170
    But what, in faith, make you from Wittenberg?
HORATIO A truant disposition, good my lord.
HAMLET I would not hear your enemy say so,
    Nor shall you do my ear that violence
    To make it truster of your own report 175
    Against yourself. I know you are no truant.
    But what is your affair in Elsinore?
    We'll teach you to drink deep ere you depart.
HORATIO My lord, I came to see your father's funeral.
HAMLET I prithee, do not mock me, fellow student. 180
    I think it was to see my mother's wedding.
HORATIO Indeed, my lord, it followed hard upon.

Like Niobe, all tears—why she, even she—
Oh, God, a beast that lacks the power to reason
Would have mourned longer. She married my uncle,
My father's brother, but no more like my father
Than I to Hercules. Within a month,   155
Before the salt in those deceitful tears
Had gone from her reddened eyes,
She married. Oh, such wicked speed, to rush
So nimbly into an incestuous bed!
It's not right and no good can come from it.   160
But, let my heart break, I must hold my tongue.
    Enter HORATIO, MARCELLUS, *and* BARNARDO
HORATIO Greetings to your lordship.
HAMLET I am glad to see you well.
  It's Horatio, if I am correct.
HORATIO The same, my lord, and your humble servant.   165
HAMLET Sir, I'll change that name with you: my good friend.
  And what brings you from Wittenberg, Horatio?
  Marcellus?
MARCELLUS My good lord.
HAMLET I am very glad to see you. [*To* BARNARDO] Good evening, sir. 170
  But what, in faith, brings you here from Wittenberg?
HORATIO An inclination to truancy, my good lord.
HAMLET I would not hear your enemy say that,
  Nor shall you offend my ears
  By hearing you give such a report   175
  Against yourself. I know you are no truant.
  But what is your business in Elsinore?
  We'll teach you to drink deep before you depart.
HORATIO My lord, I came to attend your father's funeral.
HAMLET Please, do not tease me, fellow student.   180
  I think it was to see my mother's wedding.
HORATIO Indeed, my lord, it followed very soon.

HAMLET Thrift, thrift, Horatio. The funeral baked meats
    Did coldly furnish forth the marriage tables.
    Would I had met my dearest foe in heaven   185
    Or ever I had seen that day, Horatio.
    My father—methinks I see my father—
HORATIO Where, my lord?
HAMLET In my mind's eye, Horatio.
HORATIO I saw him once; a was a goodly king.   190
HAMLET A was a man, take him for all in all,
    I shall not look upon his like again.
HORATIO My lord, I think I saw him yesternight.
HAMLET Saw? Who?
HORATIO My lord, the king your father.   195
HAMLET The king my father?
HORATIO Season your admiration for a while
    With an attent ear, till I may deliver
    Upon the witness of these gentlemen
    This marvel to you.   200
HAMLET For God's love, let me hear!
HORATIO Two nights together had these gentlemen,
    Marcellus and Barnardo, on their watch,
    In the dead waste and middle of the night,
    Been thus encountered: a figure like your father   205
    Armed at point exactly, cap-à-pie,
    Appears before them and with solemn march
    Goes slow and stately by them. Thrice he walked
    By their oppressed and fear-surprised eyes
    Within this truncheon's length, whilst they, distilled   210
    Almost to jelly with the act of fear,
    Stand dumb and speak not to him. This to me
    In dreadful secrecy impart they did,
    And I with them the third night kept the watch,
    Where, as they had delivered, both in time,   215

HAMLET Thrift, thrift, Horatio. The funeral feast
    Was served up cold for the wedding breakfast.
    Would that I met my worst enemy in heaven   185
    Before I'd seen that day, Horatio.
    My father—I think I see my father—
HORATIO Where, my lord?
HAMLET In my mind's eye, Horatio.
HORATIO I saw him once. He was a fine king.   190
HAMLET He was a man perfect in all things.
    I shall not see his kind again.
HORATIO My lord, I think I saw him last night.
HAMLET Saw? Who?
HORATIO My lord, your father the king.   195
HAMLET My father the king?
HORATIO Temper your amazement for a while
    With an attentive ear, till I describe,
    With these gentlemen as witnesses,
    This marvel to you.   200
HAMLET For God's sake, let me hear!
HORATIO For two nights in succession these gentlemen,
    Marcellus and Barnardo, on their watch,
    In the dead waste and middle of the night,
    Have been confronted thus: a figure like your father,   205
    Clad in proper armor from head to foot,
    Appears before them and walks solemnly
    With a slow and stately pace. Three times he walked
    By their astonished and overpowered eyes,
    Within this staff's length. While they—dissolved   210
    Almost to jelly with their fear—
    Stand mute and do not speak to him. This
    They told me in absolute secrecy.
    And so I joined their watch on the third night,
    Where, as they had described, both as to time   215

Form of the thing, each word made true and good,
The apparition comes. I knew your father;
These hands are not more like.

HAMLET But where was this?

MARCELLUS My lord, upon the platform where we watch.   220

HAMLET Did you not speak to it?

HORATIO My lord, I did,
But answer made it none. Yet once methought
It lifted up its head and did address
Itself to motion like as it would speak;   225
But even then the morning cock crew loud,
And at the sound it shrunk in haste away
And vanished from our sight.

HAMLET 'Tis very strange.

HORATIO As I do live, my honored lord, 'tis true.   230
And we did think it writ down in our duty
To let you know of it.

HAMLET Indeed, indeed sirs, but this troubles me.
Hold you the watch tonight?

ALL We do, my lord.   235

HAMLET Armed, say you?

ALL Armed, my lord.

HAMLET From top to toe?

ALL My lord, from head to foot.

HAMLET Then saw you not his face?   240

HORATIO O, yes, my lord, he wore his beaver up.

HAMLET What, looked he frowningly?

HORATIO A countenance more in sorrow than in anger.

HAMLET Pale, or red?

HORATIO Nay, very pale.   245

HAMLET And fixed his eyes upon you?

HORATIO Most constantly.

HAMLET I would I had been there.

And the appearance of the thing, each detail true,
The apparition came. I knew it was your father.
These hands are not more similar.

HAMLET But where was this?

MARCELLUS My lord, on the battlement where we watched.   220

HAMLET Did you not speak to it?

HORATIO My lord, I did,
But it made no reply. Yet once, I thought,
It lifted up its head and started to move
As though it were going to speak.   225
But just then the morning cock crowed loudly,
And at the sound, it shrank away in haste
And vanished from our sight.

HAMLET This is very strange.

HORATIO Upon my life, my honored lord, it's true.   230
And we felt that it was our duty
To let you know of it.

HAMLET Of course, of course, sirs, but this troubles me.
Are you on watch tonight?

ALL We are, my lord.   235

HAMLET In armor, you say?

ALL In armor, my lord.

HAMLET From top to toe?

ALL My lord, from head to foot.

HAMLET Then you didn't see his face?   240

HORATIO Oh, yes, my lord, he wore his visor up.

HAMLET How did he look, fierce?

HORATIO His face was more sorrowful than angry.

HAMLET Pale or ruddy?

HORATIO Oh, very pale.   245

HAMLET And he looked right at you.

HORATIO Almost constantly.

HAMLET I wish I had been there.

HORATIO It would have much amazed you.
HAMLET Very like, very like. Stayed it long?   250
HORATIO While one with moderate haste might tell a hundred.
MARCELLUS }   Longer, longer.
BARNARDO }
HORATIO Not when I saw 't.
HAMLET His beard was grizzled, no?
HORATIO It was as I have seen it in his life,   255
    A sable silvered.
HAMLET I will watch tonight,
    Perchance 'twill walk again.
HORATIO I warrant it will.
HAMLET If it assume my noble father's person,   260
    I'll speak to it though hell itself should gape
    And bid me hold my peace. I pray you all,
    If you have hitherto concealed this sight,
    Let it be tenable in your silence still,
    And whatsomever else shall hap tonight,   265
    Give it an understanding but no tongue.
    I will requite your loves. So fare you well:
    Upon this platform, 'twixt eleven and twelve,
    I'll visit you.
ALL Our duty to your honor.   270
HAMLET Your loves, as mine to you. Farewell.
                 Exeunt all but HAMLET
    My father's spirit, in arms! All is not well.
    I doubt some foul play. Would the night were come.
    Till then sit still my soul. Foul deeds will rise,
    Though all the earth o'erwhelm them, to men's eyes.   275
                       Exit

Scene 3 [*In Polonius's chambers*]
           Enter LAERTES *and* OPHELIA *his sister*
LAERTES My necessaries are embarked, farewell.

HORATIO It would have bewildered you.

HAMLET Very likely, very likely. Did it stay long?   250

HORATIO As long as it takes to count to a hundred.

MARCELLUS } Longer, longer.

BARNARDO }

HORATIO Not when I saw it.

HAMLET His beard was grey, correct?

HORATIO It was as I have seen it when he was alive,   255

    Black streaked with silver.

HAMLET I will watch tonight.

    Perhaps it will walk again.

HORATIO I am sure it will.

HAMLET If it takes on the appearance of my noble father,   260

    I'll speak to it, even though hell should open wide,

    Threatening me to hold my peace. I ask you all,

    If you have up to now kept secret this appearance,

    Continue to hold your silence.

    And whatever else shall happen tonight,   265

    Take it all in but don't talk about it.

    I shall repay your loyalty. So, good-bye.

    Upon this battlement, between eleven and twelve,

    I'll visit you.

ALL We'll do our duty to your honor.   270

HAMLET Your love, just as you have mine. Farewell.

Exit all but HAMLET

    My father's spirit—in armor. All is not well.

    I suspect some foul play. I wish the night were here.

    Till then, patience, my soul. Evil deeds will rise,

    No matter how deeply buried, to men's eyes.   275

Exit

Scene 3 [*In Polonius's chambers*]

Enter LAERTES *and his sister* OPHELIA

LAERTES My bags are packed. Farewell.

And, sister, as the winds give benefit
And convoy is assistant, do not sleep,
But let me hear from you.

OPHELIA Do you doubt that?   5

LAERTES For Hamlet, and the trifling of his favor,
Hold it a fashion and a toy in blood,
A violet in the youth of primy nature,
Forward, not permanent, sweet, not lasting,
The perfume and suppliance of a minute,   10
No more.

OPHELIA No more but so?

LAERTES Think it no more.
For nature crescent does not grow alone
In thews and bulk, but, as this temple waxes,   15
The inward service of the mind and soul
Grows wide withal. Perhaps he loves you now,
And now no soil nor cautel doth besmirch
The virtue of his will; but you must fear,
His greatness weighed, his will is not his own,   20
For he himself is subject to his birth.
He may not, as unvalued persons do,
Carve for himself, for on his choice depends
The sanctity and the health of this whole state.
And therefore must his choice be circumscribed   25
Unto the voice and yielding of that body
Whereof he is the head. Then if he says he loves you,
It fits your wisdom so far to believe it
As he in his peculiar sect and force
May give his saying deed, which is no further   30
Than the main voice of Denmark goes withal.
Then weigh what loss your honor may sustain
If with too credent ear you list his songs,

And, sister, when the winds are strong
And the ships ready to sail, do not sleep
Until you write to me.
OPHELIA Can you doubt that?   5
LAERTES As for Hamlet and his trifling interest in you,
    Consider it just a passing thing, a whim of passion,
    Like a violet in the springtime of life,
    Eager, but not permanent, sweet, but not lasting,
    The fragrance that fills a minute.   10
    Nothing more.
OPHELIA No more than that?
LAERTES Take it as nothing more.
    For nature grows not alone
    In muscle and size, but as the body enlarges   15
    The inward service of the mind and soul
    Grows larger at the same time. Perhaps he loves you now
    And no stain or deceit mars
    The virtue of his intentions. But you must be mindful,
    If you consider his high rank, that his will is not his own.   20
    He is subject to the duties of his birth.
    He cannot, as some ordinary person may do,
    Choose for himself, for on his choice depends
    The sanctity and the health of the whole country.
    Therefore his choice is limited   25
    By the approval and consent of those people
    Whom he rules. So, if he says that he loves you,
    You would be wise to believe it only so far
    As a man of his class and power
    May turn his words into deeds, which is no further   30
    Than the general view in Denmark would allow.
    So weigh what loss your honor might sustain,
    If you listen to his songs with gullible ears,

Or lose your heart or your chaste treasure open   35
To his unmastered importunity.
Fear it, Ophelia; fear it, my dear sister,
And keep you in the rear of your affection,
Out of shot and danger of desire.
The chariest maid is prodigal enough   40
If she unmask her beauty to the moon.
Virtue itself 'scapes not calumnious strokes.
The canker galls the infants of the spring
Too oft before their buttons be disclosed,
And in the morn and liquid dew of youth,   45
Contagious blastments are most imminent.
Be wary, then; best safety lies in fear.
Youth to itself rebels, though none else near.

OPHELIA I shall the effect of this good lesson keep
As watchman to my heart. But, good my brother,   50
Do not as some ungracious pastors do,
Show me the steep and thorny way to heaven,
Whiles, like a puffed and reckless libertine,
Himself the primrose path of dalliance treads,
And recks not his own rede.   55

LAERTES O, fear me not.

Enter POLONIUS

I stay too long. But here my father comes.
A double blessing is a double grace:
Occasion smiles upon a second leave.

POLONIUS Yet here, Laertes? Aboard, aboard for shame!   60
The wind sits in the shoulder of your sail,
And you are stayed for. There, my blessing with thee.
And these few precepts in thy memory
Look thou character. Give thy thoughts no tongue,
Nor any unproportioned thought his act.   65
Be thou familiar, but by no means vulgar.

Or lose your heart or yield your virginity 35
To his uncontrolled pleading.
Fear it, Ophelia; fear it, my dear sister,
And hold yourself back from where your feelings lead,
Out of range of the shot and danger of desire.
The most cautious maid goes almost too far 40
If she does no more than reveal her beauty to the moon.
Virtue itself has no defense against the blows of scandal.
The worm kills the flowers of spring
Too often before their buds can open,
And in the morning and bright dew of youth, 45
Blights of contagion are most likely.
Be cautious, then; security lies in being fearful.
Youth loses self-control, even without a tempter.

OPHELIA I shall keep the meaning of your good lesson
As a watchman for my heart. But, my dear brother, 50
Do not, as some ungodly preachers do,
Show me the steep and thorny way to heaven
While, like some bloated and reckless sinner,
He treads the easy path of wanton pleasure
And does not heed his own advice. 55

LAERTES Oh, don't worry about me.

Enter POLONIUS

I've stayed too long. But here comes my father.
A second blessing is a double grace:
A second farewell is a fortunate occurrence.

POLONIUS Still here, Laertes? Get going, for shame. 60
The winds are right for your sailing,
And the ship waits for you. There, you have my blessing.
And for these few precepts, engrave them
In your memory: Do not say what is on your mind
Nor utter any hasty thought. 65
Be friendly, but not overly familiar.

Those friends thou hast, and their adoption tried,
Grapple them unto thy soul with hoops of steel,
But do not dull thy palm with entertainment
Of each new-hatched, unfledged courage. Beware 70
Of entrance to a quarrel, but being in,
Bear 't that the opposed may beware of thee.
Give every man thy ear, but few thy voice.
Take each man's censure, but reserve thy judgment.
Costly thy habit as thy purse can buy, 75
But not expressed in fancy: rich, not gaudy.
For the apparel oft proclaims the man,
And they in France of the best rank and station
Are of a most select and generous choice in that.
Neither a borrower nor a lender be, 80
For loan oft loses both itself and friend,
And borrowing dulls the edge of husbandry.
This above all, to thine own self be true,
And it must follow, as the night the day,
Thou canst not then be false to any man. 85
Farewell, my blessing season this in thee.
LAERTES Most humbly do I take my leave, my lord.
POLONIUS The time invites you. Go, your servants tend.
LAERTES Farewell, Ophelia, and remember well
  What I have said to you. 90
OPHELIA 'Tis in my memory locked,
  And you yourself shall keep the key of it.
LAERTES Farewell.

Exit LAERTES

POLONIUS What is 't, Ophelia, he hath said to you?
OPHELIA So please you, something touching the Lord Hamlet. 95
POLONIUS Marry, well bethought.
  'Tis told me he hath very oft of late
  Given private time to you, and you yourself

Those friends of yours who have proved themselves,
Clasp them to your soul with bands of steel,
But do not offer the hand of friendship
To every newly made, unproven fellow. Beware   70
Of starting a quarrel, but once in,
Carry it off so that your opponent is sorry.
Listen to everyone, but don't say too much.
Take each man's opinion, but keep your own to yourself.
Buy the best clothes that you can afford,   75
But not those expressing extremes: quality, not show.
You can often tell a man by the style of his clothes,
And in France those of the highest rank and station
Have an exquisite and noble gift in choosing them.
Be neither a borrower nor a lender.   80
A lender often loses both money and a friend,
And borrowing often dulls the edge of thrift.
This above all else, be true to your own self,
And it will follow, as the night the day,
That you cannot be false to any man.   85
Farewell, may my blessing help you in all of this.
LAERTES Most humbly do I take my leave, my lord.
POLONIUS Time invites you. Go, your servants wait.
LAERTES Farewell, Ophelia, and remember
    What I have said to you.   90
OPHELIA It's locked in my memory,
    And you yourself shall keep the key.
LAERTES Farewell.
                                 Exit LAERTES
POLONIUS What was it, Ophelia, he said to you?
OPHELIA With respect, something concerning the Lord Hamlet.   95
POLONIUS Indeed, that was good thinking.
    I'm told that very often of late he has
    Spent time with you privately, and you yourself

Have of your audience been most free and bounteous.
If it be so, as so 'tis put on me, 100
And that in way of caution, I must tell you
You do not understand yourself so clearly
As it behooves my daughter and your honor.
What is between you? Give me up the truth.
OPHELIA He hath, my lord, of late made many tenders 105
Of his affection to me.
POLONIUS Affection? Puh! You speak like a green girl,
Unsifted in such perilous circumstance.
Do you believe his tenders, as you call them?
OPHELIA I do not know, my lord, what I should think. 110
POLONIUS Marry, I'll teach you. Think yourself a baby
That you have ta'en these tenders for true pay,
Which are not sterling. Tender yourself more dearly,
Or—not to crack the wind of the poor phrase,
Roaming it thus—you'll tender me a fool. 115
OPHELIA My lord, he hath importuned me with love
In honorable fashion.
POLONIUS Ay, fashion you may call it. Go to, go to!
OPHELIA And hath given countenance to his speech, my lord,
With almost all the holy vows of heaven. 120
POLONIUS Ay, springes to catch woodcocks. I do know,
When the blood burns, how prodigal the soul
Lends the tongue vows. These blazes, daughter,
Giving more light than heat, extinct in both
Even in their promise as it is a-making, 125
You must not take for fire. From this time
Be something scanter of your maiden presence.
Set your entreatments at a higher rate
Than a command to parley. For Lord Hamlet,
Believe so much in him, that he is young 130
And with a larger tether may he walk

Have been liberal and generous in your availability.
If this is so, as it is told to me,   100
By way of warning, I must tell you
That you do not understand your position as clearly
As befits my daughter and your own honor.
What's between you? Tell me the truth.

OPHELIA He has, my lord, lately given many tenders   105
Of his affection to me.

POLONIUS Affection? Pooh! You speak like a green girl,
Naive about such dangerous matters.
Do you believe these "tenders," as you call them?

OPHELIA I do not know, my lord, what I should think.   110

POLONIUS Heavens, I'll teach you. Consider yourself a baby
That you have taken these tenders for real money,
When they are not genuine at all. Tender yourself more dearly
Or—not to run the phrase, like a horse, so hard
That it becomes winded—you'll tender me a fool.   115

OPHELIA My Lord, he has wooed me
In an honorable fashion.

POLONIUS Yes, "fashion" you may call it. Come now!

OPHELIA And he has backed up his words, my lord,
With almost all the holy vows of heaven.   120

POLONIUS Yes, snares to catch stupid birds. I know
How lavish the soul is with vows
When passion is roused. These flare-ups, daughter,
Give more light than heat, dying out
Even as their promise is being made.   125
Do not mistake them for fire. From now on,
Be more sparing of your maidenly presence.
Do not yield immediately
To a command to talk. As for Lord Hamlet,
Believe only this much: that he is young   130
And has a greater freedom of action

Than may be given you. In few, Ophelia,
Do not believe his vows, for they are brokers,
Not of that dye which their investments show,
But mere implorators of unholy suits,   135
Breathing like sanctified and pious bonds,
The better to beguile. This is for all:
I would not in plain terms from this time forth
Have you slander any moment leisure
As to give words or talk with the Lord Hamlet.   140
Look to 't, I charge you. Come your ways.
OPHELIA I shall obey, my lord.

Exeunt

Scene 4 [*On the castle walls*]
        Enter HAMLET, HORATIO, *and* MARCELLUS
HAMLET The air bites shrewdly; it is very cold.
HORATIO It is a nipping and an eager air.
HAMLET What hour now?
HORATIO I think it lacks of twelve.
MARCELLUS No, it is struck.   5
HORATIO Indeed? I heard it not. It then draws near the season
    Wherein the spirit held his wont to walk.
A flourish of trumpets and two pieces go off.
    What does this mean, my lord?
HAMLET The king doth wake tonight and takes his rouse,
    Keeps wassail, and the swaggering upspring reels;   10
    And as he drains his draughts of Rhenish down,
    The kettle-drum and trumpet thus bray out
    The triumph of his pledge.
HORATIO Is it a custom?
HAMLET Ay, marry, is 't,   15
    But to my mind, though I am native here
    And to the manner born, it is a custom

Than may be given you. In short, Ophelia,
Do not believe his vows. They are peddlers,
Disguising their true colors,
Out-and-out pleaders on behalf of sin,   135
Speaking the words of the holy contracts of love,
The better to beguile. This is final:
In plain words, I would not from now on
Have you misuse any moment of leisure
Exchanging words or talking with the Lord Hamlet.   140
Do as I say. Now, come along.
OPHELIA I shall obey, my lord.

They exit

Scene 4 [*On the castle walls*]
            Enter HAMLET, HORATIO, *and* MARCELLUS
HAMLET The wind bites keenly; it is very cold.
HORATIO It is a nipping and sharp wind.
HAMLET What time is it?
HORATIO I think it's nearly twelve.
MARCELLUS No, it has struck.   5
HORATIO Indeed? I didn't hear it. It draws near the time
      When the ghost used to walk.
The sound of trumpets and cannons being fired.
      What does this mean, my lord?
HAMLET The king celebrates tonight, drinking,
      Carousing, and dancing riotously;   10
      And as he drains his draughts of Rhine wine,
      The trumpet and the kettledrum bray out
      His finishing a cup in one gulp.
HORATIO Is it a custom?
HAMLET Yes, indeed, it is.   15
      But to my mind, though I'm a native
      And born to it, it is a custom

41

More honored in the breach than the observance.
This heavy-headed revel east and west
Makes us traduced and taxed of other nations.   20
They clepe us drunkards, and with swinish phrase
Soil our addition. And, indeed, it takes
From our achievements, though performed at height,
The pith and marrow of our attribute.
So, oft it chances in particular men,   25
That for some vicious mole of nature in them,
As in their birth, wherein they are not guilty,
Since nature cannot choose his origin,
 By their o'ergrowth of some complexion,
Oft breaking down the pales and forts of reason,   30
Or by some habit that too much o'erleavens
The form of plausive manners—that these men,
Carrying, I say, the stamp of one defect,
Being nature's livery or fortune's star,
His virtues else, be they as pure as grace,   35
As infinite as man may undergo,
Shall in the general censure take corruption
From that particular fault. The dram of evil
Doth all the noble substance of a doubt
To his own scandal.   40

Enter GHOST

HORATIO Look, my lord, it comes.
HAMLET Angels and ministers of grace, defend us!
    Be thou a spirit of health, or a goblin damned,
    Bring with thee airs from heaven or blasts from hell,
    Be thy intents wicked or charitable,   45
    Thou com'st in such a questionable shape
    That I will speak to thee. I'll call thee Hamlet,
    King, father, royal Dane. O, answer me.
    Let me not burst in ignorance, but tell

More honorably broken than observed.
This drunken revelry everywhere
Makes us slandered and censured by other nations.   20
They call us drunkards, and our reputation is soiled
By calling us swine. Indeed, our fondness of drink
Robs our achievements, though performed at the height,
Of the essence of the reputation due us.
So, it often happens that particular men,   25
Because of some natural flaw in them
They have inherited— which is not their fault,
Since one cannot choose his ancestors—
Or by the excessive growth of some natural trait
That breaks down the fortifications of reason,   30
Or by some bad habit that too much alters
The form of pleasing manners—that these men,
Suffering, as I say, the stamp of one defect,
Being nature's mark or bad luck,
Their virtues otherwise pure as grace   35
Or as plentiful as a man may support,
Shall, in the general opinion, be corrupted
By that particular fault. A drop of evil
Outweighs all the good in a man,
To his own discredit.   40

Enter GHOST

HORATIO Look, my lord, it comes.

HAMLET Angels and ministers of God, defend us!
Whether you're a good spirit or a damned demon,
Bringing with you airs from heaven or blasts from hell,
Whether your intents are wicked or charitable,   45
You come as one who can be questioned,
And I will speak with you. I'll call you Hamlet,
King, father, royal Dane. Oh, answer me.
Don't let me burst with ignorance, but tell me

Why thy canonized bones, hearsed in death,   50
Have burst their cerements; why the sepulchre,
Wherein we saw thee quietly enurned,
Hath oped his ponderous and marble jaws
To cast thee up again. What may this mean,
That thou, dead corse, again in complete steel,   55
Revisits thus the glimpses of the moon,
Making night hideous, and we fools of nature
So horridly to shake our disposition
With thoughts beyond the reaches of our souls?
Say, why is this? Wherefore? What should we do?   60

                GHOST *beckons* HAMLET

HORATIO It beckons you to go away with it,
    As if it some impartment did desire
    To you alone.
MARCELLUS Look with what courteous action
    It wafts you to a more removed ground.   65
    But do not go with it.
HORATIO No, by no means.
HAMLET It will not speak. Then I will follow it.
HORATIO Do not, my lord.
HAMLET Why, what should be the fear?   70
    I do not set my life at a pin's fee.
    And for my soul, what can it do to that,
    Being a thing immortal as itself?
    It waves me forth again. I'll follow it.
HORATIO What if it tempt you toward the flood, my lord?   75
    Or to the dreadful summit of the cliff
    That beetles o'er his base into the sea,
    And there assume some other horrible form
    Which might deprive your sovereignty of reason,
    And draw you into madness? Think of it.   80

Why your consecrated bones, coffined in death,   50
Have burst from their burial shroud; why the tomb
In which we saw you quietly set to rest
Has opened its ponderous marble jaws
To cast you up again. What does this mean
When you, a dead corpse, again in full armor,   55
Come again in the pale gleams of the moon,
Making night hideous, and we creatures of nature
Upset ourselves so violently
With thoughts beyond the reach of our souls?
Speak. What is the reason? What do you want us to do?   60

        GHOST *beckons* HAMLET

HORATIO It beckons you to go away with it,
 As if it were going to impart something
 To you alone.
MARCELLUS Look, how courteously
 It waves you toward a more distant ground.   65
 But do not go with it.
HORATIO No, by no means.
HAMLET It will not speak. So, I will follow it.
HORATIO Do not, my lord.
HAMLET Why, what's to fear?   70
 I do not value my life more than a pin.
 And, as for my soul, what can it do to that,
 Being something as immortal as itself?
 It waves me on again. I'll follow it.
HORATIO What if it tempts you toward the sea, my lord?   75
 Or to the fearful summit of the cliff
 That overhangs its base in the sea,
 And there assumes some other horrible form
 That might depose reason as the ruler of your mind
 And draw you into madness? Think of it.   80

The very place puts toys of desperation,
Without more motive, into every brain
That looks so many fathoms to the sea
And hears it roar beneath.

HAMLET It wafts me still. Go on, I'll follow thee.   85

MARCELLUS You shall not go, my lord.

HAMLET Hold off your hands.

HORATIO Be ruled. You shall not go.

HAMLET My fate cries out,
And makes each petty arture in this body   90
As hardy as the Nemean lion's nerve.
Still am I called. Unhand me, gentlemen!
By heaven, I'll make a ghost of him that lets me.
I say, away!— Go on, I'll follow thee.

Exit GHOST *and* HAMLET

HORATIO He waxes desperate with imagination.   95

MARCELLUS Let's follow, 'tis not fit thus to obey him.

HORATIO Have after. To what issue will this come?

MARCELLUS Something is rotten in the state of Denmark.

HORATIO Heaven will direct it.

MARCELLUS Nay, let's follow him.   100

Exeunt

Scene 5 [*At a distance from the castle walls*]

Enter GHOST *and* HAMLET

HAMLET Whither wilt thou lead me? Speak, I'll go no further.

GHOST Mark me.

HAMLET I will.

GHOST My hour is almost come
When I to sulf'rous and tormenting flames   5
Must render up myself.

HAMLET Alas, poor ghost!

GHOST Pity me not, but lend thy serious hearing

That very site puts whims of desperation,
All by itself, into every mind
That looks from so great a height to the sea
And hears it roar beneath.
HAMLET It's still waving me on. Go on, I'll follow you.   85
MARCELLUS You shall not go, my lord.
HAMLET Take your hands away.
HORATIO Be ruled by us. You shall not go.
HAMLET My destiny is calling,
And gives the smallest artery in this body   90
The strength of the Nemean lion's sinew.
Still it calls me. Unhand me, gentlemen!
By heaven, I'll make a ghost of him that hinders me.
Get away, I say!—Go on, I'll follow you.

Exit GHOST *and* HAMLET

HORATIO His imagination has made him desperate.   95
MARCELLUS Let's follow. It's not right to obey him.
HORATIO Let's go after him. What will come of this?
MARCELLUS Something is rotten in the state of Denmark.
HORATIO Heaven will straighten it out.
MARCELLUS No, let's follow him.   100

They exit

Scene 5 [*At a distance from the castle walls*]

Enter GHOST *and* HAMLET

HAMLET Where are you leading me? Answer, I'll go no further.
GHOST Pay attention to me.
HAMLET I will.
GHOST The hour is almost come
When I to the sulfurous and tormenting flames   5
Must give myself up.
HAMLET Alas, poor ghost!
GHOST Don't pity me, but listen hard

To what I shall unfold.

HAMLET Speak. I am bound to hear. 10

GHOST So art thou to revenge, when thou shalt hear.

HAMLET What?

GHOST I am thy father's spirit,
    Doomed for a certain term to walk the night,
    And for the day confined to fast in fires, 15
    Till the foul crimes done in my days of nature
    Are burnt and purged away. But that I am forbid
    To tell the secrets of my prison house,
    I could a tale unfold whose lightest word
    Would harrow up thy soul, freeze thy young blood, 20
    Make thy two eyes, like stars, start from their spheres,
    Thy knotted and combined locks to part
    And each particular hair to stand on end,
    Like quills upon the fretful porpentine.
    But this eternal blazon must not be 25
    To ears of flesh and blood. List, list, O list!
    If thou didst ever thy dear father love—

HAMLET O God!

GHOST Revenge his foul and most unnatural murder.

HAMLET Murder? 30

GHOST Murder most foul, as in the best it is,
    But this most foul, strange, and unnatural.

HAMLET Haste me to know 't, that I, with wings as swift
    As meditation or thoughts of love,
    May sweep to my revenge. 35

GHOST I find thee apt,
    And duller shouldst thou be than the fat weed
    That rots itself in ease on Lethe wharf,
    Wouldst thou not stir in this. Now, Hamlet, hear.
    'Tis given out that, sleeping in my orchard, 40
    A serpent stung me. So the whole ear of Denmark

To what I shall reveal.
HAMLET Speak. I'm bound to hear.   10
GHOST So also are you bound to revenge, when you hear.
HAMLET What?
GHOST I am your father's spirit,
    Doomed for a certain term to walk the night,
    And during the day to fast in fires,   15
    Till the sins done during my lifetime
    Are burned and purged away. If I were not forbidden
    To tell the secrets of my prison,
    I could tell a tale whose simple word
    Would tear up your soul, freeze your young blood,   20
    Make your two eyes, like stars, bolt from their orbit,
    The tousled hair on your head to part
    And every individual hair to stand on end,
    Like quills on the fretful porcupine.
    But making known the afterlife is not for   25
    The ears of flesh and blood. Listen, listen, oh, listen!
    If ever you loved your dear father—
HAMLET Oh, God!
GHOST Revenge his foul and most unnatural murder.
HAMLET Murder?   30
GHOST Murder most foul, as at its best it is,
    But this one—most foul, strange, and unnatural.
HAMLET Tell me quickly, so that I with wings as swift
    As meditation or the thoughts of love,
    May sweep to my revenge.   35
GHOST I find you quick.
    You would be duller than the sluggish weed
    That roots in ease by the banks of Lethe
    If you were not roused by this. Now, Hamlet, hear.
    People were told that, sleeping in my garden,   40
    A snake stung me. So everyone in Denmark

Is by a forged process of my death
Rankly abused; but know, thou noble youth,
The serpent that did sting thy father's life
Now wears his crown.   45
HAMLET O, my prophetic soul!
    My uncle?
GHOST Ay, that incestuous, that adulterate beast,
    With witchcraft of his wit, with traitorous gifts—
    O wicked wit and gifts that have the power   50
    So to seduce—won to his shameful lust
    The will of my most seeming-virtuous queen.
    O Hamlet, what a falling off was there!
    From me, whose love was of that dignity
    That it went hand in hand even with the vow   55
    I made to her in marriage, and to decline
    Upon a wretch whose natural gifts were poor
    To those of mine.
    But virtue, as it never will be moved,
    Though lewdness court it in a shape of heaven,   60
    So lust, though to a radiant angel linked,
    Will sate itself in a celestial bed,
    And prey on garbage.
    But soft, methinks I scent the morning air.
    Brief let me be. Sleeping within my orchard,   65
    My custom always of the afternoon,
    Upon my secure hour thy uncle stole,
    With juice of cursed hebenon in a vial,
    And in the porches of my ears did pour
    The leprous distilment, whose effect   70
    Holds such an enmity with blood of man
    That swift as quicksilver it courses through
    The natural gates and alleys of the body,
    And with a sudden vigor it doth posset

Is by a false story of my death
Vilely misled; so know, you noble youth,
The serpent that stung away your father's life
Now wears his crown.   45
HAMLET As I felt all along!
    My uncle?
GHOST Yes, that incestuous, that adulterous beast.
    With bewitching wit, with traitorous skills—
    Oh, wicked wit and skill that have the power   50
    So to seduce—he satisfied his shameful lust
    With the will of my apparently virtuous queen.
    Oh, Hamlet, what a fall from grace that was!
    To move from me whose love was such
    That it was equal to the vow   55
    I made to her in marriage, and to descend
    To a wretch whose merits were poor
    Compared to those of mine.
    But virtue will never be seduced,
    Even though lewdness court it in a heavenly shape,   60
    And lust, though like a radiant angel,
    Will not satisfy itself in a holy bed,
    But preys on garbage.
    But enough, I think I scent the morning air.
    Let me be brief. While I slept in my garden—   65
    My custom always in the afternoon—
    Where I felt free from danger, your uncle stole in
    With a poisonous drug in a vial
    And poured it in my ears, the gates of my body.
    This leprous liquid, whose effect   70
    Is so harmful to the blood of man,
    Coursed swift as quicksilver through
    The veins and arteries of my body
    And with a sudden force it clotted

And curd, like eager droppings into milk,   75
The thin and wholesome blood. So did it mine,
And a most instant tetter barked about,
Most lazar-like, with vile and loathsome crust,
All my smooth body.
Thus was I, sleeping, by a brother's hand   80
Of life, of crown, of queen, at once dispatched;
Cut off even in the blossoms of my sin,
Unhouseled, disappointed, unaneled;
No reckoning made, but sent to my account
With all my imperfections on my head—   85
O horrible, O horrible, most horrible!
If thou hast nature in thee bear it not;
Let not the royal bed of Denmark be
A couch for luxury and damned incest.
But howsomever thou pursues this act,   90
Taint not thy mind, nor let thy soul contrive
Against thy mother aught. Leave her to heaven
And to those thorns that in her bosom lodge
To prick and sting her. Fare thee well at once.
The glowworm shows the martin to be near,   95
And 'gins to pale his uneffectual fire.
Adieu, adieu, adieu. Remember me.
                                                    Exit
HAMLET O all you host of heaven! O earth! What else?
    And shall I couple hell? O fie! Hold, hold, my heart,
    And you my sinews grow not instant old   100
    But bear me stiffly up. Remember thee?
    Ay, thou poor ghost, whiles memory holds a seat
    In this distracted globe. Remember thee?
    Yea, from the table of my memory
    I'll wipe away all trivial fond records,   105
    All saws of books, all forms, all pressures past,

And curdled, like acid dropped in milk,   75
The thin and healthy blood. It did this to me,
And in an instant my skin erupted like tree bark,
A leper's skin covered with vile and loathsome crust
Covered my whole smooth body.
Thus sleeping, I was deprived by a brother's hand   80
Of life, of crown, and of queen, all at once;
Cut off in a state of sinfulness,
Without the sacrament, unprepared, without last rites;
No settling of accounts, but sent to final reckoning
With all my sins upon my head—   85
Oh horrible, oh horrible, most horrible!
If you have natural feelings, do not stand for it;
Do not let the royal bed of Denmark be
A couch of lust and damned incest.
But however you pursue this deed,   90
Don't poison your mind nor consider
Any action against your mother. Leave her to heaven
And to the thorns of her own conscience
To prick and sting her. Farewell, quickly.
The glowworm shows the morning's near,   95
With its diminished light.
Adieu, adieu, adieu. Remember me.
                                           Exit
HAMLET Oh, all you angels! Oh, earth! What else?
          And shall I call on hell? Oh, shame! Hold, hold, my heart,
          And you, my sinews, do not grow suddenly old,   100
          But keep me from collapsing. Remember you?
          Yes, you poor ghost, so long as memory holds a seat
          In this disordered world. Remember you?
          Yes, from the slate of my memory,
          I'll wipe away all trivial, foolish records,   105
          All sayings from books, concepts, impressions past,

That youth and observation copied there,
And thy commandment all alone shall live
Within the book and volume of my brain,
Unmixed with baser matter. Yes, by heaven! 110
O most pernicious woman!
O villain, villain, smiling damned villain!
My tables—meet it is I set it down
That one may smile and smile and be a villain;
At least I'm sure it may be so in Denmark. 115
[*He writes*]
So, uncle, there you are. Now to my word.
It is "Adieu, adieu, remember me."
I have sworn 't.
HORATIO [*Within*] My lord, my lord!
MARCELLUS [*Within*] Lord Hamlet! 120
          Enter HORATIO *and* MARCELLUS
HORATIO Heavens secure him!
HAMLET So be it.
MARCELLUS Illo, ho, ho, my lord!
HAMLET Hillo, ho, ho, boy! Come, bird, come.
MARCELLUS How is 't, my noble lord? 125
HORATIO What news, my lord?
HAMLET O, wonderful!
HORATIO Good my lord, tell it.
HAMLET No, you will reveal it.
HORATIO Not I, my lord, by heaven. 130
MARCELLUS Nor I, my lord.
HAMLET How say you, then, would heart of man once think it—
    But you'll be secret?
HORATIO   }
MARCELLUS } Ay, by heaven, my lord.
HAMLET There's never a villain dwelling in all Denmark 135
    But he's an arrant knave.

That youth and dutiful attention copied there.
And your command alone shall be filed
As the books and volumes of my brain,
Unmixed with lesser stuff. Yes, by heaven!   110
Oh, that most wicked woman!
Oh, you villain, villain, smiling damned villain!
My notebook—it is right that I set down:
One may smile and smile and be a villain;
At least I'm sure it may be true in Denmark.   115
[*He writes*]
So, uncle, there you are. Now to my word.
It is "Adieu, adieu, remember me."
I have sworn it.
HORATIO [*Within*] My lord, my lord!
MARCELLUS [*Within*] Lord Hamlet!   120
                    Enter HORATIO *and* MARCELLUS
HORATIO Heaven protect him.
HAMLET So be it.
MARCELLUS Hello, ho, ho, my lord.
HAMLET Hello, ho, ho, boy! Come here, bird.
MARCELLUS Are you all right, my noble lord?   125
HORATIO What news, my lord?
HAMLET Oh, amazing!
HORATIO My good lord, tell it.
HAMLET No, you will reveal it.
HORATIO Not I, my lord, by heaven.   130
MARCELLUS Nor I, my lord.
HAMLET What would you say, then, would anyone ever think—
     But you'll keep a secret?
HORATIO   }
MARCELLUS } Yes, by heaven, my lord.
HAMLET There's not a single villain dwelling in all Denmark   135
     Who isn't a complete rogue.

HORATIO There needs no ghost, my lord, come from the grave,
    To tell us this.
HAMLET Why right, you are in the right,
    And so, without more circumstance at all,   140
    I hold it fit that we shake hands and part—
    You, as your business and desire shall point you,
    For every man hath business and desire,
    Such as it is, and for my poor part,
    Look you, I'll go pray.   145
HORATIO These are but wild and whirling words, my lord.
HAMLET I'm sorry they offend you, heartily;
    Yes faith, heartily.
HORATIO There's no offense, my lord.
HAMLET Yes, by Saint Patrick, but there is, Horatio,   150
    And much offense, too. Touching this vision here,
    It is an honest ghost, that let me tell you.
    For your desire to know what is between us,
    O'ermaster 't as you may. And now, good friends,
    As you are friends, scholars, and soldiers,   155
    Give me one poor request.
HORATIO What is 't, my lord? We will.
HAMLET Never make known what you have seen tonight.
HORATIO   }
MARCELLUS } My lord, we will not.
HAMLET Nay, but swear 't.   160
HORATIO In faith,
    My lord, not I.
MARCELLUS Nor I, my lord, in faith.
HAMLET Upon my sword.
MARCELLUS We have sworn, my lord, already.   165
HAMLET Indeed, upon my sword, indeed.
GHOST [*Cries under the stage*] Swear.

HORATIO There's no need for a ghost, my lord, come from the grave
     To tell us this.
HAMLET That's right. You're in the right,
     And so, without any further formality   140
     I feel it's right that we shake hands and part—
     You, as your business and pleasure shall direct,
     Because every man has business and pleasure,
     Such as it is, and for my poor part,
     Look, I'll go pray.   145
HORATIO These words are wild and hysterical, my lord.
HAMLET I'm sorry they offend you, really;
     Yes, in faith, really.
HORATIO There's no offense, my lord.
HAMLET Yes, by Saint Patrick, but there is, Horatio,   150
     And much offense, too. As for this vision here,
     It is a genuine ghost, let me tell you that.
     As for your desire to know what we said to each other,
     Suppress that, as best you can. And now, good friends,
     As you are friends, scholars, and soldiers,   155
     Grant me one small request.
HORATIO What is it, my lord? We will.
HAMLET Never make known what you have seen tonight.
HORATIO   }
MARCELLUS }   My lord, we will not.
HAMLET No, but swear it.   160
HORATIO In faith,
     My lord, I will not tell.
MARCELLUS Nor I, my lord, in faith.
HAMLET Swear upon the cross, my sword.
MARCELLUS We have sworn already, my lord.   165
HAMLET Indeed, upon my sword. Indeed.
GHOST [*Cries under the stage*] Swear.

HAMLET Ha, ha, boy, sayest thou so? Art thou there, truepenny?
    Come on, you hear this fellow in the cellarage.
    Consent to swear.   170
HORATIO Propose the oath, my lord.
HAMLET Never to speak of this that you have seen,
    Swear by my sword.
GHOST Swear.
HAMLET *Hic et ubique?* Then we'll shift our ground.   175
    Come hither, gentlemen,
    And lay your hands again upon my sword.
    Never to speak of this that you have heard,
    Swear by my sword.
GHOST Swear.   180
HAMLET Well said, old mole, canst work i' th' earth so fast?
    A worthy pioneer. Once more remove, good friends.
HORATIO O day and night, but this is wondrous strange.
HAMLET And therefore as a stranger give it welcome.
    There are more things in heaven and earth, Horatio,   185
    Than are dreamt of in your philosophy.
    But come—
    Here as before, never, so help you mercy,
    How strange or odd some'er I bear myself,
    (As I perchance hereafter shall think meet   190
    To put an antic disposition on)—
    That you at such times seeing me, never shall,
    With arms encumbered thus, or this headshake,
    Or by pronouncing of some doubtful phrase,
    As "Well, well, we know," or "We could an if we would,"   195
    Or "If we list to speak," or "There be an if they might,"
    Or such ambiguous giving-out, to note
    That you know aught of me: this do swear,
    So grace and mercy at your most need help you,

'

HAMLET Ha, aha, boy, do you say so? Are you there, old fellow?
 Come on, you can hear this fellow down in the cellar.
 Consent to swear.   170
HORATIO Propose the oath, my lord.
HAMLET Never to speak of what you've seen.
 Swear by my sword.
GHOST Swear.
HAMLET Here and everywhere? Now we'll shift our ground. 175
 Come here, gentlemen,
 And lay your hands again upon my sword.
 Never to speak of what you've heard,
 Swear by my sword.
GHOST Swear.   180
HAMLET Well said, old mole, can you tunnel through the earth so
 fast? A skillful digger. Let's move once more, good friends.
HORATIO Oh, night and day, but this is very strange.
HAMLET And, therefore, as it is a stranger, give it welcome.
 There are more things in heaven and earth, Horatio, 185
 Than are dreamt of in your philosophy.
 But come—
 Swear here as before, never, so help you God,
 No matter how strange or odd my behavior
 (As perhaps afterward I shall think it best 190
 To put on a zany manner),
 That you seeing me at such times, never
 With arms folded like this or a shake of the head
 Or by uttering some dubious phrase,
 Such as "Well, well, we know," or "We could, if we wished," 195
 Or "If we were to speak," or "There are those who might say,"
 Or any such ambiguous remarks, to signal
 That you know the truth of me. This do swear,
 Upon God's mercy in your hour of need.

GHOST Swear.   200
HAMLET Rest, rest, perturbed spirit. So, gentlemen,
    With all my love I do commend me to you,
    And what so poor a man as Hamlet is
    May do t' express his love and friending to you,
    God willing, shall not lack. Let us go in together,   205
    And still your finger on your lips, I pray.
    The time is out of joint. O cursed spite,
    That ever I was born to set it right.
    Nay, come, let's go together.
                           Exeunt

GHOST Swear.   200
HAMLET Rest, rest, troubled spirit. So, gentlemen,
      With all my love I entrust myself to you,
      And whatever a man so poor as Hamlet is
      May do to express his love and friendship to you,
      God willing, you shall not lack it. Let us go in together,   205
      And, please, keep your finger on your lips.
      The times are out of joint. Oh cursed plight,
      That ever I was born to set them right.
      No, come, let's go together.

                                                        They exit

Act Two

Scene 1 [*In Polonius's chambers*]

Enter POLONIUS *with his man* REYNALDO

POLONIUS Give him this money and these notes, Reynaldo.

REYNALDO I will, my lord.

POLONIUS You shall do marvelous wisely, good Reynaldo,

    Before you visit him, to make inquire

    Of his behavior.   5

REYNALDO My lord, I did intend it.

POLONIUS Marry, well said, very well said. Look you, sir,

    Inquire me first what Danskers are in Paris,

    And how, and who, what means, and where they keep,

    What company, at what expense; and finding   10

    By this encompassment and drift of question

    That they do know my son, come you more nearer

    Than your particular demands will touch it.

    Take you, as 'twere some distant knowledge of him,

    As thus, "I know his father and his friends,   15

    And, in part, him"—do you mark this, Reynaldo?

REYNALDO Ay, very well, my lord.

Act Two

Scene 1 [*In Polonius's chambers*]

Enter POLONIUS *and his servant* REYNALDO

POLONIUS Give him this money and these notes, Reynaldo.

REYNALDO I will, my lord.

POLONIUS It would be extremely wise, Reynaldo,

 Before you visit him, to inquire

 About his behavior.   5

REYNALDO I intended to, my lord.

POLONIUS Good, well said, very well said. Look here, sir,

 Find out first what Danes live in Paris,

 How they came there, who they are, what means they have,

 Where they stay, what they spend; and discovering 10

 By this roundabout and indirect way

 That they know my son, you'll come nearer

 The facts than with direct questions.

 Pretend you have some distant knowledge of him,

 Say, for instance, "I know his father and his friends 15

 And, slightly, him"—are you following this, Reynaldo?

REYNALDO Yes, very well, my lord.

POLONIUS "And in part, him, but"—you may say—"not well.
    But if 't be he I mean, he's very wild,
    Addicted so and so"—and there put on him   20
    What forgeries you please; marry, none so rank
    As may dishonor him, take heed of that,
    But sir, such wanton, wild, and usual slips
    As are companions noted and most known
    To youth and liberty.   25
REYNALDO As gaming, my lord?
POLONIUS Ay, or drinking, fencing, swearing,
    Quarreling, drabbing—you may go so far.
REYNALDO My lord, that would dishonor him.
POLONIUS Faith no, as you may season it in the charge.   30
    You must not put another scandal on him,
    That he is open to incontinency;
    That's not my meaning. But breathe his faults so quaintly
    That they may seem the taints of liberty,
    The flash and outbreak of a fiery mind,   35
    A savageness in unreclaimed blood,
    Of general assault.
REYNALDO But, my good lord—
POLONIUS Wherefore should you do this?
REYNALDO Ay, my lord,   40
    I would know that.
POLONIUS Marry, sir, here's my drift,
    And I believe it is a fetch of warrant.
    You, laying these slight sullies on my son,
    As 'twere a thing a little soiled i' th' working,   45
    Mark you,
    Your party in converse, him you would sound,
    Having ever seen in the prenominate crimes
    The youth you breathe of guilty, be assured
    He closes with you in this consequence,   50

POLONIUS "And, slightly, him, but"—you might say—"not well.
    But if he's the one I mean, he's very wild,
    Addicted to this and that"—and then accuse him   20
    Of what inventions you please; though, none so gross
    As will dishonor him, don't do that,
    But, sir, such rebellious, wild, and usual slips
    As are the known companions of
    Youth and liberty.   25
REYNALDO Like gambling, my lord?
POLONIUS Yes, or drinking, fencing, swearing,
    Quarreling, whoring—you may go that far.
REYNALDO My lord, that would dishonor him!
POLONIUS Truly, no, as you may soften it in the telling.   30
    You must not slander him in another way,
    Saying that he is given to sexual excess.
    That's not what I mean. You must speak his faults so artfully
    That they seem the blemishes of freedom,
    The impulsiveness of a lively mind,   35
    A wildness of untamed vigor,
    Which assails everyone.
REYNALDO But, my good lord—
POLONIUS Why should you do this?
REYNALDO Yes, my lord,   40
    That I would like to know.
POLONIUS Well, sir, here's my drift,
    And I believe it is a clever device.
    In imputing these slight flaws to my son,
    As it were cloth a little soiled in the handling,   45
    Listen well,
    To the person you're questioning, you sound him out,
    About having seen these named faults
    In the youth you speak of. You can be sure
    He will confide in you like this: 50

"Good sir," or so, or "friend," or "gentleman,"
According to the phrase and the addition
Of man and country.
REYNALDO Very good, my lord.
POLONIUS And then, sir, does a this—a does— what was I   55
about to say? By the mass, I was about to say something.
Where did I leave?
REYNALDO At "closes in the consequence," at "friend" or
so, and "gentleman."
POLONIUS At "closes in the consequence"—ay, marry,   60
He closes with you thus: "I know the gentleman,
I saw him yesterday," or "th' other day"
Or then, or then, with such or such, "and as you say,
There was a gaming, there o'ertook in 's rouse,
There falling out at tennis," or perchance,   65
"I saw him enter such a house of sale"—
Videlicet, a brothel— or so forth. See you now,
Your bait of falsehood take this carp of truth,
And thus do we of wisdom and of reach,
With windlasses and with assays of bias,   70
By indirections find directions out.
So, by my former lecture and advice,
Shall you my son. You have me, have you not?
REYNALDO My lord, I have.
POLONIUS God be wi' ye, fare ye well.   75
REYNALDO Good my lord.
POLONIUS Observe his inclination in yourself.
REYNALDO I shall, my lord.
POLONIUS And let him ply his music.
REYNALDO Well, my lord.   80
POLONIUS Farewell.

Exit REYNALDO

"Good sir," or something, or "friend," or "gentleman,"
According to the conventions and the status
Of the man and the country.

REYNALDO Very good, my lord.

POLONIUS And then, sir, he does this—he does—what was I   55
    about to say? By heaven, I was about to say something.
    Where did I leave off?

REYNALDO At "confide in you like this," at "friend" or
    something, and "gentleman."

POLONIUS At "confide in you like this"—yes, right,   60
    He confides in you thus: "I know the gentleman,
    I saw him yesterday," or "the other day"
    Or then or then, with so-and-so, "and, as you say,
    There he was gambling, there he was drunk,
    There squabbling at tennis," or perhaps,   65
    "I saw him enter a house of ill repute"—
    That is to say, a brothel—and so forth. Do you see?
    You use the bait of falsehood to catch the fish of truth.
    That's how we who are wise and far-seeing
    Use a roundabout and circuitous movement,   70
    Use indirections to find the way things are going.
    So shall you, if you follow my lesson and advice,
    Find out about my son. You see my meaning, do you not?

REYNALDO My lord, I do.

POLONIUS God be with you. Fare you well.   75

REYNALDO Thank you, my lord.

POLONIUS Observe how he is yourself.

REYNALDO I shall, my lord.

POLONIUS And let him go his way.

REYNALDO Of course, my lord.   80

POLONIUS Farewell.

Exit REYNALDO

Enter OPHELIA

How now, Ophelia, what's the matter?

OPHELIA O, my lord, my lord, I have been so affrighted!

POLONIUS With what, i' th' name of God?

OPHELIA My lord, as I was sewing in my closet,   85
    Lord Hamlet, with his doublet all unbraced,
    No hat upon his head, his stockings fouled,
    Ungartered, and down-gyved to his ankle,
    Pale as his shirt, his knees knocking each other,
    And with a look so piteous in purport   90
    As if he had been loosed out of hell
    To speak of horrors—he comes before me.

POLONIUS Mad for thy love?

OPHELIA My lord, I do not know,
    But truly I do fear it.   95

POLONIUS What said he?

OPHELIA He took me by the wrist, and held me hard.
    Then goes he to the length of all his arm,
    And with his other hand thus o'er his brow
    He falls to such perusal of my face   100
    As he would draw it. Long stayed he so.
    At last, a little shaking of mine arm,
    And thrice his head thus waving up and down,
    He raised a sigh so piteous and profound
    As it did seem to shatter all his bulk   105
    And end his being. That done, he lets me go,
    And, with his head over his shoulder turned,
    He seemed to find his way without his eyes,
    For out-a-doors he went without their help
    And to the last bended their light on me.   110

POLONIUS Come, go with me. I will go seek the king.
    This is the very ecstasy of love,
    Whose violent property fordoes itself,

Enter OPHELIA

Well, now, Ophelia, what's the matter?

OPHELIA Oh, my lord, my lord, I have been so frightened!

POLONIUS By what, in the name of God?

OPHELIA My lord, as I was sewing in my room,   85
    Lord Hamlet, with his jacket all unbuttoned;
    No hat upon his head; his stockings dirty,
    Ungartered, fallen down like ankle chains;
    Pale as his shirt; his knees knocking together;
    And with a look so piteous in expression   90
    As if he had been released from hell
    To speak of its horrors—that's how he comes to me.

POLONIUS Mad for love of you?

OPHELIA My lord, I do not know,
    But truly I fear he is.   95

POLONIUS What did he say?

OPHELIA He took me by the wrist and held me hard.
    Then he stretched out his arm at length,
    And with his other hand like this over his brow
    He studied my face so intently   100
    As if he would sketch it. He stayed that way some time.
    At last, shaking my arm a little,
    And nodding his head three times up and down,
    He gave a sigh so pitiful and profound
    That it seemed to shatter his body   105
    And end his life. Having done that, he let me go
    And, his head turned back over his shoulder,
    He seemed to find his way without looking,
    Because he went out-of-doors,
    His eyes always fixed on me.   110

POLONIUS Come, go with me. I will find the king.
    This is the true madness of love,
    Whose violent nature leads to suicide

And leads the will to desperate undertakings
As oft as any passion under heaven   115
That does afflict our natures. I am sorry.
What, have you given him any hard words of late?
OPHELIA No, my good lord, but as you did command,
I did repel his letters, and denied
His access to me.   120
POLONIUS That hath made him mad.
I am sorry that with better heed and judgment
I had not quoted him. I feared he did but trifle,
And meant to wrack thee, but beshrew my jealousy!
By heaven, it is as proper to our age   125
To cast beyond ourselves in our opinions
As it is common for the younger sort
To lack discretion. Come, go we to the king.
This must be known, which being kept close, might move
More grief to hide than hate to utter love.   130
Come.

Exeunt

Scene 2 *Flourish. Enter* CLAUDIUS *and* GERTRUDE, ROSENCRANTZ,
   GUILDENSTERN, *with others*

CLAUDIUS Welcome, dear Rosencrantz and Guildenstern!
Moreover that we much did long to see you,
The need we have to use you did provoke
Our hasty sending. Something have you heard
Of Hamlet's transformation—so call it,   5
Sith nor th' exterior nor the inward man
Resembles that it was. What it should be,
More than his father's death, that thus hath put him
So much from th' understanding of himself,
I cannot dream of. I entreat you both,   10

And tempts the will to desperate undertakings,
As often as any passion under heaven   115
Afflicting human nature. I am sorry.
What, have you spoken harshly to him lately?
OPHELIA No, my good lord, but as you ordered,
I returned his letters and refused
To let him visit me.   120
POLONIUS That has made him mad.
I am sorry that with closer attention and judgment
I had not observed him. I feared he was only trifling
And meant to ruin you. Shame on my suspicions!
By heaven, it is as common for our generation   125
To go too far in our suspicions
As it is for the younger ones
To lack good judgment. Come, we'll go to the king.
This must be known. Being kept secret, it might cause
More grief if hidden than offense if disclosed.   130
Come.

They exit

Scene 2 *Trumpets sound. Enter* CLAUDIUS *and* GERTRUDE,
      ROSENCRANTZ, GUILDENSTERN, *and others*

CLAUDIUS Welcome, dear Rosencrantz and Guildenstern!
As much as we longed to see you,
We had a need for your services, and that was why
We sent for you in haste. You have heard something
Of Hamlet's transformation—call it that,   5
Since neither in body nor in mind is
He like the man he was. What has happened,
Other than his father's death, to put him
So much at odds with himself,
I cannot imagine. So I ask you both,   10

71

That, being of so young days brought up with him,
And sith so neighbored to his youth and havior,
That you vouchsafe your rest here in our court
Some little time, so by your companies
To draw him on to pleasures, and to gather
So much as from occasion you may glean,   15
Whether aught to us unknown afflicts him thus,
That opened lies within our remedy.
GERTRUDE Good gentlemen, he hath much talked of you,
And sure I am, two men there is not living
To whom he more adheres. If it will please you   20
To show us so much gentry and good will
As to expend your time with us awhile,
For the supply and profit of our hope,
Your visitation shall receive such thanks
As fits a king's remembrance.   25
ROSENCRANTZ Both your majesties
Might, by the sovereign power you have of us,
Put your dread pleasures more into command
Than to entreaty.
GUILDENSTERN But we both obey,   30
And here give up ourselves in the full bent
To lay our service freely at your feet,
To be commanded.
CLAUDIUS Thanks, Rosencrantz and gentle Guildenstern.
GERTRUDE Thanks, Guildenstern and gentle Rosencrantz. 35
And I beseech you instantly to visit
My too much changed son. Go, some of you,
And bring these gentlemen where Hamlet is.
GUILDENSTERN Heavens make our presence and our practices
Pleasant and helpful to him.   40
GERTRUDE Ay, amen!

Exit ROSENCRANTZ *and* GUILDENSTERN *with some attendants*

Because you were brought up with him since childhood
And were a part of his youthful way of behaving,
That you agree to remain here in our court
For a little while, so by your company
To draw him on to enjoyment and to gather,
So far as opportunity may allow,   15
Whether something unknown to us is bothering him,
That revealed we can remedy.
GERTRUDE Good gentlemen, he has talked much of you,
    And I am sure, there are not two men alive
    With whom he is closer. If it pleases you   20
    To show us so much courtesy and good will
    As to spend your time with us awhile,
    For the aid and advancement of our hope,
    Your visit shall receive such thanks
    As befits a king's recognition.   25
ROSENCRANTZ Both your majesties
    Might, by the sovereign power you have over us,
    State your fearful wishes more as a command
    Than as a request.
GUILDENSTERN But we both obey.   30
    And here offer ourselves to full capacity
    To lay our service freely at your feet,
    Ready to be commanded.
CLAUDIUS Thanks, Rosencrantz and kind Guildenstern.
GERTRUDE Thanks, Guildenstern and kind Rosencrantz.   35
    And I ask you immediately to visit
    My too-much-altered son. Go some of you
    And take these gentlemen to where Hamlet is.
GUILDENSTERN Pray heaven that our presence and our activities
    Prove pleasing and helpful to him.   40
GERTRUDE Yes, amen to that!

Exit ROSENCRANTZ *and* GUILDENSTERN *with some attendants*

Enter POLONIUS

POLONIUS Th' ambassadors from Norway, my good lord,
    Are joyfully returned.
CLAUDIUS Thou still hast been the father of good news.
POLONIUS Have I, my lord? Assure you, my good liege,   45
    I hold my duty, as I hold my soul,
    Both to my God and to my gracious king;
    And I do think, or else this brain of mine
    Hunts not the trail of policy so sure
    As it hath used to do, that I have found   50
    The very cause of Hamlet's lunacy.
CLAUDIUS O, speak of that, that do I long to hear.
POLONIUS Give first admittance to th' ambassadors;
    My news shall be the fruit to that great feast.
CLAUDIUS Thyself do grace to them and bring them in.   55

                                    Exit POLONIUS

    He tells me, my dear Gertrude, he hath found
    The head and source of all your son's distemper.
GERTRUDE I doubt it is no other but the main—
    His father's death and our o'erhasty marriage.
CLAUDIUS Well, we shall sift him.   60

            Enter VOLTEMAND *and* CORNELIUS *with* POLONIUS

    Welcome, my good friends.
    Say, Voltemand, what from our brother Norway?
VOLTEMAND Most fair return of greetings and desires.
    Upon our first, he sent out to suppress
    His nephew's levies, which to him appeared   65
    To be a preparation 'gainst the Polack,
    But, better looked into, he truly found
    It was against your highness. Whereat, grieved
    That so his sickness, age, and impotence
    Was falsely borne in hand, sends out arrests   70
    On Fortinbras, which he, in brief, obeys,

Enter POLONIUS

POLONIUS The ambassadors from Norway, my good lord,
    Have returned with success.

CLAUDIUS You have always been the father of good news.

POLONIUS Have I, my lord? I assure your majesty   45
    I keep my duty, as I do my soul,
    Both to serve my God and my gracious king.
    And I now think, unless this brain of mine
    Does not follow the scent of politics so keenly
    As it once used to, that I have found   50
    The true cause of Hamlet's lunacy.

CLAUDIUS Oh, speak of that, that I am longing to hear.

POLONIUS First admit the ambassadors;
    My news shall be the dessert of that great feast.

CLAUDIUS Do the honors yourself and bring them in.   55

                     Exit POLONIUS
    He tells me, my dear Gertrude, that he has found
    The origin and source of your son's disorder.

GERTRUDE I suspect it is no other but this cause—
    His father's death and our over-hasty marriage.

CLAUDIUS Well, we'll examine him closely.   60

     Enter VOLTEMAND *and* CORNELIUS *with* POLONIUS
    Welcome, my good friends,
    Tell us, Voltemand, the news from our brother, Norway's king.

VOLTEMAND A favorable response to your greetings and requests.
    At our first request, he sent out orders to suppress
    His nephew's troops, which appeared to him   65
    To be an expedition against the Poles,
    But, more closely looked at, he found it was
    Really against your highness. Whereupon, grieved
    That his sickness, age, and helplessness
    Were misused by false pretenses, he ordered   70
    Fortinbras to stop, which, to conclude, he did,

Receives rebuke from Norway, and, in fine
Makes vow before his uncle never more
To give th' assay of arms against your majesty.
Whereon old Norway, overcome with joy,   75
Gives him three thousand crowns in annual fee
And his commission to employ those soldiers,
So levied as before, against the Polack;
With an entreaty, herein further shown,
That it might please you to give quiet pass   80
Through your dominions for this enterprise,
On such regards of safety and allowance
As therein are set down. [*Hands him a paper*]
CLAUDIUS It likes us well,
And at our more considered time we'll read,   85
Answer, and think upon this business.
Meantime, we thank you for your well-took labor.
Go to your rest; at night we'll feast together.
Most welcome home!
                              Exeunt AMBASSADORS
POLONIUS This business is well ended.   90
My liege, and madam, to expostulate
What majesty should be, what duty is,
Why day is day, night night, and time is time,
Were nothing but to waste night, day, and time.
Therefore, since brevity is the soul of wit   95
And tediousness the limbs and outward flourishes,
I will be brief. Your noble son is mad.
Mad call I it, for to define true madness,
What is 't but to be nothing else but mad?
But let that go.   100
GERTRUDE More matter with less art.
POLONIUS Madam, I swear I use no art at all.

Was rebuked by the king, and, to conclude,
Took a vow before his uncle to never more
Make an armed attempt against your majesty.
At that, the old king, overcome with joy,   75
Gave him three thousand crowns annually
And a commission to employ those soldiers
He had levied before, against the Poles;
Together with a request, which I have here,
That it might please you to give safe passage   80
Through your dominions for this expedition,
With such conditions and terms
As herein are set down. [*Hands him a paper*]
CLAUDIUS It pleases us,
And when we have time to consider it, we'll read,   85
Answer, and reflect upon this business.
Meanwhile, we thank you for your successful efforts.
Go get some rest; tonight, we'll feast together.
You're most welcome home!
                    Exit VOLTEMAND *and* CORNELIUS
POLONIUS This business is happily ended.   90
My king, and madam, to debate
What kingship is, what duty is,
Why day is day, night night, and time is time,
Is nothing but to waste night, day, and time.
Therefore, since brevity is the soul of wit,   95
And longwindedness only appearance and dress,
I will be brief. Your noble son is mad.
Mad I call it, for to define true madness,
What is it, but nothing else but madness?
But let that go.   100
GERTRUDE More content with less art, please.
POLONIUS Madam, I swear I use no art at all.

That he is mad, 'tis true; 'tis true, 'tis pity,
And pity 'tis 'tis true—a foolish figure,
But farewell it, for I will use no art.   105
Mad let us grant him then, and now remains
That we find out the cause of this effect,
Or, rather say, the cause of this defect,
For this effect defective comes by cause.
Thus it remains, and the remainder thus.   110
Perpend.
I have a daughter—have her while she is mine—
Who in her duty and obedience, mark,
Hath given me this. Now gather and surmise.
[*Reads the letter*]
"To the celestial, and my soul's idol, the most beautified Ophelia,"   115
That's an ill phrase, a vile phrase, "beautified" is a vile phrase,
but you shall hear. Thus: "In her excellent white bosom,
these, *et cetera*."
GERTRUDE Came this from Hamlet to her?
POLONIUS Good madam, stay awhile, I will be faithful.   120
          "Doubt thou the stars are fire,
           Doubt that the sun doth move,
           Doubt truth to be a liar,
           But never doubt I love.
"O dear Ophelia, I am ill at these numbers, I have not art to   125
reckon my groans; but I love thee best, O most best, believe
it. Adieu. Thine evermore, most dear lady, whilst this machine
is to him, Hamlet."
     This in obedience hath my daughter shown me,
     And, more above, hath his solicitings,   130
     As they fell out, by time, by means, and place
     All given to mine ear.
CLAUDIUS But how hath she
          Received his love?

That he is mad, it's true. That it's true is a pity.
And a pity that it's true—a foolish figure of speech.
But forget that, for I will use no art.   105
Then, let us say that he is mad. It now remains
That we find out the cause of this effect,
Or, rather say, the cause of this defect,
For this defect must have a cause.
Thus it remains, and it remains thus.   110
Consider.
I have a daughter—have her while she is unmarried—
Who dutifully and obediently, please note,
Has given me this. Now, draw your own conclusions.
[*Reads the letter*]
"To the celestial, and my soul's idol, the most beautified Ophelia." 115
That's a bad word, a vile word. "Beautified" is a vile word,
but you shall hear more. Thus: "In her excellent white bosom,
these, *et cetera*."
GERTRUDE Hamlet wrote this to her?
POLONIUS Good madam, wait awhile. I will be accurate.   120
                "Doubt that the stars are fire,
                Doubt that the sun does move,
                Doubt that truth be a liar,
                But never doubt I love.
"Oh, dear Ophelia, I am not good at writing verse. I have no art to 125
tell my sufferings, but I love you best, more than anyone. Believe
me. Adieu. Yours evermore, most dear lady, while this body still
belongs to me, Hamlet."
        This, out of obedience, my daughter has shown me,
        And more of his overtures,   130
        As they came about—by time, by means, and place—
        All she has told me.
CLAUDIUS But how has she
        Responded to his love?

POLONIUS What do you think of me?   135
CLAUDIUS As of a man faithful and honorable.
POLONIUS I would fain prove so. But what might you think,
    When I had seen this hot love on the wing—
    As I perceived it, I must tell you that,
    Before my daughter told me—what might you,   140
    Or my dear majesty, your queen here, think,
    If I had played the desk, or table-book,
    Or given my heart a winking, mute and dumb,
    Or looked upon this love with idle sight—
    What might you think? No, I went round to work,   145
    And my young mistress thus I did bespeak:
    "Lord Hamlet is a prince out of thy star.
    This must not be." And then I prescripts gave her,
    That she should lock herself from his resort,
    Admit no messengers, receive no tokens.   150
    Which done, she took the fruits of my advice,
    And he, repulsed—a short tale to make—
    Fell into a sadness, then into a fast,
    Thence to a watch, thence into a weakness,
    Thence to a lightness, and by this declension   155
    Into the madness wherein now he raves,
    And all we mourn for.
CLAUDIUS Do you think 'tis this?
GERTRUDE It may be, very like.
POLONIUS Hath there been such a time, I'd fain know that,   160
    That I have positively said "'Tis so,"
    When it proved otherwise?
CLAUDIUS Not that I know.
POLONIUS Take this from this, if this be otherwise.
    If circumstances lead me, I will find   165
    Where truth is hid, though it were hid indeed
    Within the center.

POLONIUS How do you think of me?   135
CLAUDIUS As a man faithful and honorable.
POLONIUS So I would gladly prove. But what would you think,
    When I had seen this hot love taking wing—
    And I recognized it, I must tell you that,
    Before my daughter told me—what would you think,   140
    Or my dear majesty, your queen here, think,
    If I had taken note, and like a diary left in a desk,
    Had closed the eyes of my heart, mute and dumb,
    And looked upon this love as if it didn't matter.
    What might you think? No, I went right to work,   145
    And to my young lady this I said:
    "Lord Hamlet is like a star in another sphere.
    This must not be." And then I gave her orders,
    That she should lock herself away from his visits,
    Admit no messengers, accept no love tokens.   150
    That done, she reaped the harvest of my advice,
    And he, rejected—to make a long story short—
    Became depressed, then could not eat,
    Then could not sleep, then became weak,
    Then light-headed, and by this descent came   155
    Into the madness in which he now raves,
    And for which we all mourn.
CLAUDIUS Do you think this is it?
GERTRUDE It may be, very likely.
POLONIUS Has there ever been a time, I'd like to know,   160
    That I have positively said, "This is so,"
    And it proved otherwise?
CLAUDIUS Not that I know.
POLONIUS Take this from this, if it be otherwise.
    If the evidence guides me, I will find   165
    Where the truth is hidden, even though it were hidden
    In the center of the earth.

CLAUDIUS How may we try it further?

POLONIUS You know sometimes he walks four hours together

    Here in the lobby. 170

GERTRUDE So he does, indeed.

POLONIUS At such time I'll loose my daughter to him.

    Be you and I behind an arras then.

    Mark the encounter: if he love her not,

    And be not from his reason fallen thereon, 175

    Let me be no assistant for a state,

    But keep a farm and carters.

CLAUDIUS We will try it.

           Enter HAMLET *reading a book*

GERTRUDE But look where sadly the poor wretch comes reading.

POLONIUS Away, I do beseech you both, away. 180

    I'll board him presently. O, give me leave.

           Exeunt CLAUDIUS *and* GERTRUDE *and* ATTENDANTS

    How does my good Lord Hamlet?

HAMLET Well, God-a-mercy.

POLONIUS Do you know me, my lord?

HAMLET Excellent well, you are a fishmonger. 185

POLONIUS Not I, my lord.

HAMLET Then I would you were so honest a man.

POLONIUS Honest, my lord?

HAMLET Ay, sir. To be honest, as this world goes, is to be one

    man picked out of ten thousand. 190

POLONIUS That's very true, my lord.

HAMLET For if the sun breed maggots in a dead dog, being a good

    kissing carrion—Have you a daughter?

POLONIUS I have, my lord.

HAMLET Let her not walk i' th' sun. Conception is a blessing, but as 195

    your daughter may conceive—Friend, look to 't.

POLONIUS [*Aside*] How say you by that? Still harping on my daughter.

    Yet he knew me not at first, a said I was a fishmonger—a is far

CLAUDIUS How can we test it further?

POLONIUS You know that he sometimes walks four hours on end
    Here in the hall. 170

GERTRUDE So he does, indeed.

POLONIUS At such a time, I'll turn loose my daughter on him.
    You and I will be behind a tapestry then,
    And watch their encounter. If he doesn't love her,
    And hasn't lost his reason as a result, 175
    Let me cease to be a minister of state,
    But keep a farm and wagons.

CLAUDIUS We will try it.

Enter HAMLET *reading a book*

GERTRUDE But look, how sadly the poor wretch comes, reading.

POLONIUS Away, both of you, please, away. 180
    I'll speak to him immediately. Oh, allow me.

Exit CLAUDIUS, GERTRUDE, *and* ATTENDANTS

    How is my good Lord Hamlet?

HAMLET Well, God be thanked.

POLONIUS Do you know me, my lord?

HAMLET Extremely well. You are a fish peddler. 185

POLONIUS Not I, my lord.

HAMLET Then I wish you were so honest a man.

POLONIUS Honest, my lord?

HAMLET Yes, sir. To be honest, as this world goes, is to be one
    in ten thousand men. 190

POLONIUS That's very true, my lord.

HAMLET If the sun can breed maggots in a dead dog by kissing
    the carrion—Have you a daughter?

POLONIUS I have, my lord.

HAMLET Let her not walk in the sun. Conception is a blessing, but as 195
    your daughter may conceive—Friend, watch it.

POLONIUS [*Aside*] Why do you say that? Still harping on my daughter.
Yet he didn't know me at first. He said I was a fish peddler—he is far

gone, far gone. And truly, in my youth I suffered much
extremity for love, very near this. I'll speak to him again.— 200
What do you read, my lord?

HAMLET Words, words, words.

POLONIUS What is the matter, my lord?

HAMLET Between who?

POLONIUS I mean the matter that you read, my lord. 205

HAMLET Slanders, sir, for the satirical rogue says here that old
men have grey beards, that their faces are wrinkled, their eyes
purging thick amber and plum-tree gum, and that they have a
plentiful lack of wit, together with most weak hams. All of
which, sir, though I most powerfully and potently believe, yet I 210
hold it not honesty to have it thus set down. For yourself, sir,
shall grow old as I am, if like a crab you could go backward.

POLONIUS [*Aside*] Though this be madness, yet there is a method
in 't.—Will you walk out of the air, my lord?

HAMLET Into my grave? 215

POLONIUS Indeed, that's out of the air. [*Aside*] How pregnant
sometimes his replies are! A happiness that often madness hits
on, which reason and sanity could not so prosperously be
delivered of. I will leave him, and suddenly contrive the means
of meeting between him and my daughter.—My honorable lord, 220
I will most humbly take my leave of you.

HAMLET You cannot, sir, take from me anything that I will more
willingly part withal; except my life, except my life, except
my life.

POLONIUS Fare you well, my lord. 225

HAMLET [*Aside*] These tedious old fools!

               Enter GUILDENSTERN *and* ROSENCRANTZ

POLONIUS You go to seek the Lord Hamlet. There he is.

ROSENCRANTZ God save you, sir.

                     Exit POLONIUS

GUILDENSTERN My honored lord!

gone, far gone. And in my youth, truly, I suffered extremely
for love, much like this. I'll speak to him again.— 200
What are you reading, my lord?

HAMLET Words, words, words.

POLONIUS What is the matter, my lord?

HAMLET Between who?

POLONIUS I mean the subject matter of what you read, my lord. 205

HAMLET Slanders, sir. The satirical rogue says here that old
men have grey beards, that their faces are wrinkled, their eyes
oozing a thick discharge, amber and resin, and that they have a
plentiful lack of brains, together with very weak thighs. All of
which, sir, I most fervently believe. But I hold it not honorable 210
to have written it down like this. As for yourself, sir, you shall
grow old like me, if you can go backward like a crab.

POLONIUS [*Aside*] Though this is madness, there is still some sense
in it.—Will you come out in the air, my lord?

HAMLET Into my grave? 215

POLONIUS Indeed, that's out in the air. [*Aside*] How meaningful
his replies sometimes are! An aptness that madness often
hits on that reason and sanity could not give birth to. I will
leave him and immediately arrange the means by which he
and my daughter may meet.—My honorable lord, I will 220
most humbly take my leave of you.

HAMLET You cannot, sir, take from me anything that I will
more willingly part with. Except my life, except my life,
except my life.

POLONIUS Farewell, my lord. 225

HAMLET [*Aside*] These tedious old fools!

        Enter GUILDENSTERN *and* ROSENCRANTZ

POLONIUS You come to seek the Lord Hamlet. There he is.

ROSENCRANTZ God save you, sir.

              Exit POLONIUS

GUILDENSTERN My honored lord!

ROSENCRANTZ My most dear lord!   230
HAMLET My excellent good friends! How dost thou, Guildenstern?
    Ah, Rosencrantz. Good lads, how do you both?
ROSENCRANTZ As the indifferent children of the earth.
GUILDENSTERN Happy in that we are not overhappy. On Fortune's
    cap, we are not the very button.   235
HAMLET Nor the soles of her shoe?
ROSENCRANTZ Neither, my lord.
HAMLET Then you live about her waist, or in the middle of her
    favors?
GUILDENSTERN Faith, her privates we.   240
HAMLET In the secret parts of Fortune? O, most true. She is
    a strumpet. What news?
ROSENCRANTZ None, my lord, but that the world's grown honest.
HAMLET Then is doomsday near—but your news is not true. Let me
    question more in particular. What have you, my good friends,   245
    deserved at the hands of Fortune, that she sends you to prison hither?
GUILDENSTERN Prison, my lord?
HAMLET Denmark's a prison.
ROSENCRANTZ Then is the world one.
HAMLET A goodly one, in which there are many confines,   250
    wards, and dungeons, Denmark being one o' th' worst.
ROSENCRANTZ We think not so, my lord.
HAMLET Why, then, 'tis none to you, for there is nothing either
    good or bad but thinking makes it so. To me, it is a prison.
ROSENCRANTZ Why then your ambition makes it one; 'tis too   255
    narrow for your mind.
HAMLET O God, I could be bounded in a nutshell and count myself
    a king of infinite space, were it not that I have bad dreams.
GUILDENSTERN Which dreams indeed are ambition, for the very
    substance of the ambitious is merely the shadow of a dream.   260
HAMLET A dream itself is but a shadow.
ROSENCRANTZ Truly, and I hold ambition of so airy and light a

ROSENCRANTZ My most dear lord.   230

HAMLET My excellent good friends! How are you Guildenstern?
    Ah, Rosencrantz. Good lads, how are you both?

ROSENCRANTZ Like the general run of men.

GUILDENSTERN Happy in that we are not too happy. On the
    cap of Fortune, we're not the button on the top.   235

HAMLET Nor the soles of her shoes?

ROSENCRANTZ Neither, my lord.

HAMLET Then you live around her waist, or at the middle
    of her favors?

GUILDENSTERN Faith, we're her privates.   240

HAMLET In the secret parts of Fortune? Oh, most true. She is
    a whore. What's the news?

ROSENCRANTZ None, my lord, except that the world's grown honest.

HAMLET Then doomsday is near. But your news is not true. Let me
    question you in particular. What have you, my good friends,   245
    deserved from the hand of Fortune that she sends you to prison here?

GUILDENSTERN Prison, my lord?

HAMLET Denmark's a prison.

ROSENCRANTZ Then so is the world.

HAMLET A large one, in which there are many jails, cells, and   250
    dungeons, Denmark being one of the worst.

ROSENCRANTZ We don't think so, my lord.

HAMLET Why, then, it's not one for you. Things are neither good nor
    bad; they are what you think they are. To me, Denmark's a prison.

ROSENCRANTZ Why, then, your ambition makes it one; it's too   255
    limiting for your mind.

HAMLET Oh, God, I could be enclosed in a nutshell and count myself
    a king of infinite space, if it were not that I have bad dreams.

GUILDENSTERN Those dreams, indeed, are ambition; for the food of
    the ambitious is merely the shadow of a dream.   260

HAMLET A dream itself is only a shadow.

ROSENCRANTZ True, and I regard ambition as so airy and light a quality that it is but a shadow's shadow.

HAMLET Then are our beggars bodies, and our monarchs and out-
stretched heroes the beggars' shadows. Shall we to th' court?   265
For, by my fay, I cannot reason.

ROSENCRANTZ }

GUILDENSTERN } We'll wait upon you.

HAMLET No such matter. I will not sort you with the rest of my
servants; for to speak to you like an honest man, I am most
dreadfully attended. But in the beaten way of friendship,   270
what make you at Elsinore?

ROSENCRANTZ To visit you, my lord, no other occasion.

HAMLET Beggar that I am, I am even poor in thanks, but I thank
you—and sure, dear friends, my thanks are too dear a halfpenny.
Were you not sent for? Is it your own inclining? Is it a free   275
visitation? Come, deal justly with me. Come, come. Nay, speak.

GUILDENSTERN What should we say, my lord?

HAMLET Why, anything but to the purpose. You were sent for—and
there is a kind of confession in your looks which your modesties
have not craft enough to color. I know the good king and queen   280
have sent for you.

ROSENCRANTZ To what end, my lord?

HAMLET That you must teach me. But let me conjure you, by the
rights of our fellowship, by the consonancy of our youth, by
the obligation of our ever-preserved love, and by what more dear   285
a better proposer can charge you withal, be even and direct with
me, whether you were sent for or no.

ROSENCRANTZ [To GUILDENSTERN] What say you?

HAMLET [Aside] Nay, then, I have an eye of you.—If you love me,
hold not off.   290

GUILDENSTERN My lord, we were sent for.

HAMLET I will tell you why. So shall my anticipation prevent your
discovery, and your secrecy to the king and queen molt no
feather. I have of late, but wherefore I know not, lost all my

thing, it is only a shadow's shadow.

HAMLET Then beggars have real bodies, and our kings and
    oversized heroes are the beggars' shadows. Shall we take   265
    it to court? For, by my faith, I cannot argue further.

ROSENCRANTZ }

GUILDENSTERN }   We'll serve you.

HAMLET No such thing. I will not have you classed as my
    servants, for, to tell the truth, I am most dreadfully looked
    after. But in the well-worn path of friendship, what brings   270
    you to Elsinore?

ROSENCRANTZ To visit you, my lord. No other reason.

HAMLET Being a beggar, I am even poor in thanks, but I thank
    you. And, truly, dear friends, my thanks are too costly at a
    halfpenny. Were you not sent for? Was it your own wish? Is this   275
    a free visit? Come, deal justly with me. Come, come. Now, speak.

GUILDENSTERN What should we say, my lord?

HAMLET Why, anything. But come to the point. You were sent for
    —there is a kind of confession in your looks which your sense
    of shame is not artful enough to cover. I know the good king   280
    and queen have sent for you.

ROSENCRANTZ For what purpose, my lord?

HAMLET You must teach me that. But let me solemnly entreat you
    by the bonds of our fellowship, by the harmony of our youthful
    days, by the claims of our long-standing love, and by whatever   285
    is more precious that could be proposed, be straightforward and
    direct with me whether you were sent for or not.

ROSENCRANTZ [*To* GUILDENSTERN] What will you say?

HAMLET [*Aside*] Now, I have an eye on you.—If you're my friends,
    do not hold back.   290

GUILDENSTERN My lord, we were sent for.

HAMLET I will tell you why. And so shall my answer prevent your
    discovery and your secret remain intact with the king and the
    queen. I have lately, but I don't know why, lost all my

mirth, forgone all custom of exercises; and indeed it goes   295
so heavily with my disposition that this goodly frame, the
earth, seems to me a sterile promontory; this most excellent
canopy, the air, look you, this brave o'erhanging firmament,
this majestical roof, fretted with golden fire—why, it appeareth
no other thing to me but a foul and pestilent congregation   300
of vapors. What a piece of work is a man, how noble in
reason, how infinite in faculties, in form and moving how
express and admirable; in action how like an angel, in
apprehension how like a god! The beauty of the world,
the paragon of animals—and yet to me, what is this quintessence   305
of dust? Man delights not me—no, nor woman neither, though
by your smiling you seem to say so.

ROSENCRANTZ My lord, there was no such stuff in my thoughts.

HAMLET Why did ye laugh then, when I said "man delights not me"?

ROSENCRANTZ To think, my lord, if you delight not in man, what   310
Lenten entertainment the players shall receive from you. We
coted them on the way, and hither are they coming to offer
you service.

HAMLET He that plays the king shall be welcome—his majesty shall
have tribute of me; the adventurous knight shall use his foil and   315
target, the lover shall not sigh gratis, the humorous man shall end
his part in peace, the clown shall make those laugh whose lungs
are tickle o' th' sere, and the lady shall say her mind freely—or
the blank verse shall halt for 't. What players are they?

ROSENCRANTZ Even those you were wont to take such delight in,   320
the tragedians of the city.

HAMLET How chances it they travel? Their residence, both in
reputation and profit, was better both ways.

ROSENCRANTZ I think their inhibition comes by the means of the late
innovation.   325

HAMLET Do they hold the same estimation they did when I was in the
city? Are they so followed?

cheerfulness, given up all usual pastimes; and, indeed, 295
my spirits are so weighed down that this goodly frame,
the earth, seems to me a barren point of rock; this
admirable canopy, the air, look, this splendid overhanging
sky, this majestic roof, laced with golden fire—why, it
appears to me nothing but a foul and poisonous collection 300
of vapors. What a piece of work is a man! How noble in
his reason; how infinite in powers; in form and movement,
how exact and admirable; in action, how like an angel; in
understanding, how like a god! The world's most beautiful
creature, a paragon of animals—and yet to me, what is this 305
very essence of dust? Man gives me no pleasure—no, nor
woman either, though by your smiles you seem to say so.

ROSENCRANTZ My lord, I was thinking no such thing.

HAMLET Why did you laugh when I said "man gives me no pleasure"?

ROSENCRANTZ I thought, my lord, if you take no pleasure in men, 310
what a meager reception the actors shall receive from you. We
overtook them on the way, and they are coming here to offer
you their services.

HAMLET He that plays the king shall be welcome—his majesty shall
receive my tribute; the wandering knight shall use his sword and 315
shield; the lover shall not sigh for nothing; the ill-tempered man
shall say his lines unchecked; the clown shall make those who
laugh easily, laugh; and the lady shall speak her mind openly—
or the blank verse will sound lame. What actors are these?

ROSENCRANTZ They are the same actors you used to take such 320
delight in, the tragedians from the city.

HAMLET How does it happen they are traveling? They did better in
reputation and profit when they stayed at home.

ROSENCRANTZ I think they are forbidden to play in the city because
of recent disturbances. 325

HAMLET Do they have as good a reputation as they did when I was
in the city? Are they as popular?

ROSENCRANTZ No, indeed are they not.

HAMLET How comes it? Do they grow rusty?

ROSENCRANTZ Nay, their endeavor keeps in the wonted pace, but   330
    there is, sir, an aerie of children, little eyases, that cry out on
    the top of question and are most tyrannically clapped for 't.
    These are now the fashion, and so berattle the common stages
    (so they call them) that many wearing rapiers are afraid of goose
    quills, and dare scarce come thither.   335

HAMLET What, are they children? Who maintains 'em? How are
    they escoted? Will they pursue the quality no longer than they
    can sing? Will they not say afterwards, if they should grow
    themselves to common players—as it is most like, if their means
    are no better—their writers do them wrong to make them
    exclaim against their own succession?   340

ROSENCRANTZ Faith, there has been much to-do on both sides, and
    the nation holds it no sin to tar them to controversy. There was
    for a while no money bid for argument unless the poet and the
    player went to cuffs in the question.   345

HAMLET Is 't possible?

GUILDENSTERN O, there has been much throwing about of brains.

HAMLET Do the boys carry it away?

ROSENCRANTZ Ay, that they do, my lord, Hercules and his load too.

HAMLET It is not very strange, for my uncle is a king of Denmark,   350
    and those that would make mouths at him while my father lived
    give twenty, forty, fifty, a hundred ducats apiece for his picture
    in little. 'Sblood, there is something in this more than natural, if
    philosophy could find it out.

A flourish.

GUILDENSTERN There are the players.   355

HAMLET Gentlemen, you are welcome to Elsinore. Your hands, come
    then. Th' appurtenance of welcome is fashion and ceremony. Let
    me comply with you in this garb, lest my extent to the players,
    which I tell you must show fairly outwards, should more appear

ROSENCRANTZ No, indeed they are not.

HAMLET How's that? Have they grown rusty?

ROSENCRANTZ No, they've kept up their standards, but there   330
    is, sir, a nest of child actors, little hawks, who speak their lines
    in loud, shrill voices and are excessively applauded for it. These
    are now the fashion, and so shake the common stages (as they
    call them) that many men-about-town, afraid of being satirized,
    dare not be seen there.   335

HAMLET What, are they children? Who runs them? How are they
    paid? Will they pursue the profession only until their voices
    change? Will they not say later, if they themselves grow up to
    be "common actors"—as is most likely, since it's all they can
    do—that their writers wronged them by making them denounce   340
    their own profession?

ROSENCRANTZ Faith, there has been much protest on both sides, and
    the public thinks it's no sin to incite them to controversy. At one
    time, there was no money for a new play unless the story had the
    children's writers and the common actors come to blows.   345

HAMLET Is it possible?

GUILDENSTERN Oh, there was much intellectual debate.

HAMLET Do the boys carry off the victory?

ROSENCRANTZ Yes, they do, my lord, even over the Globe.

HAMLET It is not so strange. My uncle is king of Denmark, and those   350
    who used to make faces at him when my father was alive give
    twenty, forty, fifty, a hundred ducats apiece for a portrait of him
    in miniature. God's blood! There is something in this that's not
    natural, if only science could find it out.

Trumpets sound.

GUILDENSTERN There are the actors.   355

HAMLET Gentlemen, you are welcome to Elsinore. Come, give me
    your hands. The accompaniment to welcome is show and ceremony.
    Let me pay the usual courtesies in this way in case what I show the
    actors—which I tell you will appear very cordial—seems superior

like entertainment than yours. You are welcome—but my   360
uncle-father and aunt-mother are deceived.

GUILDENSTERN In what, my dear lord?

HAMLET I am but mad north-north-west. When the wind is southerly,
I know a hawk from a handsaw.

Enter POLONIUS

POLONIUS Well be with you, gentlemen.   365

HAMLET Hark you, Guildenstern, and you too—at each ear a hearer.
That great baby you see there is not yet out of his swaddling clouts.

ROSENCRANTZ Happily he's the second time come to them, for they
say an old man is twice a child.

HAMLET I will prophesy he comes to tell me of the players; mark   370
it.—You say right, sir, a Monday morning, 'twas then indeed.

POLONIUS My lord, I have news to tell you.

HAMLET My lord, I have news to tell you. When Roscius was an
actor in Rome—

POLONIUS The actors are come hither, my lord.   375

HAMLET Buzz, buzz!

POLONIUS Upon my honor—

HAMLET Then came each actor on his ass.

POLONIUS The best actors in the world, either for tragedy, comedy,
history, pastoral, pastoral-comical, historical-pastoral, tragical-   380
historical, tragical-comical, historical-pastoral, scene individable
or poem unlimited. Seneca cannot be too heavy, nor Plautus
too light. For the law of writ and the liberty, these are the
only men.

HAMLET O Jephthah, judge of Israel, what a treasure hadst thou!   385

POLONIUS What a treasure had he, my lord?

HAMLET Why—
"One fair daughter and no more,
The which he loved passing well."

POLONIUS [*Aside*] Still on my daughter.   390

HAMLET Am I not i' th' right, old Jephthah?

to the welcome I give you. You are welcome—but my   360
    uncle-father and aunt-mother are deceived.

GUILDENSTERN In what, my dear lord?

HAMLET I am only mad north-north-west. When the wind is
    southerly, I can tell a hawk from a handsaw.

Enter POLONIUS

POLONIUS I hope you are well, gentlemen.   365

HAMLET Listen, Guildenstern, and you too—one at each ear. That
    great baby you see there is not yet out of his swaddling clothes.

ROSENCRANTZ Perhaps it's the second time around. They say an old
    man is in his second childhood.

HAMLET I will prophesy he comes to tell me about the actors; take   370
    note.—You are right, sir, a Monday morning. It was then, indeed.

POLONIUS My lord, I have news to tell you.

HAMLET My lord, I have news to tell you. When Roscius was an
    actor in Rome—

POLONIUS The actors have come here, my lord.   375

HAMLET Buzz, buzz!

POLONIUS Upon my honor—

HAMLET Then came each actor on his ass—

POLONIUS The best actors in the world, either for tragedy, comedy,
    history, pastoral, pastoral-comical, historical-pastoral, tragical-   380
    historical, tragical-comical, historical-pastoral, plays that
    observe classical unities and those that don't. Seneca's plays are
    not too serious nor Plautus' too light. For plays that follow the
    rules and those that do not, these are the only men.

HAMLET Oh, Jephthah, judge of Israel, what a treasure you had!   385

POLONIUS What treasure did he have, my lord?

HAMLET Why—

      "One fair daughter and no more,
      The which he loved passing well."

POLONIUS [*Aside*] Still thinking of my daughter.   390

HAMLET Am I not right, old Jephthah?

POLONIUS If you call me "Jephthah," my lord, I have a daughter
    that I love passing well.
HAMLET Nay, that follows not.
POLONIUS What follows then, my lord?   395
HAMLET Why—
          "As by lot, God wot"
    And then you know—
          "It came to pass, as most like it was"—
    The first row of the pious chanson will show you more, for   400
    look where my abridgment comes.
                     Enter the PLAYERS
    Y'are welcome, masters, welcome all. I am glad to see thee well.
    Welcome, good friends. O my old friend! Why, thy face is valanced
    since I saw thee last. Com'st thou to beard me in Denmark? What,
    my young lady and mistress—by'r lady, your ladyship is nearer to   405
    heaven than when I saw you last by the altitude of a chopine. Pray
    God your voice, like a piece of uncurrent gold, be not cracked within
    the ring. Masters, you are all welcome. We'll e'en to 't like French
    falconers, fly at anything we see. We'll have a speech straight. Come
    give us a taste of your quality. Come, a passionate speech.   410
FIRST PLAYER What speech, my good lord?
HAMLET I heard thee speak me a speech once, but it was never acted, or,
    if it was, not above once, for the play, I remember, pleased not the
    million: 'twas caviary to the general. But it was, as I received it,
    and others whose judgments in such matters cried in the top of   415
    mine, an excellent play, well digested in the scenes, set down
    with as much modesty as cunning. I remember one said there
    were no sallets in the lines to make the matter more savory, nor
    no matter in the phrase that might indict the author of affectation,
    but called it an honest method, as wholesome as sweet and, by
    very much, more handsome than fine. One speech in 't I   420
    chiefly loved, 'twas Aeneas' tale to Dido, and thereabout of it
    especially where he speaks of Priam's slaughter. If it live in your
    memory, begin at this line, let me see, let me see—

POLONIUS Since you call me "Jephthah," my lord, I have a daughter
    that I love very much.
HAMLET No, that doesn't follow.
POLONIUS Then what follows, my lord?   395
HAMLET Why—
        "As by chance, God knows"
    And then you know—
        "It came to pass, as it should"—
    The first verse of the pious ballad will tell you more, but   400
    look, I am cut short.

Enter the ACTORS

    You are welcome, masters, welcome all. I am glad to see you well.
    Welcome, good friends. Oh, my old friend! Why, your face has
    sprouted a beard since I saw you last. Have you come to beard me
    in Denmark? What, my young lady—by our Lady, you have grown   405
    a little nearer heaven with those high heels. Pray God your voice
    has not broken, making you unfit for your parts, like a damaged coin.
    Masters, you are all welcome. We'll have a go at anything we see,
    like French falconers. We'll have a speech right away. Come, give
    us a taste of your skill. Come, a passionate speech.   410
FIRST ACTOR Which speech, my lord?
HAMLET I heard you deliver a speech once, but it was never acted—or,
    if it was, not more than once. The play, I remember, did not please
    the crowd: it was like caviar to the masses. But it was, in my opinion
    and that of others whose judgments in such matters were better than   415
    mine, an excellent play, well-crafted in the scenes, and written with
    as much restraint as skill. I remember someone said there was no
    spice in the lines to make them sharp, nor anything in the
    expression that might make the author guilty of affectation. It
    was called an honest style, as wholesome as it was sweet and
    more natural than showy. One speech in it I chiefly loved.   420
    It was the story Aeneas told to Dido, particularly when he
    speaks of the slaughter of Priam. If it lives in your memory,
    begin at this line. Let me see, let me see—

"The rugged Pyrrhus, like th' Hyrcanian beast"—
'Tis not so, it begins with Pyrrhus—   425
"The rugged Pyrrhus, he whose sable arms,
Black as his purpose, did the night resemble
When he lay couched in th' ominous horse,
Hath now this dread and black complexion smeared
With heraldy more dismal. Head to foot   430
Now is he total gules, horridly tricked
With blood of fathers, mothers, daughters, sons,
Baked and impasted with the parching streets,
That lend a tyrannous and a damned light
To their lord's murder. Roasted in wrath and fire,   435
And thus o'ersized with coagulate gore,
With eyes like carbuncles, the hellish Pyrrhus
Old grandsire Priam seeks—"
So, proceed you.
POLONIUS 'Fore God, my lord, well spoken, with good accent   440

and good discretion.
FIRST PLAYER "Anon he finds him,
Striking too short at Greeks. His antique sword,
Rebellious to his arm, lies where it falls,
Repugnant to command. Unequal matched,   445
Pyrrhus at Priam drives, in rage strikes wide,
But with the whiff and wind of his fell sword
Th' unnerved father falls. Then senseless Ilium,
Seeming to feel this blow, with flaming top
Stoops to his base, and with a hideous crash   450
Takes prisoner Pyrrhus' ear; for lo, his sword,
Which was declining on the milky head
Of reverend Priam, seemed i' th' air to stick.
So, as a painted tyrant, Pyrrhus stood,
And, like a neutral to his will and matter,   455
Did nothing.

"The rugged Pyrrhus, like a Hyrcanian tiger"—
That's not right. It begins with Pyrrhus—   425
"The rugged Pyrrhus, he whose sable armor,
Black as his purpose, looked like the night
When he lay hidden in the Trojan horse,
Has now this fearful, black appearance smeared
With a pattern more sinister. Head to foot,   430
He is now all red, horridly covered
With blood of fathers, mothers, daughters, sons,
Baked and crusted by the heat of the flaming streets
That give a ferocious and a damned light
To their lord's murder. Roasted in wrath and fire,   435
And covered over with congealed gore,
With eyes like carbuncles, the hellish Pyrrhus
Old grandfather Priam seeks—"
So, you proceed.
POLONIUS By God, my lord, well spoken, good delivery and   440
good judgment.
FIRST ACTOR "Soon he finds him,
Striking short at Greeks. His antique sword,
Too heavy for his arm, lies where it falls,
Resisting command. Unequally matched,   445
Pyrrhus drives at Priam, and enraged strikes wide,
But with the gust and wind of his cruel sword
The weakened father falls. Then the tower of Ilium,
Seeming to feel this blow, its top aflame,
Falls to the ground, and with a hideous crash   450
Deafens Pyrrhus' ear; for lo, his sword,
Which was descending on the white-haired head
Of esteemed Priam, seemed to stick in mid-air.
So, like a picture of a tyrant, Pyrrhus stood,
And, indifferent to will and task,   455
Did nothing.

But as we often see against some storm
A silence in the heavens, the rack stand still
The bold winds speechless, and the orb below
As hush as death, anon the dreadful thunder   460
Doth rend the region; so, after Pyrrhus' pause,
Aroused vengeance sets him new a-work,
And never did the Cyclops' hammers fall
On Mars's armor, forged for proof eterne,
With less remorse than Pyrrhus' bleeding sword   465
Now falls on Priam.
Out, out, thou strumpet Fortune! All you gods,
In general synod take away her power,
Break all the spokes and fellies from her wheel,
And bowl the round nave down the hill of heaven   470
As low as to the fiends."

POLONIUS This is too long.

HAMLET It shall to th' barber's with your beard. Prithee say on.
He's for a jig or a tale of bawdry, or he sleeps. Say on,
come to Hecuba.   475

FIRST PLAYER "But who—ah woe—had seen the mobled queen—"

HAMLET "The mobled queen"?

POLONIUS That's good, "mobled queen" is good.

FIRST PLAYER "Run barefoot up and down, threat'ning the flames
With bisson rheum, a clout upon that head   480
Where late the diadem stood, and, for a robe,
About her lank and all o'erteemed loins
A blanket, in th' alarm of fear caught up—
Who this had seen, with tongue in venom steeped,
'Gainst Fortune's state would treason have pronounced.   485
But if the gods themselves did see her then,
When she saw Pyrrhus make malicious sport
In mincing with his sword her husband's limbs,
The instant burst of clamor that she made,

But as we often see before a storm,
A silence in the heavens, the clouds stand still,
The bold winds silent, and the earth below
As calm as death; at last the dreadful thunder   460
Rends the sky; so, after Pyrrhus' pause,
Renewed vengeance sets him to work again,
And never did Cyclops' hammers fall
On Mars's armor, forged to last forever,
With less pity than Pyrrhus' bleeding sword   465
Now falls on Priam.
Away, away, you whore Fortune! All you gods
In general council, take away her power,
Break all the spokes and rim of her wheel,
And bowl the round hub down the hill of heaven   470
To the devils in hell."

POLONIUS This is too long.

HAMLET It shall be trimmed at the barber's with your beard. Please
continue. He favors a dance or a dirty story, or he goes
to sleep. Continue, come to Hecuba.   475

FIRST ACTOR "But who—ah woe—had seen the muffled queen—"

HAMLET "The muffled queen"?

POLONIUS That's good, "muffled queen" is good.

FIRST ACTOR "Run barefoot up and down, threatening the flames
With blinding tears, a cloth upon that head   480
Where late a crown had stood, and, for a robe,
Around her thin and wasted loins
A blanket, caught up in the alarm of fear—
Whoever had seen this, his tongue steeped in venom,
Against Fortune's rule would have treason pronounced.   485
But if the gods themselves did see her then,
When she saw Pyrrhus make malicious sport
Of chopping with his sword her husband's limbs,
The sudden burst of howling that she made,

101

Unless things mortal move them not at all,   490
Would have made milch the burning eyes of heaven,
And passion in the gods."
POLONIUS Look where he has not turned his color, and has tears
in's eyes. Prithee, no more.
HAMLET 'Tis well, I'll have thee speak out the rest of this soon.—   495
Good my lord, will you see the players well bestowed? Do
you hear, let them be well used, for they are the abstract and
brief chronicles of the time. After your death, you were better
have a bad epitaph than their ill report while you live.
POLONIUS My lord, I will use them according to their desert.   500
HAMLET God's bodkin, man, much better! Use every man after
his desert, and who shall 'scape whipping? Use them after your
own honor and dignity; the less they deserve, the more merit is
in your bounty. Take them in.
POLONIUS Come, sirs.   505

Exit POLONIUS

HAMLET Follow him, friends, we'll hear a play tomorrow.— Dost
thou hear me, old friend? Can you play *The Murder of Gonzago?*
FIRST PLAYER Ay, my lord.
HAMLET We'll ha' t tomorrow night. You could for a need study a
speech of some dozen or sixteen lines, which I would set   510
down and insert in 't, could you not?
FIRST PLAYER Ay, my lord.
HAMLET Very well. Follow that lord, and look you mock him not.

Exeunt PLAYERS

My good friends, I'll leave you till night. You are welcome to
Elsinore.   515
ROSENCRANTZ Good my lord.

Exeunt ROSENCRANTZ and GUILDENSTERN

HAMLET Ay so, God bye to you. Now I am alone.
O what a rogue and peasant slave am I!

Unless things mortal do not move them at all,   490
Would have made the stars of heaven weep milky tears,
And caused a violent sorrow in the gods."

POLONIUS Look, how his color has changed, and there are tears in
his eyes. Please, no more.

HAMLET That's good. I'll have you recite the rest of this soon.—   495
My good lord, you will see the actors lodged and provided for?
Do you hear, let them be well cared for. They are the record and
summing up of our time. After your death, you'd be better off
with a bad epitaph than their bad report while you live.

POLONIUS My lord, I will treat them as they deserve.   500

HAMLET By God's body, man, much better! Treat every man as he
deserves and who shall escape a whipping? Treat them according
to your own honor and dignity: the less they deserve, the more
your merit in being generous. Take them in.

POLONIUS Come, sirs.   505

Exit POLONIUS

HAMLET Follow him, friends, we'll hear a play tomorrow.—May I
have a word, old friend? Can you play *The Murder of Gonzago?*

FIRST ACTOR Yes, my lord.

HAMLET We'll have it tomorrow night. If need be, you could learn a
speech of some dozen or sixteen lines that I would write   510
and insert in it, couldn't you?

FIRST ACTOR Yes, my lord.

HAMLET Good. Follow that lord and see that you don't make fun of him.

Exit ACTORS

My good friends, I'll leave you till tonight. You are welcome to
Elsinore.   515

ROSENCRANTZ Good my lord.

Exit ROSENCRANTZ *and* GUILDENSTERN

HAMLET And so, goodbye to you. Now I am alone.
Oh, what a scoundrel and peasant slave am I!

Is it not monstrous that this player here,
But in a fiction, in a dream of passion,   520
Could force his soul so to his own conceit
That from her working all his visage wanned,
Tears in his eyes, distraction in 's aspect,
A broken voice, and his whole function suiting
With forms to his conceit? And all for nothing!   525
For Hecuba!
What's Hecuba to him, or he to Hecuba,
That he should weep for her? What would he do,
Had he the motive and the cue for passion
That I have? He would drown the stage with tears,   530
And cleave the general ear with horrid speech,
Make mad the guilty and appall the free,
Confound the ignorant and amaze indeed
The very faculties of eyes and ears. Yet I,
A dull and muddy-mettled rascal, peak   535
Like John-a-dreams, unpregnant of my cause,
And can say nothing—no, not for a king,
Upon whose property and most dear life
A damned defeat was made. Am I a coward?
Who calls me "villain," breaks my pate across,   540
Plucks off my beard and blows it in my face,
Tweaks me by the nose, gives me the lie i' th' throat
As deep as to the lungs? Who does me this?
Ha! 'Swounds, I should take it! For it cannot be
But I am pigeon-livered and lack gall   545
To make oppression bitter, or ere this
I should ha' fatted all the region kites
With this slave's offal. Bloody, bawdy villain!
Remorseless, treacherous, lecherous, kindless villain!
O vengeance!   550
Why, what an ass am I! This is most brave,

Is it not amazing that this actor here,
In a mere story, in a dream of passion,   520
Could force his soul so to his own idea
That from its working his whole face grew pale,
Tears in his eyes, grief in his face,
A broken voice, all his bodily powers producing
Expressions of his thought? And all for nothing!   525
For Hecuba!
What's Hecuba to him, or he to Hecuba,
That he should weep for her? What would he do
Had he the motive and the cue for passion
That I have? He would drown the stage with tears,   530
Split open the ears of the people with horrid speech,
Make mad the guilty and terrify the innocent,
Silence the ignorant and dazzle indeed
The senses of sight and hearing. Yet I,
A slow and hesitant rascal, droop   535
Like Johnny-the-dreamer, unready for my cause,
And unable to say a word—no, not for a king,
Whose kingdom and most dear life
Were cruelly destroyed. Am I a coward?
Does anyone call me a "villain," hit me on the head,   540
Pull off my beard and blow it in my face,
Tweak me by the nose, accuse me of being a liar,
Seriously and deeply? Does anyone?
Ha! By God's wounds, I should take it! For it must be
That I am pigeon-livered and lack the gall   545
To make this king's oppression bitter to him, or by now,
I should have fattened all the vultures of the region
With the guts of this wretch. Bloody, bawdy villain!
Remorseless, treacherous, lecherous, unfeeling villain!
O vengeance!   550
Why, what an ass I am! This is most noble:

That I, the son of a dear father murdered,
Prompted to my revenge by heaven and hell,
Must like a whore unpack my heart with words,
And fall a-cursing like a very drab,   555
A scullion! Fie upon 't, foh!
About, my brains! Hum, I have heard
That guilty creatures sitting at a play
Have by the very cunning of the scene
Been struck so to the soul, that presently   560
They have proclaimed their malefactions.
For murder, though it have no tongue, will speak
With most miraculous organ. I'll have these players
Play something like the murder of my father
Before mine uncle. I'll observe his looks,   565
I'll tent him to the quick. If a do blench,
I know my course. The spirit that I have seen
May be a devil—and the devil hath power
T' assume a pleasing shape. Yea, and perhaps,
Out of my weakness and my melancholy,   570
As he is very potent with such spirits,
Abuses me to damn me. I'll have grounds
More relative than this. The play's the thing
Wherein I'll catch the conscience of the king.

He exits

That I, the son of a dear, murdered father,
Stirred to my revenge by heaven and hell,
Must like a whore relieve my heart with words
And fall to cursing like a true slut,   555
A kitchen maid! A blight upon it! A blight!
Use your brains! Hmm, I have heard
That guilty persons attending a play
Have by a skillful presentation
Been so struck to the soul that instantly   560
They have confessed their crimes.
For murder, though it's mute, will speak
With a most miraculous power. I'll have these actors
Act out something like the murder of my father
In front of my uncle. I'll observe his looks,   565
I'll probe him where it hurts. If he turns pale,
I know my course. The ghost that I have seen
May be a devil—and the devil has the power
To assume a pleasing form. Yes, and perhaps,
Out of my weakness and my melancholy—   570
The devil is very powerful with such people—
He deceives me to damn me. I'll have proof
More pertinent than this. The play's the thing
Whereby I'll trap the conscience of the king.

He exits

Act Three

Scene 1 [*The king's apartments*] *Enter* CLAUDIUS, GERTRUDE,
    POLONIUS, OPHELIA, ROSENCRANTZ, GUILDENSTERN, *and* LORDS

CLAUDIUS And can you no drift of conference
    Get from him why he puts on this confusion,
    Grating so harshly all his days of quiet
    With turbulent and dangerous lunacy?
ROSENCRANTZ He does confess he feels himself distracted,   5
    But from what cause a will by no means speak.
GUILDENSTERN Nor do we find him forward to be sounded,
    But with a crafty madness keeps aloof
    When we would bring him on to some confession
    Of his true state.   10
GERTRUDE Did he receive you well?
ROSENCRANTZ Most like a gentleman.
GUILDENSTERN But with much forcing of his disposition.
ROSENCRANTZ Niggard of question, but of our demands
    Most free in his reply.   15
GERTRUDE Did you assay him
    To any pastime?
ROSENCRANTZ Madam, it so fell out that certain players
    We o'erraught on the way. Of these we told him,
    And there did seem in him a kind of joy   20
    To hear of it. They are about the court,
    And as I think, they have already order
    This night to play before him.
POLONIUS 'Tis most true,
    And he beseeched me to entreat your majesties   25
    To hear and see the matter.

Act Three

Scene 1 [*The king's apartments*] *Enter* CLAUDIUS, GERTRUDE,
    POLONIUS, OPHELIA, ROSENCRANTZ, GUILDENSTERN, *and* LORDS

CLAUDIUS And can you not by directing the conversation
    Learn from him why he wears this guise of madness,
    Disturbing so harshly his peace of mind
    With turbulent and dangerous lunacy?

ROSENCRANTZ He does admit he feels himself unsettled,   5
    But from what cause he will by no means speak.

GUILDENSTERN Nor did we find him ready to be questioned,
    But with a crafty madness kept aloof
    When we tried to lead him to some admission
    Of his true state.   10

GERTRUDE Did he welcome you warmly?

ROSENCRANTZ In a gentlemanly fashion.

GUILDENSTERN But with a great effort.

ROSENCRANTZ He was sparing in asking questions, but replied
    To ours most freely.   15

GERTRUDE Did you ask him
    About any pastimes?

ROSENCRANTZ Madam, it so happened that we overtook
    Certain actors on our way here. We told him of them,
    And he seemed pleased to hear it.   20
    They are here at court,
    And I believe, they have already been ordered
    To play before him tonight.

POLONIUS That's quite true,
    And he asked me to entreat your majesties   25
    To hear and see the play.

CLAUDIUS With all my heart, and it doth much content me
    To hear him so inclined.
    Good gentlemen, give him a further edge,
    And drive his purpose into these delights.   30
ROSENCRANTZ We shall, my lord.
                    Exeunt ROSENCRANTZ *and* GUILDENSTERN
CLAUDIUS Sweet Gertrude, leave us too,
    For we have closely sent for Hamlet hither,
    That he, as 'twere by accident, may here
    Affront Ophelia. Her father and myself,   35
    Lawful espials,
    Will so bestow ourselves that, seeing unseen,
    We may of their encounter frankly judge,
    And gather by him, as he is behaved,
    If 't be th' affliction of his love or no   40
    That thus he suffers for.
GERTRUDE I shall obey you.
    And for your part, Ophelia, I do wish
    That your good beauties be the happy cause
    Of Hamlet's wildness. So shall I hope your virtues   45
    Will bring him to his wonted way again,
    To both your honors.
OPHELIA Madam, I wish it may.
                    Exit GERTRUDE *with* LORDS
POLONIUS Ophelia, walk you here.—Gracious, so please you,
    We will bestow ourselves.—Read on this book,   50
    That show of such an exercise may color
    Your loneliness.—We are oft to blame in this:
    'Tis too much proved, that with devotion's visage,
    And pious action, we do sugar o'er
    The devil himself.   55
CLAUDIUS [*Aside*] O, 'tis too true.

CLAUDIUS With all my heart. And I am pleased
    To hear him so disposed.
    Good gentlemen, encourage him further
    And steer him into these pleasures.   30
ROSENCRANTZ We shall, my lord.
Exit ROSENCRANTZ and GUILDENSTERN
CLAUDIUS Sweet Gertrude, leave us too.
    We have contrived to send for Hamlet
    So that he, as it were by accident, may here
    Confront Ophelia. Her father and I,   35
    As lawful observers,
    Will place ourselves so we can see, but not be seen,
    And make a frank judgment of their encounter,
    To deduce from his behavior
    Whether or not it is from love   40
    That he suffers.
GERTRUDE I shall obey you.
    As for you, Ophelia, I do hope
    That your good charms are the happy cause
    Of Hamlet's wildness. So also I hope that your virtues   45
    Will restore him to his usual behavior,
    For the sake of both of you.
OPHELIA Madam, I hope so too.
Exit GERTRUDE with LORDS
POLONIUS Ophelia, walk over here.—Your majesty, if you please,
    We will conceal ourselves.—Read this prayer book   50
    So that your appearance will provide an excuse
    For being alone.—We are often guilty of this:
    As we know from experience, with the face of devotion
    And pious actions, we can sugar over
    The devil himself.   55
CLAUDIUS [*Aside*] Oh, that's very true.

How smart a lash that speech doth give my conscience!
The harlot's cheek, beautied with plastering art,
Is not more ugly to the thing that helps it
Than is my deed to my most painted word.   60
O heavy burden!
POLONIUS I hear him coming. Let's withdraw, my lord.
                              Exeunt CLAUDIUS *and* POLONIUS
                              Enter HAMLET
HAMLET To be or not to be, that is the question—
    Whether 'tis nobler in the mind to suffer
    The slings and arrows of outrageous fortune,   65
    Or to take arms against a sea of troubles,
    And, by opposing, end them. To die, to sleep—
    No more? And by a sleep to say we end
    The heartache and the thousand natural shocks
    That flesh is heir to—'tis a consummation   70
    Devoutly to be wished. To die, to sleep—
    To sleep, perchance to dream. Ay, there's the rub,
    For in that sleep of death what dreams may come,
    When we have shuffled off this mortal coil,
    Must give us pause. There's the respect   75
    That makes calamity of so long life.
    For who would bear the whips and scorns of time,
    Th' oppressor's wrong, the proud man's contumely,
    The pangs of despised love, the law's delay,
    The insolence of office, and the spurns   80
    That patient merit of th' unworthy takes,
    When he himself might his quietus make
    With a bare bodkin? Who would fardels bear,
    To grunt and sweat under a weary life,
    But that the dread of something after death,   85
    The undiscovered country from whose bourn
    No traveler returns, puzzles the will,

What a stinging lash his remark gives my conscience!
The harlot's face, made pretty with paint and art,
Is not more ugly in its artificiality
Than is my deed to my colored words.   60
Oh, what a heavy burden!

POLONIUS I hear him coming. Let's withdraw, my lord.

Exit CLAUDIUS *and* POLONIUS

Enter HAMLET

HAMLET To be or not to be, that is the question.
Is it nobler for the mind to endure
The slings and arrows of outrageous fortune   65
Or to take arms against a sea of troubles
And, by opposing, end them? To die is to sleep—
Nothing more? And if by sleep we could end
The heartache and the thousand natural shocks
That humans are heir to—that's a completion   70
Devoutly to be wished. To die, to sleep—
To sleep, perhaps to dream. Yes, there's the catch.
For in that sleep of death what dreams may come,
When we have sloughed off life's turmoil,
Must give us pause. That's what makes us   75
Tolerate suffering for so long.
Who would bear the whips and scorns of the times,
The oppressor's wrong, the proud man's arrogance,
The pangs of despised love, the law's delay,
The insolence of officials, the insults   80
That patient merit receives from the unworthy,
When he might settle everything himself
With a mere knife? Who would bear burdens,
Grunt and sweat under a weary life,
But for the dread of something after death,   85
The undiscovered country from whose border
No traveler returns, confuses the will,

And makes us rather bear those ills we have
Than fly to others that we know not of?
Thus conscience does make cowards of us all,   90
And thus the native hue of resolution
Is sicklied o'er with the pale cast of thought,
And enterprises of great pitch and moment
With this regard their currents turn awry
And lose the name of action. Soft you now,   95
The fair Ophelia.—Nymph, in thy orisons
Be all my sins remembered.
OPHELIA Good my lord,
    How does your honor for this many a day?
HAMLET I humbly thank you, well, well, well.   100
OPHELIA My lord, I have remembrances of yours
    That I have longed to redeliver.
    I pray you now receive them.
HAMLET No, not I,
    I never gave you aught.   105
OPHELIA My honored lord, you know right well you did,
    And with them these words of so sweet breath composed
    As made the things more rich. Their perfume lost,
    Take these again, for to the noble mind
    Rich gifts wax poor when givers prove unkind.   110
    There, my lord.
HAMLET Ha, ha, are you honest?
OPHELIA My lord?
HAMLET Are you fair?
OPHELIA What means your lordship?   115
HAMLET That if you be honest and fair, your honesty should
    admit no discourse to your beauty.
OPHELIA Could beauty, my lord, have better commerce than with
    honesty?
HAMLET Ay, truly, for the power of beauty will sooner transform   120

And makes us rather bear those ills we have
Than fly to others we know nothing of?
That's why thinking makes cowards of us all, 90
And why the natural color of determination
Is unhealthily covered with the pale hue of thought,
And ventures of the highest importance,
On this account, turn away from their proper course
And lose their impetus. Wait a moment, 95
The lovely Ophelia.—Young lady, in your prayers
Remember all my sins.

OPHELIA My lord,
How does it go for your honor these last few days?

HAMLET I humbly thank you—well, well, well. 100

OPHELIA My lord, I have keepsakes of yours
That I have longed to return.
I ask you to take them now.

HAMLET No, not I.
I never gave you anything. 105

OPHELIA My honored lord, you know quite well that you did,
And with them these words of such sweet fragrance
As made them more precious. Since their scent has faded,
Take them back again. To the sensitive mind,
Rich gifts grow poor when the giver proves unkind. 110
There, my lord.

HAMLET Ah, ha, are you chaste?

OPHELIA My lord?

HAMLET Are you beautiful?

OPHELIA What does your lordship mean? 115

HAMLET That if you are chaste and beautiful, your chastity
should permit no communication with your beauty.

OPHELIA Could beauty, my lord, have a better relationship than
with chastity?

HAMLET Yes, truly. Beauty can more easily corrupt 120

honesty from what it is to a bawd than the force of honesty
can translate beauty into his likeness. This was sometime a
paradox, but now the time gives it proof. I did love you once.

OPHELIA Indeed, my lord, you made me believe so.

HAMLET You should not have believed me, for virtue cannot so   125
inoculate our old stock but we shall relish of it. I loved
you not.

OPHELIA I was the more deceived.

HAMLET Get thee to a nunnery—why wouldst thou be a breeder
of sinners? I am myself indifferent honest, but yet I could   130
accuse me of such things that it were better my mother had
not borne me. I am very proud, revengeful, ambitious, with
more offenses at my beck than I have thoughts to act them in,
imagination to give them shape, or time to act them in. What
should such fellows as I do crawling between earth and heaven?   135
We are arrant knaves all; believe none of us. Go thy ways to a
nunnery. Where's your father?

OPHELIA At home, my lord.

HAMLET Let the doors be shut upon him, that he may play the
fool nowhere but in 's own house. Farewell.   140

OPHELIA O, help him, you sweet heavens.

HAMLET If thou dost marry, I'll give thee this plague for thy
dowry: be thou as chaste as ice, as pure as snow, thou shalt
not escape calumny. Get thee to a nunnery, go. Farewell. Or
if thou needs marry, marry a fool, for wise men know well   145
enough what monsters you make of them. To a nunnery, go,
and quickly too. Farewell.

OPHELIA O heavenly powers, restore him!

HAMLET I have heard of your paintings too, well enough. God hath
given you one face, and you have made yourself another. You jig,   150
you amble, you lisp, you nickname God's creatures, and make
your wantonness your ignorance. Go to, I'll no more on 't, it hath
made me mad. I say we will have no mo marriages. Those that are

chastity from what it is to a whore than the force of chastity
can transform beauty into its likeness. This used to be
unthinkable, but these days it's proved true. I loved you once.

OPHELIA Indeed, my lord, you made me believe so.

HAMLET You should not have believed me, for virtue cannot   125
graft onto an old stock without leaving a taste behind. I
never loved you.

OPHELIA I was the more deceived.

HAMLET Get yourself to a nunnery—why would you become a
breeder of sinners? I am myself reasonably moral, but I could   130
accuse myself of such things that it were better my mother had
not borne me. I am very proud, revengeful, ambitious, with
more offenses at my command than my thoughts can conceive,
my imagination can shape, or I have time to act out. What
right have such as me to life? We are all out-and-out scoundrels; 135
believe none of us. Take yourself off to a nunnery. Where's
your father?

OPHELIA At home, my lord.

HAMLET Lock him in so that he may play the fool nowhere but in
his own house. Farewell.   140

OPHELIA Oh, help him, you sweet heavens.

HAMLET If you do marry, I'll give you this curse for your dowry:
be you as chaste as ice, as pure as snow, you shall not escape
false slander. Take yourself off to a nunnery, go on.
Farewell. Or if you do marry, marry a fool, for wise men know   145
how you deceive them. To a nunnery, go, and quickly too.
Farewell.

OPHELIA Oh, heavenly powers, make him well again!

HAMLET I know all about your face painting too. God has given
you one face, and you have made yourself another. You dance, you 150
saunter, you lisp, you give God's creatures pet names, you
pretend your behavior is just simplicity. Enough. I'll have no more
of it. It has made me mad. I say no more marriages. Those who are

married already, all but one, shall live, the rest shall keep as
they are. To a nunnery, go.   155
                              Exit HAMLET
OPHELIA O, what a noble mind is here o'erthrown!
    The courtier's, soldier's, scholar's, eye, tongue, sword,
    Th' expectancy and rose of the fair state,
    The glass of fashion and the mould of form,
    Th' observed of all observers, quite, quite down!   160
    And I, of ladies most deject and wretched,
    That sucked the honey of his music vows,
    Now see that noble and most sovereign reason,
    Like sweet bells jangled, out of time and harsh;
    That unmatched form and feature of blown youth   165
    Blasted with ecstasy. O, woe is me
    T' have seen what I have seen, see what I see.
                    Enter CLAUDIUS *and* POLONIUS
CLAUDIUS Love? His affections do not that way tend;
    Nor what he spake, though it lacked form a little,
    Was not like madness. There's something in his soul   170
    O'er which his melancholy sits on brood,
    And I do doubt the hatch and the disclose
    Will be some danger; which for to prevent,
    I have in quick determination
    Thus set it down: he shall with speed to England   175
    For the demand of our neglected tribute.
    Haply the seas, and countries different,
    With variable objects, shall expel
    This something-settled matter in his heart,
    Whereon his brains still beating puts him thus   180
    From fashion of himself. What think you on 't?
POLONIUS It shall do well. But yet do I believe
    The origin and commencement of his grief
    Sprung from neglected love. How now, Ophelia?

married already—all except one—may remain. The rest
shall stay as they are. To a nunnery, go.   155

Exit HAMLET

OPHELIA Oh, what a noble mind has lost its reason!
    The courtier's, soldier's, scholar's, eye, tongue, and sword,
    The hope and ornament of the state,
    The mirror of fashion and the model of conduct,
    The observed of all observers, completely ruined!   160
    And I, the most dejected and wretched of women,
    Who fed upon the honey of his musical words,
    Now see that noble and supreme reason,
    Like sweet bells rung in discord, harsh and out of tune;
    That unmatched form of youth in full bloom   165
    Destroyed by madness. Oh, bitter grief for me
    To have seen what I have seen, see what I see.

Enter CLAUDIUS *and* POLONIUS

CLAUDIUS Love? His emotions do not run that way;
    Nor was what he spoke, though it lacked logic a little,
    Anything like madness. There's something in his soul   170
    Over which his melancholy sits brooding,
    And I suspect that when it hatches, it will disclose
    Something quite dangerous. To prevent that,
    I have just decided this:
    He shall be sent to England immediately   175
    To collect our outstanding payments.
    Perhaps a sea voyage and different countries
    And a changing scene will dispel
    This disease settled in his heart,
    Which disturbs his mind and keeps him from   180
    Behaving in his own proper way. What do you think?

POLONIUS It will work. But still I believe
    The origin and beginning of his grief
    Sprung from unrequited love. All right, Ophelia,

You need not tell us what Lord Hamlet said, 185
We heard it all. My lord, do as you please,
But if you hold it fit, after the play,
Let his queen-mother all alone entreat him
To show his grief. Let her be round with him,
And I'll be placed, so please you, in the ear 190
Of all their conference. If she find him not,
To England send him; or confine him where
Your wisdom best shall think.

CLAUDIUS It shall be so.
Madness in great ones must not unwatched go. 195

Exeunt

Scene 2 [*The Palace*] *Enter* HAMLET *and some* PLAYERS

HAMLET Speak the speech I pray you as I pronounced it to you,
trippingly on the tongue; but if you mouth it, as many of our
players do, I had as lief the town-crier spoke my lines. Nor do
not saw the air too much with your hand, thus, but use all gently;
for in the very torrent, tempest, and, as I may say, whirlwind 5
of your passion, you must acquire and beget a temperance that
may give it smoothness. O, it offends me to the soul to hear a
robustious, periwig-pated fellow tear a passion to tatters, to
very rags, to split the ears of the groundlings, who for the most
part are capable of nothing but inexplicable dumb-shows and 10
noise. I would have such a fellow whipped for o'erdoing
Termagant—it out-Herods Herod. Pray you, avoid it.

FIRST PLAYER I warrant your honor.

HAMLET Be not too tame neither, but let your own discretion be
your tutor. Suit the action to the word, the word to the action, 15
with this special observance, that you o'erstep not the modesty
of nature. For anything so o'erdone is from the purpose of
playing, whose end, both at the first and now, was and is, to hold, as

You need not tell us what Lord Hamlet said,   185
We heard it all. My lord, do as you please,
But if you approve, then after the play,
Let his mother in private persuade him
To reveal the cause of his grief. Let her be blunt,
And I'll be concealed, if it please you, within   190
Hearing of all that they say. If she doesn't find the truth,
Send him to England—or lock him up where
You in your wisdom think best.
CLAUDIUS It shall be so.
Madness in great ones should not unheeded go.   195

They exit

Scene 2 [*The Palace*] *Enter* HAMLET *and some* ACTORS

HAMLET Speak the speech, please, as I read it to you, running
lightly off the tongue. If you overdo it, as many actors do, I
would just as soon the town crier spoke my lines. And don't
saw the air too much with your hand, like this, but use restraint.
In the very torrent, tempest, and, as I say, the whirlwind of   5
your passion, you must acquire and produce a balance that will
give it smoothness. Oh, it offends me to the soul to hear a loud,
crude, bewigged fellow tear a passion to shreds, to very rags, and
split the ears of the groundlings, who for the most part appreciate
nothing but meaningless pantomime or noise. I would have such   10
a fellow whipped for overdoing the part of a heathen god—he
out-Herods even the tyrant Herod. Please, avoid that.
FIRST ACTOR I guarantee it, your honor.
HAMLET Don't be too tame either. Let your discretion guide you.
Suit your actions to the words, your words to the actions—   15
with this special proviso, that you don't overstep the moderation
of nature. Because anything so overdone is contrary to the
purpose of acting, whose goal was and is to hold, as

'twere, the mirror up to nature; to show virtue her own feature, scorn her own image, and the very age and body of the time his 20
form and pressure. Now this overdone or come tardy off, though it makes the unskillful laugh, cannot but make the judicious grieve, the censure of the which one must in your allowance o'erweigh a whole threatre of others. O, there be players that I have seen play and heard others praise and that highly, not 25
to speak it profanely, that, neither having th' accent of Christians, nor the gait of Christian, pagan, nor man, have so strutted and bellowed that I have thought some of nature's journeymen had made men, and not made them well, they imitated humanity so abominably. 30

FIRST PLAYER I hope we have reformed that indifferently with us, sir.

HAMLET O, reform it altogether. And let those that play your clowns speak no more than is set down for them, for there be of them that will themselves laugh, to set on some quantity of 35
barren spectators to laugh too, though in the meantime some necessary question of the play be then to be considered. That's villainous, and shows a most pitiful ambition in the fool that uses it. Go make you ready.

Exeunt PLAYERS

Enter POLONIUS, ROSENCRANTZ, *and* GUILDENSTERN

How now, my lord, will the king hear this piece of work? 40

POLONIUS And the queen too, and that presently.

HAMLET Bid the players make haste.

Exit POLONIUS

Will you two help to hasten them?

ROSENCRANTZ Ay, my lord.

Exeunt ROSENCRANTZ *and* GUILDENSTERN

HAMLET What ho, Horatio! 45

Enter HORATIO

it were, the mirror up to nature; to show what's virtuous,
what's to be scorned, to depict the shape of our times in   20
the clearest detail. Now all this overdone or badly executed,
though the ignorant may laugh, cannot help but make the
knowing grieve, and their opinion, you must allow, outweighs
an entire theatre of the others. Oh, there are actors I've seen
act—and heard others praise and praise highly—that, not to   25
speak profanely, have neither the voice of Christians nor the
walk of Christians, pagans, or whatever. They have so strutted
and bellowed that I had thought that some journeyman of
nature had made them, and not made them well, they
imitated humanity so abominably.   30

FIRST ACTOR I hope we have reformed that reasonably
well, sir.

HAMLET Oh, reform it altogether. And let those who take your
comic parts speak no more than is set down for them. There
are some who will laugh themselves in order to set off laughter 35
among witless spectators and cause, in the meantime, some
necessary part of the plot to be delayed. That's villainous
and shows a contemptible ambition in the comic who uses
it. Go and get ready.

Exit ACTORS

Enter POLONIUS, ROSENCRANTZ, *and* GUILDENSTERN

Well now, my lord, will the king hear this play?   40

POLONIUS And the queen too, and immediately.

HAMLET Ask the actors to hurry.

Exit POLONIUS

Will you two help hurry them?

ROSENCRANTZ Yes, my lord.

Exit ROSENCRANTZ *and* GUILDENSTERN

HAMLET Well hello, Horatio!   45

Enter HORATIO

HORATIO Here, sweet lord, at your service.
HAMLET Horatio, thou art e'en as just a man
    As e'er my conversation coped withal.
HORATIO O, my dear lord—
HAMLET Nay, do not think I flatter, 50
    For what advancement may I hope from thee,
    That no revenue hast but thy good spirits
    To feed and clothe thee? Why should the poor be flattered?
    No, let the candied tongue lick absurd pomp
    And crook the pregnant hinges of the knee 55
    Where thrift may follow fawning. Dost thou hear?
    Since my dear soul was mistress of her choice,
    And could of men distinguish, her election
    Sh'hath sealed thee for herself, for thou hast been
    As one in suffering all that suffers nothing, 60
    A man that Fortune's buffets and rewards
    Hast tane with equal thanks. And blest are those
    Whose blood and judgment are so well commeddled
    That they are not a pipe for Fortune's finger
    To sound what stop she please. Give me that man 65
    That is not passion's slave, and I will wear him
    In my heart's core, ay, in my heart of heart,
    As I do thee.— Something too much of this.—
    There is a play tonight before the king.
    One scene of it comes near the circumstance 70
    Which I have told thee of my father's death.
    I prithee, when thou seest that act afoot,
    Even with the very comment of thy soul
    Observe my uncle. If his occulted guilt
    Do not itself unkennel in one speech, 75
    It is a damned ghost that we have seen,
    And my imaginations are as foul
    As Vulcan's stithy. Give him heedful note,

HORATIO Here, sweet lord, at your service.
HAMLET Horatio, you are as upright a man
    As ever I encountered in all my dealings.
HORATIO Oh, my dear lord—
HAMLET No, do not think I flatter,   50
    For what advancement may I hope from you,
    Who have no assets but your good spirits
    To feed and clothe you? Who would flatter the poor?
    No, let the sugared tongue lick the hand of absurd pomp
    And bend the ready hinges of the knee   55
    Where profit may follow fawning. Do you hear?
    Ever since my precious soul was in command of her choice
    And had the power to discriminate among men, her preference
    Has sealed you for herself, for you have been
    As one who has undergone all things but is harmed by none,   60
    A man that has taken Fortune's blows and rewards
    With equal thanks. And blessed are those
    Whose passion and judgment are so commingled
    That they are not an instrument for Fortune
    To play what tune she pleases. Give me that man   65
    That is not passion's slave, and I will wear him
    In my heart's core, yes, in my heart of hearts,
    As I do you.—That's enough of this.—
    There is a play being performed tonight before the king.
    One scene in it comes near the circumstance   70
    Which I have told you of my father's death.
    Please, when you see that part beginning,
    With your most critical attention,
    Observe my uncle. If his hidden guilt
    Does not come into the open with one speech,   75
    It is a damned ghost that we have seen,
    And my imaginings are as foul
    As Vulcan's forge. Take careful note of him,

For I mine eyes will rivet to his face;
And, after, we will both our judgments join 80
In censure of his seeming.
HORATIO Well, my lord,
If he steal aught the whilst this play is playing
And scape detecting, I will pay the theft.

Trumpets and kettledrums. Danish march. Sound a flourish. Enter
CLAUDIUS, GERTRUDE, POLONIUS, OPHELIA,
ROSENCRANTZ, GUILDENSTERN, *and other* LORDS
with the king's GUARD *carrying torches*
HAMLET They are coming to the play. I must be idle. 85
Get you a place.
CLAUDIUS How fares our cousin Hamlet?
HAMLET Excellent, i' faith, of the chameleon's dish. I eat the air,
promise-crammed. You cannot feed capons so.
CLAUDIUS I have nothing with this answer, Hamlet. These words 90
are not mine.
HAMLET No, nor mine now. [*To* POLONIUS] My lord, you played
once i' th' university, you say?
POLONIUS That I did, my lord, and was accounted a good actor.
HAMLET What did you enact? 95
POLONIUS I did enact Julius Caesar. I was killed i' th' Capitol.
Brutus killed me.
HAMLET It was a brute part of him to kill so capital a calf there. Be
the players ready?
ROSENCRANTZ Ay, my lord. They stay upon your patience. 100
GERTRUDE Come hither, my dear Hamlet, sit by me.
HAMLET No, good mother. Here's metal more attractive.
POLONIUS [*Aside to* CLAUDIUS] O, ho! Do you mark that?
HAMLET Lady, shall I lie in your lap?
OPHELIA No, my lord. 105
HAMLET I mean, my head upon your lap.

And I will rivet my eyes on his face.
And, later, we will join our judgments   80
In forming an opinion of his demeanor.
HORATIO Indeed, my lord,
    If he steals anything while this play is playing,
    And escapes detection, I will pay for the theft.

Trumpets and kettledrums. Danish march. Sound a flourish. Enter
        CLAUDIUS, GERTRUDE, POLONIUS, OPHELIA,
        ROSENCRANTZ, GUILDENSTERN, *and other* LORDS
        with the king's GUARD *carrying torches*
HAMLET They are coming to the play. I must look mad.   85
    Find yourself a place.
CLAUDIUS How is our kinsman Hamlet?
HAMLET Excellent, indeed, eating the same food as the chameleon,
    air filled with promises. You cannot feed chickens like that.
CLAUDIUS This answer makes no sense to me, Hamlet. These words   90
    have nothing to do with my words.
HAMLET No, nor are they my words now. [*To* POLONIUS] My lord,
    you acted once in the university, you say?
POLONIUS That I did, my lord, and was said to be a good actor.
HAMLET What did you play?   95
POLONIUS I played Julius Caesar. I was killed in the Capitol.
    Brutus killed me.
HAMLET What a brute he was to kill so capital a fool there. Are
    the actors ready?
ROSENCRANTZ Yes, my lord. They wait for your permission.   100
GERTRUDE Come here, my dear Hamlet, and sit by me.
HAMLET No, good mother, I'm drawn to more precious metal.
POLONIUS [*Aside to* CLAUDIUS] Oh, ho! Did you hear that?
HAMLET Lady, shall I lie in your lap?
OPHELIA No, my lord.   105
HAMLET I mean, with my head upon your lap.

OPHELIA Ay, my lord.

HAMLET Did you think I meant country matters?

OPHELIA I think nothing, my lord.

HAMLET That's a fair thought to lie between maids' legs.   110

OPHELIA What is, my lord?

HAMLET Nothing.

OPHELIA You are merry, my lord.

HAMLET Who, I?

OPHELIA Ay, my lord.   115

HAMLET O God, your only jig-maker. What should a man do but be
     merry? For look you how cheerfully my mother looks and my
     father died within's two hours.

OPHELIA Nay, 'tis twice two months, my lord.

HAMLET So long? Nay, then, let the devil wear black, for I'll have   120
     a suit of sables. O heavens, die two months ago and not
     forgotten yet! Then there's hope a great man's memory may
     outlive his life half a year. But, by'r Lady, a must build
     churches then, or else shall a suffer not thinking on, with the
     hobby-horse, whose epitaph is "For O, for O, the   125
     hobby-horse is forgot."

The trumpets sound. A dumb-show follows.

Enter a KING *and a* QUEEN *very lovingly, the* QUEEN *embracing him
and he her. She kneels and makes show of protestation unto him. He
takes her up and declines his head upon her neck. He lies him down
on a bank of flowers. She, seeing him asleep, leaves him. Anon comes
in another* MAN, *takes off his crown, kisses it, pours poison in the
sleeper's ears, and leaves him. The* QUEEN *returns, finds the* KING
dead, makes passionate action. The POISONER *with some* THREE *or*
FOUR *comes in again. They seem to condole with her. The dead body
is carried away. The* POISONER *woos the* QUEEN *with gifts. She seems
harsh awhile, but in the end accepts his love.*

Exeunt

OPHELIA What means this, my lord?

OPHELIA Yes, my lord.

HAMLET Did you think I meant sexual matters?

OPHELIA I thought nothing, my lord.

HAMLET It's pleasing to think of that lying between maidens' legs.   110

OPHELIA What is, my lord?

HAMLET Nothing.

OPHELIA You are merry, my lord?

HAMLET Who, I?

OPHELIA Yes, my lord.   115

HAMLET Oh God, your writer of light comedy. But what else should
a man be but merry? Look how cheerful my mother looks and
my father's dead less than two hours.

OPHELIA No, it's twice two months, my lord.

HAMLET That long? Well, then, let the devil wear black, for I'll   120
wear a suit of sable. Oh, heavens, died two months ago and not
forgotten yet! Then there's hope that a great man's memory may
outlive his life by half a year. But, by Our Lady, he must build
churches then or else resign himself to be forgotten, like the
hobbyhorses they used to have at country fairs, whose   125
refrain is "For oh, for oh, the hobbyhorse is forgot."

The trumpets sound. A scene without words follows.

Enter a KING *and a* QUEEN *showing affection, the* QUEEN *embracing
him and he her. She kneels and expresses her love for him. He raises her
from her knees and lays his head upon her shoulder. He lies down upon
a bank of flowers. She, seeing him asleep, leaves him. Soon a* MAN
comes in, removes the KING'S *crown, kisses it, and then pours poison
into the sleeping* KING'S *ears, and leaves him. The* QUEEN *returns, finds
the* KING *dead, and expresses her grief. The* POISONER *with* THREE *or*
FOUR OTHERS *enter again. They seem to share her grief. The dead body
is carried away. The* POISONER *woos the* QUEEN *with gifts. She resists at
first, but in the end accepts his love.*

They exit

OPHELIA What does this mean, my lord?

HAMLET Marry, this is miching malicho. It means mischief.
OPHELIA Belike this show imports the argument of the play?
Enter PROLOGUE
HAMLET We shall know by this fellow. The players cannot keep   130
    counsel. They'll tell all.
OPHELIA Will a tell us what this show meant?
HAMLET Ay, or any show that you will show him. Be not
    you ashamed to show, he'll not shame to show you what
    it means.   135
OPHELIA You are naught, you are naught. I'll mark the play.
PROLOGUE For us and for our tragedy,
    Here stooping to your clemency,
    We beg your hearing patiently.
Exit
HAMLET Is this a prologue, or the posy of a ring?   140
OPHELIA 'Tis brief, my lord.
HAMLET As woman's love.
Enter the PLAYER KING *and* QUEEN
PLAYER KING Full thirty times hath Phoebus' cart gone round
    Neptune's salt wash and Tellus' orbed ground,
    And thirty dozen moons with borrowed sheen   145
    About the world have times twelve thirties been
    Since love our hearts and Hymen did our hands
    Unite commutual in most sacred bands.
PLAYER QUEEN So many journeys may the sun and moon
    Make us again count o'er, ere love be done!   150
    But woe is me, you are so sick of late
    So far from cheer and from your former state,
    That I distrust you. Yet, though I distrust,
    Discomfort you, my lord, it nothing must;
    For women's fear and love hold quantity,   155
    In neither aught, or in extremity.
    Now what my love is, proof hath made you know,

HAMLET By God, this is a sneaky trick. It means mischief.

OPHELIA It's likely this mime shows the plot of the play.

Enter SPEAKER

HAMLET We shall know by this fellow. These actors can't keep   130
a secret. They'll tell all.

OPHELIA Will he tell us what this show meant?

HAMLET Yes, or anything that you will show him. If you're
not ashamed to show him, he'll not be ashamed to tell what
it's for.   135

OPHELIA You are naughty, naughty. I'll watch the play.

SPEAKER For us and for our tragedy,
We bow in hope of leniency,
And beg you hear us patiently.

Exit

HAMLET Is this a prologue or a verse engraved in a ring?   140

OPHELIA It is brief, my lord.

HAMLET As woman's love.

Enter the ACTOR KING and QUEEN

ACTOR KING For thirty years now has the sun gone round
The ocean waves and the orbed ground,
And thirty dozen moons with reflected light   145
Have twelve times thirty shone out at night,
Since love our hearts and marriage our hands
Did unite together in most sacred bands.

ACTOR QUEEN And so many years may the sun and the moon
Be counted again before our love is done!   150
But I am grieved. You are so sick of late—
So far from your normal, healthy state—
That you alarm me. Yet, though I feel distress,
This must not, my lord, spoil your happiness;
For woman's fear and love are always running near: 155
When they love, they also fear.
Now, what my love is, I have proved to you,

131

And, as my love is sized, my fear is so.
Where love is great, the littlest doubts are fear;
Where little fears grow great, great love grows there.   160
PLAYER KING Faith, I must leave thee, love, and shortly too:
My operant powers their functions leave to do.
And thou shalt live in this fair world behind,
Honored, beloved; and haply one as kind
For husband shalt thou—   165
PLAYER QUEEN O, confound the rest!
Such love must needs be treason in my breast.
In second husband let me be accurst.
None wed the second but who killed the first.
HAMLET [Aside] That's wormwood.   170
PLAYER QUEEN The instances that second marriage move
Are base respects of thrift, but none of love.
A second time I kill my husband dead,
When second husband kisses me in bed.
PLAYER KING I do believe you think what now you speak;   175
But what we do determine, oft we break.
Purpose is but the slave to memory,
Of violent birth but poor validity,
Which now, the fruit unripe, sticks on the tree
But fall unshaken when they mellow be.   180
Most necessary 'tis that we forget
To pay ourselves what to ourselves is debt.
What to ourselves in passion we propose,
The passion ending, doth the purpose lose.
The violence of either grief or joy   185
Their own enactures with themselves destroy.
Where joy most revels, grief doth most lament;
Grief joys, joy grieves, on slender accident.
The world is not for aye, nor 'tis not strange
That even our loves should with our fortunes change,   190

And, as my love is, so is my fear too.
Where love is great, small worries lead to fear.
Where little fears grow great, great love grows there.   160
ACTOR KING In faith, I must leave you, love, and shortly too:
My faculties no longer work as they should do.
And you in this fair world shall stay behind,
Honored, beloved; with luck, you will find
A new husband whom you'll—   165
ACTOR QUEEN Oh, don't say the rest!
Such a love is treason in my breast.
To take a second husband, let me be accursed.
None wed twice but those who killed the first.
HAMLET [*Aside*] That has a bitter taste.   170
ACTOR QUEEN The examples that second marriage prove
Are base matters of greed, but not of love.
A second time I'd kill my husband dead
Were I to kiss another husband in his bed.
ACTOR KING I think that you believe what you say now,   175
But though we don't intend it, we often break a vow.
Resolve is only a slave to memory,
Though strong at first, it's bound to flee;
Like unripe fruit clinging to the tree,
But once mellow, falling quite free.   180
It's inevitable that we forget
To pay ourselves what is our debt.
What we to ourselves in a passion propose,
The passion cooled, the purpose slows.
The violence of either grief or joy   185
In their fulfillment does the passion destroy.
Where joy is greatest, grief greatly rants;
Grief joys, joy grieves, almost by chance.
The world is not for always, so it's not strange
That even our loves should with fortune change,   190

For 'tis a question left us yet to prove,
Whether love lead fortune or else fortune love.
The great man down, you mark his favorite flies;
The poor, advanced, makes friends of enemies;
And hitherto doth love on fortune tend,   195
For who not needs shall never lack a friend,
And who in want a hollow friend doth try
Directly seasons him his enemy.
But orderly to end where I begun,
Our wills and fates do so contrary run   200
That our devices still are overthrown:
Our thoughts are ours, their ends none of our own.
So think thou wilt no second husband wed,
But die thy thoughts when thy first lord is dead.
PLAYER QUEEN Nor earth to me give food, nor heaven light,   205
Sport and repose lock from me day and night,
To desperation turn my trust and hope,
An anchor's cheer in prison be my scope,
Each opposite, that blanks the face of joy,
Meet what I would have well and it destroy.   210
Both here and hence pursue me lasting strife,
If, once a widow, ever I be wife.
HAMLET If she should break it now!
PLAYER KING 'Tis deeply sworn. Sweet, leave me here awhile.
My spirits grow dull, and fain I would beguile   215
The tedious day with sleep.
                                                        He sleeps
PLAYER QUEEN Sleep rock thy brain,
And never come mischance between us twain.
                                                        She exits
HAMLET Madam, how like you this play?
GERTRUDE The lady doth protest too much, methinks.   220
HAMLET O, but she'll keep her word.

It is a question left for us to prove
Whether love decides our fate or fate our love.
When a great man falls, note that his favorite flies,
But those on the rise find friends among their enemies.
And so also does love on fortune depend: 195
Those who have no needs shall never lack a friend,
And he who's in want, a false friend will try
And directly change him to his enemy.
But logically, to end where I had begun:
Our wills with fate do so contrary run   200
That our plans are always overthrown.
Our thoughts are ours, but the ends are not our own.
So you think you will no second husband wed,
But your thoughts will change when your first lord is dead.
ACTOR QUEEN May earth give me no food, nor heaven light,   205
Leisure withheld by day and sleep by night,
To desperation turn my hope and trust,
A hermit's prison food be my only crust;
The force that pales the face of joy
Meet all that I would have and it destroy.   210
In this world and the next punish me with strife,
Should I, once a widow, again be a wife.
HAMLET If she should break her vow!
ACTOR KING That's deeply sworn. Sweet, leave me for awhile.
I grow tired and would now beguile   215
The tedious day with sleep.
                                                      He sleeps
ACTOR QUEEN Sleep soothe your brain,
And never let bad luck divide us again.
                                                      She exits
HAMLET Madam, what do you think of this play?
GERTRUDE The lady protests too much, I think.   220
HAMLET Oh, but she'll keep her word.

CLAUDIUS Have you heard the argument? Is there no offense
    in 't?

HAMLET No, no, they do but jest—poison in jest. No offense
    i' th' world.   225

CLAUDIUS What do you call the play?

HAMLET *The Mousetrap*—marry, how? Tropically. This play is
    the image of a murder done in Vienna—Gonzago is the
    Duke's name, his wife Baptista—you shall see anon. 'Tis
    a knavish piece of work, but what of that? Your Majesty,   230
    and we that have free souls, it touches us not. Let the galled
    jade wince, our withers are unwrung.

                        Enter LUCIANUS

    This is one Lucianus, nephew to the king.

OPHELIA You are as good as a chorus, my lord.

HAMLET I could interpret between you and your love if I could   235
    see the puppets dallying.

OPHELIA You are keen, my lord, you are keen.

HAMLET It would cost you a groaning to take off my edge.

OPHELIA Still better, and worse.

HAMLET So you mis-take your husbands.—Begin, murderer. Leave   240
    thy damnable faces and begin. Come, "The croaking raven doth
    bellow for revenge."

LUCIANUS Thoughts black, hands apt, drugs fit, and time agreeing,
    Confederate season, else no creature seeing,
    Thou mixture rank, of midnight weeds collected,   245
    With Hecate's ban thrice blasted, thrice infected,
    Thy natural magic and dire property
    On wholesome life usurps immediately.

[*He pours poison in the sleeper's ear*]

HAMLET A poisons him i' th' garden for his estate. His name's
    Gonzago. The story is extant, and written in very choice   250
    Italian. You shall see anon how the murderer gets the love
    of Gonzago's wife.

CLAUDIUS Do you know the plot? Is there any offense
    in it?
HAMLET No, no, they only joke—the poison isn't real. No
    offense in the world.   225
CLAUDIUS What do you call the play?
HAMLET *The Mousetrap.* Why? That's a metaphor. The play is
    about a true story of a murder done in Vienna. Gonzago is
    the duke's name. His wife is Baptista. You shall soon see.
    It's a vulgar sort of story, but what of that? Your Majesty,   230
    and we that have clear consciences—it doesn't concern us.
    Let the guilty squirm, we are not touched.
                      Enter LUCIANUS
    This is one Lucianus, nephew to the king.
OPHELIA You are as good as a guide, my lord.
HAMLET I could supply dialogue between you and your love if   235
    I could see you both performing.
OPHELIA You are sharp, my lord, you are sharp.
HAMLET It would cost you a great effort to dull my edge.
OPHELIA Better still—and worse.
HAMLET Those are words used to deceive husbands.—Begin,   240
    murderer. Stop making your awful faces and begin. Come,
    "The croaking raven is bellowing for revenge."
LUCIANUS Evil thoughts, ready hands, poison, and privacy,
    The time conspires, and no one else to see.
    This mixture of rank weeds, at midnight collected   245
    With a witch's curse thrice blasted, thrice infected,
    Whose natural feature and baleful quality
    Steals the wholesome life immediately.
[*He pours poison in the sleeper's ear*]
HAMLET He poisons him in the garden for his position. His
    name's Gonzago. The story is current and written in very   250
    choice Italian. You shall see soon how the murderer gets
    the love of Gonzago's wife.

OPHELIA The king rises.
HAMLET What, frighted with false fire?
GERTRUDE How fares my lord?   255
POLONIUS Give o'er the play.
CLAUDIUS Give me some light. Away!
LORDS Lights, lights, lights!

Exeunt all but HAMLET *and* HORATIO

HAMLET Why, let the strucken deer go weep,
   The hart ungalled play,   260
  For some must watch while some must sleep,
   Thus runs the world away.
 Would not this, sir, and a forest of feathers, if the rest of my
 fortunes turn Turk with me, with two Provincial roses on my
 razed shoes, get me a fellowship in a cry of players, sir?   265
HORATIO Half a share.
HAMLET A whole one, I.
  For thou dost know, O Damon dear,
   This realm dismantled was
  Of Jove himself, and now reigns here   270
   A very, very—pajock.
HORATIO You might have rhymed.
HAMLET O good Horatio, I'll take the ghost's word for a thousand
 pound. Didst perceive?
HORATIO Very well, my lord.   275
HAMLET Upon the talk of the poisoning?
HORATIO I did very well note him.
HAMLET Ah ha!—Come, some music! Come, the recorders!
  For if the king like not the comedy,
  Why then—belike he likes it not, perdy.   280
 Come, some music!

Enter ROSENCRANTZ *and* GUILDENSTERN

GUILDENSTERN Good my lord, vouchsafe a word with you.
HAMLET Sir, a whole history.

OPHELIA The king is on his feet.
HAMLET What, frightened by blank shots?
GERTRUDE How is my lord?   255
POLONIUS Stop the play.
CLAUDIUS Give me some light. Leave!
LORDS Lights, lights, lights!
                    Exit all but HAMLET *and* HORATIO
HAMLET Why, let the wounded deer go weep,
        The hart, uninjured, plays,   260
    For some must guard while some must sleep,
        Thus runs the world always.
    Would not this play, sir, should fortune turn on me, earn me a
    share in a company of actors, with plumes on my hat and
    rosettes on my fashionable shoes, sir?   265
HORATIO Half a share.
HAMLET A whole share for me.
        For you do know, my old friend,
            This realm lost Jove himself, alas.
        Its ruler now is nothing   270
            But a true—peacock.
HORATIO You might have rhymed.
HAMLET Oh, good Horatio. I'll wager a thousand pounds on
    the ghost's word. Did you notice?
HORATIO Very clearly, my lord.   275
HAMLET When there was talk of poisoning?
HORATIO I watched him very closely.
HAMLET Ah ha! Come, let's have music. Come, play the recorders!
        For, if the king dislikes the comic plot,
        Why then, by God, he likes it not.   280
    Come, some music!
                    Enter ROSENCRANTZ *and* GUILDENSTERN
GUILDENSTERN Good my lord, grant me a word with you.
HAMLET Sir, a whole history.

GUILDENSTERN The king, sir—
HAMLET Ay, sir, what of him?   285
GUILDENSTERN Is in his retirement marvelous distempered.
HAMLET With drink, sir?
GUILDENSTERN No, my lord, rather with choler.
HAMLET Your wisdom should show itself more richer to signify
    this to his doctor, for, for me to put him to his purgation   290
    would perhaps plunge him into far more choler.
GUILDENSTERN Good my lord, put your discourse into some
    frame and start not so wildly from my affair.
HAMLET I am tame, sir. Pronounce.
GUILDENSTERN The queen your mother, in most great affliction   295
    of spirit, hath sent me to you.
HAMLET You are welcome.
GUILDENSTERN Nay, good my lord, this courtesy is not of the
    right breed. If it will please you to make me a wholesome
    answer, I will do your mother's commandment. If not, your   300
    pardon, and my return shall be the end of my business.
HAMLET Sir, I cannot.
ROSENCRANTZ What, my lord?
HAMLET Make you a wholesome answer. My wit's diseased. But,
    sir, such an answer as I can make, you shall command, or   305
    rather, as you say, my mother. Therefore no more, but to the
    matter. My mother, you say—
ROSENCRANTZ Then thus she says. Your behavior hath struck her
    into amazement and admiration.
HAMLET O wonderful son that can so 'stonish a mother! But is there   310
    no sequel at the heels of this mother's admiration? Impart.
ROSENCRANTZ She desires to speak with you in her closet ere you
    go to bed.
HAMLET We shall obey, were she ten times our mother. Have
    you any further trade with us?   315
ROSENCRANTZ My lord, you once did love me.

GUILDENSTERN The king, sir—
HAMLET Yes, sir, what about him?   285
GUILDENSTERN Has retired to his apartments greatly upset.
HAMLET With drink, sir?
GUILDENSTERN No, my lord, rather with anger.
HAMLET You ought to have more sense and tell this to his doctor,
    for if I were to treat him, he might be plunged deeper into   290
    his anger.
GUILDENSTERN My good lord, restrain your speech and do not
    bolt so wildly at my remarks.
HAMLET I am tame, sir. Go on.
GUILDENSTERN Your mother the queen, who is in great distress,   295
    has sent me to you.
HAMLET You are welcome.
GUILDENSTERN No, my good lord, this courtesy is not good
    manners. If it please you to give me a sensible answer, I will
    carry out your mother's command. If not, give me your   300
    permission to leave, and I will return to conclude my business.
HAMLET Sir, I cannot.
ROSENCRANTZ Cannot what, my lord?
HAMLET Give you a sensible answer. My brain's scrambled. But,
    sir, such an answer as I can give you, you shall have, or   305
    rather as you say, my mother shall have. So, enough said.
    Back to the subject. My mother, you say—
ROSENCRANTZ This is what she says: your behavior has shocked
    and astonished her.
HAMLET Oh, wonderful son that can so astonish a mother! But   310
    is there no sequel in this mother's astonishment? Tell all.
ROSENCRANTZ She wants to speak with you in her apartment
    before you go to bed.
HAMLET We shall obey, even if she were ten times our mother.
    Have you any further business with us?   315
ROSENCRANTZ My lord, you once liked me very much.

HAMLET And do still, by these pickers and stealers.

ROSENCRANTZ Good my lord, what is your cause of distemper?
  You do surely bar the door upon your own liberty if you deny
  your griefs to your friend.   320

HAMLET Sir, I lack advancement.

ROSENCRANTZ How can that be, when you have the voice of the
  king himself for your succession in Denmark?

HAMLET Ay, sir, but "While the grass grows"—the proverb is
  something musty.   325

  Enter the PLAYERS *with recorders*

  O, the recorders! Let me see one. To withdraw with you—Why
  do you go about to recover the wind of me, as if you would drive
  me into a toil?

GUILDENSTERN O, my lord, if my duty be too bold, my love is too
  unmannerly.   330

HAMLET I do not well understand that. [*Handing him the recorder*]
  Will you play upon this pipe?

GUILDENSTERN My lord, I cannot.

HAMLET I pray you.

GUILDENSTERN Believe me, I cannot.   335

HAMLET I do beseech you.

GUILDENSTERN I know no touch of it, my lord.

HAMLET 'Tis as easy as lying. Govern these ventages with your
  fingers and thumb, give it breath with your mouth, and it will
  discourse most eloquent music. Look you, these are the stops.   340

GUILDENSTERN But these cannot I command to any utterance of
  harmony. I have not the skill.

HAMLET Why, look you now how unworthy a thing you make of me.
  You would play upon me, you would seem to know my stops,
  you would pluck out the heart of my mystery, you would   345
  sound me from my lowest note to the top of my compass— and there is
  much music, excellent voice, in this little organ, yet cannot you make it
  speak. 'Sblood, do you think I am easier to be played on than a pipe?

HAMLET And do still, by these hands.

ROSENCRANTZ My good lord, what is the cause of your disorder?
    You surely bar the door to a cure if you won't tell what
    troubles you to your friend.   320

HAMLET Sir, my ambitions are thwarted.

ROSENCRANTZ How can that be, when you have the word of the
    king himself for your succession in Denmark?

HAMLET Yes, sir, but "While the grass grows, the horse starves"—
    the proverb is a little musty.   325

Enter the ACTORS *with recorders*

Oh, the recorders! Let me see one. To speak in confidence,
why do you, like a hunter, get downwind of me to draw me
to your trap?

GUILDENSTERN Oh, my lord, if I am being too bold, it is my
    love that has made me unmannerly.   330

HAMLET I do not follow that. [*Handing him the recorder*] Will
    you play something?

GUILDENSTERN My lord, I cannot.

HAMLET Please.

GUILDENSTERN Believe me, I can't.   335

HAMLET I beg you.

GUILDENSTERN I don't know how to finger it, my lord.

HAMLET It's as easy as lying. You control these holes with your
    fingers and thumb, blow with your mouth, and it will deliver
    most pleasing music. Look here, there are the stops.   340

GUILDENSTERN But I cannot make them sound harmonious. I don't
    have the skill.

HAMLET Why, look now how you belittle me. You want to play
    me, you seem to know where my stops are, you would learn
    the innermost secret of my working, you would sound me   345
    from my lowest note to the top of my range—and there is much
    music, excellent melody, in this little instrument, yet you cannot
    make it speak. God's blood, do you think I am easier to be played

Call me what instrument you will, though you can fret me,
you cannot play upon me.   350

Enter POLONIUS

God bless you, sir.
POLONIUS My lord, the queen would speak with you, and presently.
HAMLET Do you see yonder cloud that's almost in shape of a camel?
POLONIUS By th' Mass, and 'tis like a camel indeed.
HAMLET Methinks it is like a weasel.   355
POLONIUS It is backed like a weasel.
HAMLET Or like a whale?
POLONIUS Very like a whale.
HAMLET Then I will come to my mother by and by. [*Aside*] They
    fool me to the top of my bent.—I will come by and by.   360
POLONIUS I will say so.

Exits

HAMLET "By and by" is easily said.—Leave me, friends.

Exeunt all but HAMLET

'Tis now the very witching time of night,
When churchyards yawn, and hell itself breathes out
Contagion to this world. Now could I drink hot blood,   365
And do such bitter business as the day
Would quake to look on. Soft, now to my mother.
O heart, lose not thy nature; let not ever
The soul of Nero enter this firm bosom.
Let me be cruel, not unnatural.   370
I will speak daggers to her but use none.
My tongue and soul in this be hypocrites:
How in my words somever she be shent,
To give them seals never my soul consent.

Exits

Scene 3 [*The Palace*] *Enter* CLAUDIUS, ROSENCRANTZ, *and*
    GUILDENSTERN
CLAUDIUS I like him not, nor stands it safe with us

than a little pipe? Call me what you will, even fret me,
you cannot sound me out.   350

Enter POLONIUS

God bless you, sir.

POLONIUS The queen would speak with you, and soon.

HAMLET Do you see that far cloud that's shaped almost like a camel?

POLONIUS By the Holy Mass, it's like a camel, indeed.

HAMLET I think it's like a weasel.   355

POLONIUS It has a back like a weasel.

HAMLET Or like a whale?

POLONIUS Very like a whale.

HAMLET Then I will visit my mother by and by. [*Aside*] They tax
me to my limit.—I will come by and by.   360

POLONIUS I will say so.

Exits

HAMLET "By and by" is easily said.—Leave me, friends.

Exit all but HAMLET

It's now the bewitching time of night,
When churchyard graves open wide, and hell itself breathes out
Evil to this world. Now could I drink hot blood   365
And do such cruel deeds as the day
Would shudder to see. Enough, now to my mother.
Oh, heart don't lose your natural feeling; never let
The soul of Nero enter this firm bosom.
Let me be cruel, but not unnatural.   370
I will speak daggers to her but use none.
My tongue and soul in this be two-faced:
However my words put her to shame,
To turn them to deeds, never my soul inflame.

Exits

Scene 3 [*The Palace*] *Enter* CLAUDIUS, ROSENCRANTZ, *and*
GUILDENSTERN

CLAUDIUS I do not like the way he acts, nor is it safe for us

To let his madness range. Therefore prepare you.
I your commission will forthwith dispatch,
And he to England shall along with you.
The terms of our estate may not endure   5
Hazard so near us as doth hourly grow
Out of his brows.
GUILDENSTERN We will ourselves provide.
    Most holy and religious fear it is
    To keep those many many bodies safe   10
    That live and feed upon your majesty.
ROSENCRANTZ The single and peculiar life is bound
    With all the strength and armor of the mind
    To keep itself from noyance; but much more
    That spirit upon whose weal depends and rests   15
    The lives of many. The cess of majesty
    Dies not alone, but like a gulf doth draw
    What's near it with it. It is a massy wheel
    Fixed on the summit of the highest mount,
    To whose huge spokes ten thousand lesser things   20
    Are mortised and adjoined, which, when it falls,
    Each small annexment, petty consequence,
    Attends the boisterous ruin. Never alone
    Did the king sigh, but with a general groan.
CLAUDIUS Arm you, I pray you to this speedy voyage,   25
    For we will fetters put about this fear,
    Which now goes too free-footed.
ROSENCRANTZ We will haste us.
                 Exeunt ROSENCRANTZ *and* GUILDENSTERN
                      Enter POLONIUS
POLONIUS My lord, he's going to his mother's closet.
    Behind the arras I'll convey myself   30
    To hear the process. I'll warrant she'll tax him home,
    And as you said, and wisely was it said,

To let his madness range free. Therefore, prepare yourselves.
I will issue your commission at once,
And he shall go along with you to England.
Our position as king cannot permit   5
The dangers so near us that hourly grow
Out of his mind.
GUILDENSTERN We will make ourselves ready.
It is a sacred and religious duty
To keep those many, many persons safe   10
That depend upon your majesty.
ROSENCRANTZ The single individual is bound
With all the strength and armor of the mind
To keep himself from harm; so how much more
A king, upon whose well-being depend and rest   15
The lives of many. A king does not die
Alone, but like a whirlpool, his death draws
In whatever's near it. Majesty is a massive wheel,
Placed at the summit of the highest mountain,
To whose huge spokes ten thousand minor parts   20
Are fitted together and attached. When it rolls,
Every small insignificant piece joined to it,
Is involved in the monumental ruin. Never alone
Does a king sigh, but the people also groan.
CLAUDIUS Make yourselves ready for this hasty voyage.   25
For we will fetter this fear
That's now so footloose.
ROSENCRANTZ We will hurry.
                  Exit ROSENCRANTZ *and* GUILDENSTERN
                      Enter POLONIUS
POLONIUS My lord, he's going to his mother's rooms.
I'll conceal myself behind a curtain   30
To hear what is said. I'm sure she'll reproach him,
And as you said, and wisely was it said,

'Tis meet that some more audience than a mother,
Since nature makes them partial, should o'erhear
The speech of vantage. Fare you well, my liege.   35
I'll call upon you ere you go to bed
And tell you what I know.
CLAUDIUS Thanks, dear my lord.

Exit POLONIUS

O, my offense is rank, it smells to heaven;
It hath the primal eldest curse upon 't,   40
A brother's murder. Pray can I not,
Though inclination be as sharp as will.
My stronger guilt defeats my strong intent,
And like a man to double business bound,
I stand in pause where I shall first begin,   45
And both neglect. What if this cursed hand
Were thicker than itself with brother's blood?
Is there not rain enough in the sweet heavens
To wash it white as snow? Whereto serves mercy
But to confront the visage of offense?   50
And what's in prayer but this twofold force,
To be forestalled ere we come to fall,
Or pardoned being down? Then I'll look up.
My fault is past. But, O, what form of prayer
Can serve my turn? "Forgive me my foul murder?"   55
That cannot be, since I am still possessed
Of those effects for which I did the murder,
My crown, mine own ambition, and my queen.
May one be pardoned and retain th' offense?
In the corrupted currents of this world,   60
Offense's gilded hand may shove by justice,
And oft 'tis seen the wicked prize itself
Buys out the law. But 'tis not so above;
There is no shuffling, there the action lies

It's better that someone other than a mother,
Since nature makes them partial, should overhear
Their speech besides. Farewell, my liege.   35
I'll call on you before you go to bed
And tell you what I learn.
CLAUDIUS Thanks, my dear lord.

                                        Exit POLONIUS

Oh, my crime is rank. It smells to heaven.
It has the original curse of Cain upon it—   40
A brother's murder. I cannot pray,
Though my desire is as sharp as my will.
My stronger sense of guilt defeats my strong intent,
And like a man drawn between two actions,
I hesitate and do not know where to begin,   45
And so neglect both. What if this cursed hand
Were even thicker with a brother's blood?
Is there not rain enough in the sweet heavens
To wash it white as snow? What is mercy for
If not to meet crime face to face?   50
And what's in prayer if not this double power—
To be prevented from doing wrong
And to pardon us if we have? Then I'll be hopeful.
My crime is past. But, oh, what kind of prayer
Would suit my needs? "Forgive me my foul murder?"   55
That would not do, since I still possess
Those things for which I did the murder—
My crown, my own ambition, and my queen.
Can one be pardoned and keep the spoils of a crime?
In the corrupted course of this world's events,   60
A hand of gold may shove aside justice,
And often it is seen that ill-gotten gains
Buy out the law. But it's not that way in heaven.
There is no trickery, there the deed lies

In his true nature, and we ourselves compelled   65
Even to the teeth and forehead of our faults
To give in evidence. What then? What rests?
Try what repentance can. What can it not?
Yet what can it, when one cannot repent?
O wretched state! O bosom black as death!   70
O limed soul, that, struggling to be free
Art more engaged! Help, angels!—Make assay.
Bow stubborn knees, and heart with strings of steel
Be soft as sinews of the newborn babe.
All may be well.   75
      [He kneels]

Enter HAMLET
HAMLET Now might I do it pat, now a is a-praying,
And now I'll do 't—and so a goes to heaven,
And so am I revenged. That would be scanned.
A villain kills my father, and for that,
I his sole son, do this same villain send   80
To heaven.
Why, this is hire and salary, not revenge.
A took my father grossly, full of bread,
With all his crimes broad blown, as flush as May,
And how his audit stands who knows save heaven?   85
But in our circumstance and course of thought
'Tis heavy with him. And am I then revenged
To take him in the purging of his soul,
When he is fit and seasoned for his passage?
No.   90
Up sword, and know thou a more horrid hent,
When he is drunk asleep, or in his rage,
Or in th' incestuous pleasure of his bed,
At game a-swearing, or about some act
That has no relish of salvation in 't—   95

In its true nature, and we ourselves are compelled,   65
In face-to-face confrontation with our faults,
To give evidence. What then? What remains?
Try what repentance can do. What can it not do?
Yet what can it do, when one cannot repent.
Oh, wretched state! Oh, heart as black as death!   70
Oh, trapped soul that, struggling to be free,
Is more entangled. Help, angels! Make the attempt.
Bow stubborn knees, and heart with strings of steel
Be soft as the sinews of a newborn baby.
All may be well.   75
            [*He kneels*]
                    Enter HAMLET
HAMLET Now might I do it quick, now he's praying.
        And now I'll do it—and then he goes to heaven,
        And thus I am revenged. That should be examined.
        A villain kills my father, and for that,
        I, his sole son, now send this same villain   80
        To heaven.
        Why, this is something to be paid for, not revenge.
        He killed my father shamefully, full fed,
        With all his sins in bloom, as lusty as May,
        And how his account stands only heaven knows.   85
        But in our situation and mortal way of thinking,
        It looks bad for him. And then am I revenged
        To kill him while he is purging his sins,
        When he is fit and ready for his judgment?
        No.   90
        Down sword, and find a more horrid occasion,
        When he is drunk asleep, in a rage,
        Or in the incestuous pleasure of his bed,
        Gambling and cursing, or in some act
        That has no trace of salvation in it.   95

Then trip him, that his heels may kick at heaven,
And that his soul may be as damned and black
As hell whereto it goes. My mother stays.
This physic but prolongs thy sickly days.

Exits

CLAUDIUS My words fly up, my thoughts remain below. 100
Words without thoughts never to heaven go.

Exits

Scene 4 [*The queen's apartments*] *Enter* GERTRUDE *and* POLONIUS

POLONIUS A will come straight. Look you lay home to him.
Tell him his pranks have been too broad to bear with,
And that your Grace hath screened and stood between
Much heat and him. I'll silence me even here.
Pray you, be round with him. 5
GERTRUDE I'll warrant you, fear me not. Withdraw, I hear him
coming.
HAMLET [*Within*] Mother, mother, mother!
[POLONIUS *hides himself behind the arras*]

Enter HAMLET

HAMLET Now, mother, what's the matter?
GERTRUDE Hamlet, thou hast thy father much offended. 10
HAMLET Mother, you have my father much offended.
GERTRUDE Come, come, you answer with an idle tongue.
HAMLET Go, go, you question with a wicked tongue.
GERTRUDE Why, how now, Hamlet?
HAMLET What's the matter now? 15
GERTRUDE Have you forgot me?
HAMLET No, by the rood, not so.
You are the queen, your husband's brother's wife,
And, would it were not so, you are my mother.
GERTRUDE Nay, then I'll set those to you that can speak. 20
HAMLET Come, come and sit down, you shall not budge.

Then I'll trip him, so that his heels may kick at heaven
And his soul may be as damned and black
As the hell to which it goes. My mother waits.
His prayer just prolongs his final fate.

Exits

CLAUDIUS My words rise up, my thoughts remain below.   100
    Words without thoughts can never to heaven go.

Exits

Scene 4 [*The queen's apartments*] *Enter* GERTRUDE *and* POLONIUS

POLONIUS He's on his way. Be sure you reprove him to the full.
    Tell him his pranks have been too gross to bear with,
    And that your Grace has been the fire screen between
    Much heat and him. I'll hide myself back here.
    Please, be direct with him.   5
GERTRUDE I promise you, don't fear me. Hide, I hear him
    coming.
HAMLET [*Within*] Mother, mother, mother!
[POLONIUS *conceals himself behind a tapestry*]

Enter HAMLET

HAMLET Now, mother. What's the matter?
GERTRUDE Hamlet, you have deeply offended your father.   10
HAMLET Mother, you have deeply offended my father.
GERTRUDE Come, come, you answer with a foolish tongue.
HAMLET Go, go, you question with a wicked tongue.
GERTRUDE How is that, Hamlet?
HAMLET What's the matter now?   15
GERTRUDE Have you forgotten who I am?
HAMLET No, by the holy Cross, not at all.
    You are the queen, your husband's brother's wife.
    And, would it were not so, you are my mother.
GERTRUDE No, I'll send people to you that are more persuasive.   20
HAMLET Come, come and sit down. You shall not budge.

You go not till I set you up a glass
Where you may see the inmost part of you.
GERTRUDE What wilt thou do? Thou wilt not murder me?
     Help, help, ho.   25
POLONIUS [*Behind*] What ho! Help, help, help!
HAMLET [*Draws*] How now, a rat? [*Kills* POLONIUS] Dead for a
     ducat, dead.
POLONIUS [*Behind*] O, I am slain!
GERTRUDE O me, what hast thou done?   30
HAMLET Nay, I know not. Is it the king?
GERTRUDE O, what a rash and bloody deed is this!
HAMLET A bloody deed? Almost as bad, good mother,
     As kill a king and marry with his brother.
GERTRUDE As kill a king?   35
HAMLET Ay, lady, 'twas my word.
[*Lifts up the arras and reveals the body of* POLONIUS]
     Thou wretched, rash, intruding fool, farewell.
     I took thee for thy better. Take thy fortune.
     Thou find'st to be too busy is some danger.—
     Leave wringing of your hands. Peace, sit you down   40
     And let me wring your heart, for so I shall
     If it be made of penetrable stuff,
     If damned custom have not brazed it so,
     That it be proof and bulwark against sense.
GERTRUDE What have I done, that thou dar'st wag thy tongue   45
     In noise so rude against me?
HAMLET Such an act
     That blurs the grace and blush of modesty,
     Calls virtue hypocrite, takes off the rose
     From the fair forehead of an innocent love   50
     And sets a blister there, makes marriage vows
     As false as dicers' oaths. O, such a deed
     As from the body of contraction plucks

You will not go till I've put up a mirror
In which you can see your inner self.
GERTRUDE What are you going to do? You're not going to murder me?
Help, help, oh.   25
POLONIUS [*From behind the tapestry*] What ho! Help, help, help!
HAMLET [*Draws his sword*] What, a rat? [*Thrusts through the tapestry*]
Dead, I'll bet a ducat on it.
POLONIUS [*From behind the tapestry*] Oh, he's killed me.
GERTRUDE Oh me, what have you done?   30
HAMLET I don't know. Is it the king?
GERTRUDE Oh, what a rash and bloody deed is this!
HAMLET A bloody deed? Almost as bad, dear mother,
As to kill a king and marry his brother.
GERTRUDE As to kill a king?   35
HAMLET Yes, lady, that was what I said.
[*Lifts up the tapestry and reveals the body of* POLONIUS]
You wretched, rash, intruding fool—farewell.
I mistook you for your better. Accept your bad luck.
You've found being nosey puts you in danger.—
Quit wringing your hands. Be quiet, sit down,   40
And let me wring your heart, for so I shall,
If it be made of penetrable stuff,
If wicked habits have not hardened it so
That it is tempered and fortified against feeling.
GERTRUDE What have I done, that you dare to wag your tongue   45
So harshly against me?
HAMLET For such an act
That defiles the grace and blush of modesty,
Calls virtue a hypocrite, takes the bloom
From the fair forehead of innocent love   50
And sets a blister there, makes marriage vows
As false as gamblers' oaths. Oh, such a deed
As from the body of solemn promises plucks

The very soul, and sweet religion makes
A rhapsody of words. Heaven's face doth glow; 55
Yea, this solidity and compound mass,
With tristful visage, as against the doom,
Is thought-sick at the act.
GERTRUDE Ay me, what act
That roars so loud and thunders in the index? 60
HAMLET Look here upon this picture and on this,
The counterfeit presentment of two brothers.
See what a grace was seated on this brow;
Hyperion's curls, the front of Jove himself,
An eye like Mars' to threaten and command, 65
A station like the herald Mercury
New-lighted on a heaven-kissing hill;
A combination and a form indeed,
Where every god did seem to set his seal
To give the world assurance of a man. 70
This was your husband. Look you now what follows.
Here is your husband, like a mildewed ear
Blasting his wholesome brother. Have you eyes?
Could you on this fair mountain leave to feed
And batten on this moor? Ha! Have you eyes? 75
You cannot call it love, for at your age
The heyday in the blood is tame, it's humble
And waits upon the judgment; and what judgment
Would step from this to this? Sense sure you have,
Else you could not have motion, but sure that sense 80
Is apoplexed, for madness would not err,
Nor sense to ecstasy was ne'er so thralled,
But it reserved some quantity of choice
To serve in such a difference. What devil was 't
That thus cozened you at hoodman-blind? 85
Eyes without feeling, feeling without sight,

Its very soul and turns sweet religion
Into a jumble of words. The skies are red with shame;   55
Yes, the huge earth itself,
With an expression as sad as doomsday
Is thought-sick at your act.
GERTRUDE Oh me, what act is it
That receives such a violent introduction?   60
HAMLET Look here at this picture and at this,
The portraits of two brothers.
See what a grace is evident in these features—
Curls like the sun god, the brow of Jove himself,
An eye like Mars' to threaten and command,   65
A bearing like the winged messenger of the gods,
New-alighted on a high hill;
An image and a form indeed,
Where every god did seem to set his stamp
To give the world the realization of a man.   70
This was your husband. Now look what follows.
Here is your husband, like a mildewed ear of corn
Infecting his healthy brother. Are you blind?
Could you leave this fair mountain to feed
And fatten on this wasteland? Ha! Are you blind?   75
You cannot call it love, for at your age
The high point of passion is tame, it's humble
And controlled by judgment; and what judgment
Would lead you from this to this? Surely, you have your senses
Or else you could not move, but surely those senses   80
Are paralyzed. Madness would not err
Nor your senses to madness be so enslaved
That you could not retain some small choice
To be used in so great a difference. What devil was it
That tricked you at blindman's bluff?   85
Sight without touch, touch without sight,

Ears without hands or eyes, smelling sans all,
Or but a sickly part of one true sense
Could not so mope.
O shame, where is thy blush? Rebellious hell,   90
If thou canst mutine in a matron's bones,
To flaming youth let virtue be as wax
And melt in her own fire. Proclaim no shame
When the compulsive ardor gives the charge,
Since frost as actively doth burn,   95
And reason panders will.
GERTRUDE O Hamlet, speak no more!
Thou turn'st my eyes into my very soul,
And there I see such black and grained spots
As will not leave their tinct.   100
HAMLET Nay, but to live
In the rank sweat of an enseamed bed,
Stewed in corruption, honeying and making love
Over the nasty sty!
GERTRUDE O, speak to me no more!   105
These words like daggers enter in my ears.
No more, sweet Hamlet.
HAMLET A murderer and a villain,
A slave that is not twentieth part the tithe
Of your precedent lord, a vice of kings,   110
A cutpurse of the empire and the rule,
That from a shelf the precious diadem stole
And put it in his pocket—
GERTRUDE No more!
      Enter GHOST
HAMLET A king of shreds and patches—   115
Save me and hover o'er me with your wings,
You heavenly guards!—What would your gracious figure?
GERTRUDE Alas, he's mad!

Hearing without sight or touch, smell without the others—
Just a sickly part of one true sense
Would keep you from being so foolish.
Oh, shame. Where is your blush? Rebellious hell,   90
If you can mutiny in a matron's bones,
Then the virtue of flaming youth is like wax
And melts in its own flame. There is no shame,
When the compelling fire of passion explodes,
Since the frost of age burns as actively,   95
And reason supports lust.
GERTRUDE Oh, Hamlet, say no more!
You turn my eyes into my very soul,
And there I see black and indelible spots
That will not lose their color.   100
HAMLET Imagine, to live
In the stinking sweat of a greasy bed,
Stewed in corruption, sweetly talking love
In that filthy sty!
GERTRUDE Oh, say no more to me!   105
These words are like daggers that enter my ears.
No more, sweet Hamlet.
HAMLET A murderer and a villain,
A vile person not worth a twentieth of a tenth
Of your former husband, a buffoon of kings,   110
A thief of the empire and the rule,
Who stole the precious crown from a shelf
And put it in his pocket—
GERTRUDE No more!
                      Enter GHOST
HAMLET A king of scraps and patches—   115
Save me and protect me with your wings,
You heavenly angels!—What does your majesty wish?
GERTRUDE Alas, he's gone mad!

HAMLET Do you not come your tardy son to chide,
    That, lapsed in time and passion, lets go by   120
    Th' important acting of your dread command? O, say!
GHOST Do not forget. This visitation
    Is but to whet thy almost blunted purpose.
    But look, amazement on thy mother sits.
    O, step between her and her fighting soul: 125
    Conceit in weakest bodies strongest works.
    Speak to her, Hamlet.
HAMLET How is it with you, lady?
GERTRUDE Alas, how is 't with you,
    That you do bend your eye on vacancy,   130
    And with th' incorporal air do hold discourse?
    Forth at your eyes your spirits wildly peep,
    And, as the sleeping soldiers in th' alarm,
    Your bedded hair, like life in excrements,
    Start up and stand an end. O gentle son,   135
    Upon the heat and flame of thy distemper
    Sprinkle cool patience. Whereon do you look?
HAMLET On him, on him! Look you how pale he glares.
    His form and cause conjoined, preaching to stones,
    Would make them capable.—Do not look upon me,   140
    Lest with this piteous action you convert
    My stern effects. Then what I have to do
    Will want true color—tears perchance for blood.
GERTRUDE To whom do you speak this?
HAMLET Do you see nothing there?   145
GERTRUDE Nothing at all, yet all that is I see.
HAMLET Nor did you nothing hear?
GERTRUDE No, nothing but ourselves.
HAMLET Why, look you there—look how it steals away—
    My father in his habit as he lived—   150
    Look where he goes, even now out at the portal.

HAMLET Have you not come to scold your slow-moving son,
    Who, having allowed time and passion to cool, let slip   120
    The urgent acting of your fearful command? Tell me.
GHOST Do not forget. This visit
    Is only to sharpen your almost blunted purpose.
    But look. Your mother is bewildered.
    Oh, step between her and her fighting soul: 125
    Weak people have the strongest imaginations.
    Speak to her, Hamlet.
HAMLET How are you, madam?
GERTRUDE No, how are you?
    What makes you turn your eye on nothing   130
    And with the empty air hold conversation?
    Your eyes bulge with excitement,
    And like sleeping soldiers at an alarm,
    The hair lying flat on your head, as if it were alive,
    Starts up and stands on end. Oh, gentle son,   135
    Upon the heat and flame of your illness,
    Sprinkle cool patience. What are you looking at?
HAMLET On him, on him! Look how pale his stare is.
    His looks and his cause together, were they to preach to stones,
    Would move them to act.—Do not look at me,   140
    Lest with this piteous act you turn aside
    My stern purposes. Then what I have to do
    Would lack true color—tears instead of blood.
GERTRUDE To whom are you speaking?
HAMLET Do you see nothing there?   145
GERTRUDE Nothing at all, yet I can see all there is to see.
HAMLET And you heard nothing?
GERTRUDE No, nothing but ourselves.
HAMLET Why, look there—see how it slips away—
    My father in the gown he wore when he was alive—   150
    Look where he goes, out through the door.

Exit GHOST

GERTRUDE This is the very coinage of your brain.
    This bodiless creation ecstasy
    Is very cunning in.
HAMLET Ecstasy?   155
    My pulse as yours doth temperately keep time,
    And makes as healthful music. It is not madness
    That I have uttered. Bring me to the test,
    And I the matter will reword, which madness
    Would gambol from. Mother, for love of grace,   160
    Lay not that flattering unction to your soul,
    That not your trespass but my madness speaks;
    It will but skin and film the ulcerous place,
    Whiles rank corruption, mining all within,
    Infects unseen. Confess yourself to heaven,   165
    Repent what's past, avoid what is to come,
    And do not spread the compost on the weeds
    To make them ranker. Forgive me this my virtue,
    For, in the fatness of these pursy times,
    Virtue itself of vice must pardon beg,   170
    Yea, curb and woo for leave to do him good.
GERTRUDE O Hamlet, thou hast cleft my heart in twain!
HAMLET O, throw away the worser part of it
    And live the purer with the other half!
    Good night—but go not to my uncle's bed.   175
    Assume a virtue if you have it not.
    That monster custom, who all sense doth eat,
    Of habits devil, is an angel yet in this,
    That to the use of actions fair and good
    He likewise gives a frock or livery   180
    That aptly is put on. Refrain tonight,
    And that shall lend a kind of easiness
    To the next abstinence, the next more easy,

Exit GHOST

GERTRUDE This is the mere invention of your brain.
    Madness is very good at
    Such imaginary creations.
HAMLET Madness?   155
    My pulse beats as regularly as yours,
    Making healthful music. It is not madness
    That I have uttered. Put me to the test,
    And I will repeat what I said, which a mad person
    Could not do. Mother, for the love of grace,   160
    Do not apply that soothing balm to your soul—
    That it is my madness and not your sin that speaks.
    That will only cover the ulcer with a thin layer,
    While the foul corruption, festering within,
    Infects unseen. Confess yourself to heaven,   165
    Repent what you have done, avoid what is to come,
    And do not spread manure on weeds
    To make them bigger. Forgive my way of speaking,
    But in the grossness of these self-indulgent times,
    Even virtue must beg vice's pardon,   170
    Yes, bow and ask permission to do good.
GERTRUDE Oh Hamlet, you have split my heart in two!
HAMLET Then throw away the worse part of it
    And live the purer with the other half!
    Good night—but don't go to my uncle's bed.   175
    Assume a virtue even if you don't have it.
    That monster custom, which devours good sense
    And leads to devilish habits, is also an angel
    In that it can make us used to good actions,
    And provide us with a uniform or clothes   180
    That are easy to put on. Refrain tonight,
    And that will make the next abstinence easier,
    And the one after that, easier still.

For use almost can change the stamp of nature,
And either throw the devil or cast him out
With wondrous potency. Once more, good night,   185
And when you are desirous to be blest,
I'll blessing beg of you. For this same lord,
I do repent; but heaven hath pleased it so,
To punish me with this and this with me,
That I must be their scourge and minister.   190
I will bestow him and will answer well
The death I gave him. So, again, good night.
I must be cruel only to be kind.
Thus bad begins, and worse remains behind.
One word more, good lady.   195
GERTRUDE What shall I do?
HAMLET Not this by no means that I bid you do:
    Let the bloat king tempt you again to bed,
    Pinch wanton on your cheek, call you his mouse,
    And let him for a pair of reechy kisses   200
    Or paddling in your neck with his damned fingers,
    Make you to ravel all this matter out,
    That I essentially am not in madness,
    But mad in craft. 'Twere good you let him know,
    For who that's but a queen, fair, sober, wise,   205
    Would from a paddock, from a bat, a gib,
    Such dear concernings hide? Who would do so?
    No, in despite of sense and secrecy,
    Unpeg the basket on the house's top,
    Let the birds fly, and like the famous ape,   210
    To try conclusions, in the basket creep
    And break your own neck down.
GERTRUDE Be thou assured, if words be made of breath,
    And breath of life, I have no life to breathe
    What thou hast said to me.   215

Habit can almost change natural character,
And either shape the devil or cast him out
Quite effectively. Once more, good night,   185
And when you seek God's blessing for yourself,
I'll beg a blessing of you. As for this lord,
I do repent. It has pleased heaven so
To punish me with this and him through me,
As heaven's whip and instrument.   190
I will dispose of his body and acknowledge
The death I caused. So, again, good night.
I must be cruel only to be kind.
A bad beginning, and worse yet to find.
One word more, good lady.   195
GERTRUDE What shall I do?
HAMLET Not, by any means, what I told you not to do:
Don't let the bloated king tempt you to his bed,
Pinch your cheek lewdly, call you his mouse,
Or let him for a pair of greasy kisses,   200
Fondling your neck with his damned fingers,
Make you explain all that has happened:
That, essentially, I am not mad,
But only pretending to be. Your duty is to tell him.
Could a mere queen—fair, sober, wise—   205
Conceal from a toad, from a bat, a tomcat
Important matters that affect one closely? Who would?
No, contrary to common sense and caution,
You could open the basket on the house top,
Let the birds fly out, and like the ape in the story,   210
To test the result, creep into the basket,
Fall down, and break your neck.
GERTRUDE Be assured, if words are made of breath,
And breath made of life, I have no life to breathe
After what you have said to me.   215

HAMLET I must to England, you know that?
GERTRUDE Alack,
    I had forgot. 'Tis so concluded on.
HAMLET There's letters sealed, and my two schoolfellows,
    Whom I will trust as I will adders fanged,   220
    They bear the mandate. They must sweep my way
    And marshal me to knavery. Let it work,
    For 'tis the sport to have the engineer
    Hoist with his own petard, and 't shall go hard
    But I will delve one yard below their mines   225
    And blow them at the moon. O, 'tis most sweet
    When in one line two crafts directly meet.
    This man [*turning to* POLONIUS] shall set me packing.
    I'll lug the guts into the neighbor room.
    Mother, good night. Indeed, this counselor   230
    Is now most still, most secret, and most grave,
    Who was in life a foolish prating knave.
    Come, sir, to draw toward an end with you.
    Good night, mother.

Exit HAMLET *dragging* POLONIUS

HAMLET I must go to England. You know that?
GERTRUDE Oh, Lord,
    I had forgotten. It's already settled.
HAMLET There are official letters, and my two schoolmates—
    Whom I trust like fanged vipers—   220
    They bear the royal commission. They must clear the path
    And guide me to mischief. Let it be,
    For it will be fun to have the plotters
    Blown up by their own bomb. Though difficult,
    I will dig a yard below their mines   225
    And blow them to the moon. Oh, it's nice
    To have two crafty schemes meet head on.
    This man [*turning to* POLONIUS] shall send me packing.
    I'll lug the guts into the next room.
    Mother, good night. Indeed, this counselor   230
    Is now most quiet, most secret, and most grave,
    Who never in life knew how to behave.
    Come, sir, to end my business with you.
    Good night, mother.

Exit HAMLET *dragging* POLONIUS

Act Four

Scene 1 [CLAUDIUS *joins* GERTRUDE *in her apartments.* ROSENCRANTZ
and GUILDENSTERN *follow him*]

CLAUDIUS There's matter in these sighs, these profound heaves.
      You must translate, 'tis fit we understand them.
      Where is your son?
GERTRUDE Bestow this place on us a little while.

Exeunt ROSENCRANTZ *and* GUILDENSTERN

CLAUDIUS What, Gertrude? How does Hamlet?   5
GERTRUDE Mad as the sea and wind, when both contend
      Which is the mightier. In his lawless fit,
      Behind the arras hearing something stir,
      Whips out his rapier, cries "A rat, a rat,"
      And in this brainish apprehension kills   10
      The unseen good old man.

Act Four

Scene 1 [CLAUDIUS *joins* GERTRUDE *in her apartments.* ROSENCRANTZ
    and GUILDENSTERN *follow him*]

CLAUDIUS There's a reason for these sighs, these deep sobs.
    You must explain. It's right that we understand.
    Where is your son?
GERTRUDE Leave us alone for a while.

                Exit ROSENCRANTZ *and* GUILDENSTERN

CLAUDIUS What now, Gertrude? How is Hamlet?   5
GERTRUDE As mad as the sea and the wind, when they fight
    To see which is the mightier. In his lawless fit,
    Hearing something stir behind the curtain,
    He whips out his rapier, crying "A rat, a rat."
    And in this mad illusion, he kills   10
    The hidden, good old man.

CLAUDIUS O heavy deed!
    It had been so with us, had we been there.
    His liberty is full of threats to all—
    To you yourself, to us, to everyone.   15
    Alas, how shall this bloody deed be answered?
    It will be laid to us, whose providence
    Should have kept short, restrained, and out of haunt,
    This mad young man. But so much was our love,
    We would not understand what was most fit,   20
    But, like the owner of a foul disease,
    To keep it from divulging, let it feed
    Even on the pith of life. Where is he gone?
GERTRUDE To draw apart the body he hath killed,
    O'er whom his very madness, like some ore   25
    Among a mineral of metals base,
    Shows itself pure: a weeps for what is done.
CLAUDIUS O Gertrude, come away!
    The sun no sooner shall the mountains touch
    But we will ship him hence, and this vile deed   30
    We must with all our majesty and skill
    Both countenance and excuse. Ho, Guildenstern!

Enter ROSENCRANTZ *and* GUILDENSTERN

    Friends both, go join you with some further aid.
    Hamlet in madness hath Polonius slain,
    And from his mother's closet hath he dragged him.   35
    Go seek him out, speak fair, and bring the body
    Into the chapel. I pray you, haste in this.

Exeunt ROSENCRANTZ *and* GUILDENSTERN

CLAUDIUS Oh, dreadful deed!
    It could have happened to me, had I been there.
    His liberty threatens us all—
    You, me, everyone.   15
    Alas, how shall we explain this bloody deed?
    It will be blamed on me. I should have had the foresight
    To have kept this mad young man on a leash
    And away from the haunts of men. But so great was my love,
    I could not accept what was best.   20
    But like someone with a foul disease,
    To keep it from being known, let it feed
    On the very core of life. Where has he gone?
GERTRUDE To remove the body that he has killed,
    Over which his very madness, like some gold   25
    In a mine of base metals,
    Shines pure: he weeps for what he has done.
CLAUDIUS Oh, Gertrude, come away!
    The sun shall no sooner touch the mountains
    Than we will ship him from here, and this vile deed,   30
    Using all my authority and skill,
    I will both support and excuse. Come here, Guildenstern!

Enter ROSENCRANTZ and GUILDENSTERN

    Friends, go get some others to help you.
    Hamlet in his madness has killed Polonius
    And has dragged him from his mother's room.   35
    Go look for him, humor him, and bring the body
    Into the chapel. I ask you, hurry.

Exit ROSENCRANTZ *and* GUILDENSTERN

Come, Gertrude, we'll call up our wisest friends
And let them know both what we mean to do
And what's untimely done. So haply slander— 40
Whose whisper o'er the world's diameter,
As level as the cannon to his blank,
Transports his poisoned shot—may miss our name
And hit the woundless air. O, come away!
My soul is full of discord and dismay. 45

Exeunt

Scene 2 [*In another part of the palace*] *Enter* HAMLET
HAMLET Safely stowed.
GENTLEMEN [*Within*] Hamlet! Lord Hamlet!
HAMLET But soft, what noise? Who calls on Hamlet? O, here
  they come.
        Enter ROSENCRANTZ, GUILDENSTERN, and OTHERS
ROSENCRANTZ What have you done, my lord, with the dead body? 5
HAMLET Compounded it with dust, whereto 'tis kin.
ROSENCRANTZ Tell us where 'tis, that we may take it thence
  and bear it to the chapel.
HAMLET Do not believe it.
ROSENCRANTZ Believe what? 10
HAMLET That I can keep your counsel and not mine own. Besides,
  to be demanded of a sponge, what replication should be made
  by the son of a king?
ROSENCRANTZ Take you me for a sponge, my lord?
HAMLET Ay, sir, that soaks up the king's countenance, his rewards, 15
  his authorities. But such officers do the king best service in
  the end. He keeps them like an ape an apple in the corner of his
  jaw, first mouthed, to be last swallowed. When he needs what
  you have gleaned, it is but squeezing you, and, sponge, you
  shall be dry again. 20
ROSENCRANTZ I understand you not, my lord.

Come, Gertrude, we'll summon our wisest friends
And let them know both what we mean to do
And what's unfortunately happened. Perhaps slander—   40
Whose whisper across the world's diameter
Travels as straight as poisonous shot
To its target—may miss our name
And hit the empty air. Oh, come away!
My soul is full of discord and dismay.   45

They exit

Scene 2 [*In another part of the palace*] *Enter* HAMLET
HAMLET Safely hidden.
GENTLEMEN [*Within*] Hamlet! Lord Hamlet!
HAMLET Wait, what is that noise? Who's calling Hamlet?
 Oh, here they come.
   Enter ROSENCRANTZ, GUILDENSTERN, *and* OTHERS
ROSENCRANTZ What have you done, my lord, with the dead body?   5
HAMLET Put it in a dusty place, which is appropriate.
ROSENCRANTZ Tell us where it is, so we may take it from there
 and carry it to the chapel.
HAMLET Do not believe it.
ROSENCRANTZ Believe what?   10
HAMLET That I can keep your secrets and not my own. Besides,
 to be questioned by a sponge! What answer should be made
 by the son of a king?
ROSENCRANTZ Do you take me for a sponge, my lord?
HAMLET Yes, sir, one that soaks up the king's favor, his rewards, 15
 his influence. But such officers do serve the king best in the
 end, like an ape storing an apple in the corner of his mouth—
 to be swallowed last. When he needs to know what you've
 found out, he just squeezes you, and, like a sponge, you'll be
 dry again.   20
ROSENCRANTZ I don't understand you, my lord.

HAMLET I am glad of it. A knavish speech sleeps in a foolish ear.

ROSENCRANTZ My lord, you must tell us where the body is, and
    go with us to the king.

HAMLET The body is with the king, but the king is not with the   25
    body. The king is a thing—

GUILDENSTERN "A thing," my lord?

HAMLET Of nothing. Bring me to him. Hide fox, and all after!

Exeunt

Scene 3 *Enter* CLAUDIUS *and two or three lords*

CLAUDIUS I have sent to seek him, and to find the body.
    How dangerous is it that this man goes loose!
    Yet must not we put the strong law on him.
    He's loved of the distracted multitude,
    Who like not in their judgment, but in their eyes;   5
    And, where 'tis so, th' offender's scourge is weighed,
    But never the offense. To bear all smooth and even,
    This sudden sending him away must seem
    Deliberate pause. Diseases desperate grown
    By desperate appliance are relieved,   10
    Or not at all.

Enter ROSENCRANTZ

    How now, what hath befallen?

ROSENCRANTZ Where the dead body is bestowed, my lord,
    We cannot get from him.

CLAUDIUS But where is he?   15

ROSENCRANTZ Without, my lord, guarded, to know your pleasure.

CLAUDIUS Bring him before us.

ROSENCRANTZ Ho! Bring in the lord.

Enter HAMLET *and* GUILDENSTERN

CLAUDIUS How now, Hamlet, where's Polonius?

HAMLET At supper.   20

CLAUDIUS At supper? Where?

HAMLET I am glad of it. Insults are wasted on the ears of fools.

ROSENCRANTZ My lord, you must tell us where the body is and
    go with us to the king.

HAMLET The king has a body, but the body of people is not with   25
    the king. The king is a thing—

GUILDENSTERN "A thing," my lord?

HAMLET Of no importance. Take me to him. Let's play hide-and-seek.

                                                            They exit

Scene 3 *Enter* CLAUDIUS *and some lords*

CLAUDIUS I have sent them to seek him and to find the body.
    How dangerous it is to have this man run loose.
    But we must not invoke the full strength of the law on him.
    He's loved by the confused multitudes,
    Who judge not by reason, but by appearances;   5
    And, when this is so, the offender's punishment is weighed,
    But never the offense. To keep everything smooth and calm,
    This sudden departure of his must seem
    The result of careful consideration. Desperate illness
    Is cured only by desperate remedy.   10
    Or not at all.

                      Enter ROSENCRANTZ

    Well now, what has happened?

ROSENCRANTZ Where he has hidden the dead body, my lord,
    We cannot learn from him.

CLAUDIUS But where is he?   15

ROSENCRANTZ Outside, my lord, under guard, awaiting your pleasure.

CLAUDIUS Bring him before us.

ROSENCRANTZ Ho! Bring in the lord.

             Enter HAMLET *and* GUILDENSTERN

CLAUDIUS Well now, Hamlet, where's Polonius?

HAMLET At supper.   20

CLAUDIUS At supper? Where?

HAMLET Not where he eats, but where a is eaten. A certain
convocation of politic worms are e'en at him. Your worm is
your only emperor for diet. We fat all creatures else to fat us,
and we fat ourselves for maggots. Your fat king and your lean   25
beggar is but variable service—two dishes, but to one table.
That's the end.

CLAUDIUS Alas, alas!

HAMLET A man may fish with the worm that hath eat of a king,
and eat of the fish that hath fed of that worm.   30

CLAUDIUS What dost thou mean by this?

HAMLET Nothing but to show you how a king may go a progress
through the guts of a beggar.

CLAUDIUS Where is Polonius?

HAMLET In heaven. Send thither to see. If your messenger find him   35
not there, seek him i' th' other place yourself. But if, indeed,
you find him not within this month, you shall nose him as you
go up the stairs into the lobby.

CLAUDIUS Go, seek him there.

HAMLET A will stay till you come.   40

Exeunt attendants

CLAUDIUS Hamlet, this deed, for thine especial safety,
Which we do tender, as we dearly grieve
For that which thou hast done, must send thee hence
With fiery quickness. Therefore prepare thyself.
The bark is ready, and the wind at help,   45
Th' associates tend, and everything is bent
For England.

HAMLET For England?

CLAUDIUS Ay, Hamlet.

HAMLET Good.   50

CLAUDIUS So is it, if thou knew'st our purposes.

HAMLET I see a cherub that sees them. But come, for England!
Farewell, dear mother.

HAMLET Not where he eats, but where he is eaten. A certain
    assembly of political worms are busy with him even now.
    A worm is the emperor of eaters. We fatten up animals to
    make us fat, and we fatten ourselves to feed maggots. Your   25
    fat king and your lean beggar are different courses served at
    the same meal—two dishes, but one table. That's the end.
CLAUDIUS Alas, alas!
HAMLET A man may fish with a worm that has fed off a king,
    and then eat the fish that ate that worm.   30
CLAUDIUS What do you mean by this?
HAMLET Nothing, just to show you how a king may make a
    state journey through the guts of a beggar.
CLAUDIUS Where is Polonius?
HAMLET In heaven. Look for him there. If your messenger cannot   35
    find him there, look for him in the other place yourself. But if,
    indeed, you cannot find him within a month, you shall smell
    him as you go up the stairs into the lobby.
CLAUDIUS Go, look for him there.
HAMLET He will stay till you come.   40

                              Exit attendants
CLAUDIUS This deed, Hamlet, for your own safety,
    Which we care for, as we deeply grieve
    Over what you have done, makes necessary your departure
    Instantly. Therefore, prepare yourself.
    The ship is ready, and the wind is right,   45
    The escorts await, and everything is set
    For England.
HAMLET For England?
CLAUDIUS Yes, Hamlet.
HAMLET Good.   50
CLAUDIUS So it is, if you knew my intentions.
HAMLET I see an angel that sees them. But come, for England!
    Farewell, dear mother.

CLAUDIUS Thy loving father, Hamlet.

HAMLET My mother. Father and mother is man and wife, man   55
    and wife is one flesh, and so, my mother. Come, for England.

                                            Exit

CLAUDIUS Follow him at foot, tempt him with speed abroad.
    Delay it not, I'll have him hence tonight.
    Away, for everything is sealed and done
    That else leans on th' affair. Pray you make haste.   60

                    Exeunt ROSENCRANTZ *and* GUILDENSTERN

    And England, if my love thou hold'st at aught,
    As my great power thereof may give thee sense,
    Since yet thy cicatrice looks raw and red
    After the Danish sword, and thy free awe
    Pays homage to us—thou mayst not coldly set   65
    Our sovereign process, which imports at full,
    By letters congruing to that effect,
    The present death of Hamlet. Do it England,
    For like the hectic in my blood he rages,
    And thou must cure me. Till I know 'tis done,   70
    Howe'er my haps, my joys were ne'er begun.

                                            Exit

Scene 4   *Enter* FORTINBRAS *with his army over the stage*

FORTINBRAS Go, captain, from me greet the Danish king.
    Tell him that by his license Fortinbras
    Craves the conveyance of a promised march
    Over his kingdom. You know the rendezvous.
    If that his majesty would aught with us,   5
    We shall express our duty in his eye,
    And let him know so.

CAPTAIN I will do 't, my lord.

FORTINBRAS Go softly on.

                    Exit FORTINBRAS *with the army*

CLAUDIUS Your loving father, Hamlet.

HAMLET My mother! Father and mother are man and wife, man   55
    and wife are one flesh, and so, my mother. Come, for England.

Exits

CLAUDIUS Follow him closely, get him abroad quickly.
    Don't delay. I want him gone tonight.
    Away! Everything is sealed and done
    That relates to this business. Please, make haste.   60

Exit ROSENCRANTZ *and* GUILDENSTERN

    And king of England, if you value my good will at all—
    As my great power may give you a sense of it,
    Since your scar still looks raw and red
    After the Danish sword—and your unforced tribute
    Pays homage to us, you will not take lightly   65
    Our royal commission, which conveys exactly
    With letters agreeing to that effect,
    The immediate death of Hamlet. See it done, king.
    He rages like a fever in my blood,
    And you must cure me. Till I know it's done,   70
    Whatever happens, my joys have not begun.

Exit

Scene 4   *Enter* FORTINBRAS *and* CAPTAIN *with an army*

FORTINBRAS Go, captain, give my greetings to the Danish king.
    Tell him that by his permission Fortinbras
    Asks safe conduct for a promised march
    Through his kingdom. You know the rendezvous.
    If his majesty has any business with us,   5
    We shall pay our respects in person.
    Tell him so.

CAPTAIN I will do it, my lord.

FORTINBRAS Be cautious.

Exit FORTINBRAS *with the army*

Enter HAMLET, ROSENCRANTZ, GUILDENSTERN, *and others*

HAMLET Good sir, whose powers are these?   10

CAPTAIN They are of Norway, sir.

HAMLET How purposed, sir, I pray you?

CAPTAIN Against some part of Poland.

HAMLET Who commands them, sir?

CAPTAIN The nephew of old Norway, Fortinbras.   15

HAMLET Goes it against the main of Poland, sir,
    Or for some frontier?

CAPTAIN Truly to speak, and with no addition,
    We go to gain a little patch of ground
    That hath in it no profit but the name.   20
    To pay five ducats, five, I would not farm it;
    Nor will it yield to Norway or the Pole
    A ranker rate, should it be sold in fee.

HAMLET Why, then, the Polack never will defend it.

CAPTAIN Yes, it is already garrisoned.   25

HAMLET Two thousand souls and twenty thousand ducats
    Will not debate the question of this straw.
    This is th' impostume of much wealth and peace,
    That inward breaks, and shows no cause without
    Why the man dies. I humbly thank you, sir.   30

CAPTAIN God be wi' you, sir.

ROSENCRANTZ Will 't please you go, my lord?

HAMLET I'll be with you straight. Go a little before.

                      Exeunt all but HAMLET

    How all occasions do inform against me,
    And spur my dull revenge! What is a man   35
    If his chief good and market of his time
    Be but to sleep and feed? A beast, no more.
    Sure He that made us with such large discourse,
    Looking before and after, gave us not

Enter HAMLET, ROSENCRANTZ, GUILDENSTERN, *and others*

HAMLET Good sir, whose forces are these?   10

CAPTAIN They are from Norway, sir.

HAMLET What's their objective, sir?

CAPTAIN They march against a part of Poland.

HAMLET Who commands them, sir?

CAPTAIN Fortinbras, the nephew of the old king of Norway.   15

HAMLET Do you attack the whole of Poland, sir,
    Or some frontier?

CAPTAIN To speak frankly and without exaggeration,
    We go to gain a little patch of ground
    That has no value but the name.   20
    I would not pay five ducats, five, to farm it;
    Nor will it yield to Norway or the Pole
    A higher rate if it were sold outright.

HAMLET Why, then, the king of Poland won't defend it.

CAPTAIN Yes, it is already garrisoned.   25

HAMLET Two thousand killed and twenty thousand ducats spent
    Will not settle this trifling issue.
    This is like an abscess of much substance
    That bursts inside a man and shows no outward sign
    Of why he died. I humbly thank you, sir.   30

CAPTAIN God be with you, sir.

ROSENCRANTZ Are you ready, my lord?

HAMLET I'll be with you right away. Go on ahead.

                      Exit all but HAMLET

    How every chance event tells against me
    And spurs my dull revenge! What is a man   35
    If his main aim and business is to spend his life
    Sleeping and eating? A beast, nothing more.
    Surely the God that made us with such wide-ranging powers,
    Able to examine the past and the future, didn't give us

That capability and godlike reason   40
To fust in us unused. Now whether it be
Bestial oblivion, or some craven scruple
Of thinking too precisely on th' event—
A thought which quartered hath but one part wisdom
And ever three parts coward—I do not know   45
Why yet I live to say "This thing's to do,"
Sith I have cause, and will, and strength, and means
To do 't. Examples gross as earth exhort me.
Witness this army of such mass and charge,
Led by a delicate and tender prince,   50
Whose spirit with divine ambition puffed
Makes mouths at the invisible event,
Exposing what is mortal and unsure
To all that fortune, death, and danger dare,
Even for an eggshell. Rightly to be great   55
Is not to stir without great argument,
But greatly to find a quarrel in a straw
When honor's at the stake. How stand I, then,
That have a father killed, a mother stained,
Excitements of my reason and my blood,   60
And let all sleep, while to my shame I see
The imminent death of twenty thousand men
That for a fantasy and trick of fame
Go to their graves like beds, fight for a plot
Whereon the numbers cannot try the cause,   65
Which is not tomb enough and continent
To hide the slain? O, from this time forth,
My thoughts be bloody or be nothing worth.
                                                Exit

Scene 5 *Enter* HORATIO, GERTRUDE, *and a* GENTLEMAN
GERTRUDE I will not speak with her.

That prudence and godlike reason   40
To grow mouldy and unused. Now whether it is
Animal-like forgetfulness or cowardly doubt
From thinking too intently of the consequences—
Thinking which divides itself into one part wisdom
And three parts cowardice—I do not know.   45
Yet I keep saying "This is what I must do,"
And I have the motive, the will, the strength, and the means
To do it. Examples as plain as earth inspire me.
Witness this army, huge and costly,
Led by a properly brought up prince,   50
Whose spirit swollen with divine ambition
Defies unseen consequences,
Exposing what is mortal and unsure
To all that fortune, death, and danger can do—
For an empty shell. True greatness   55
Lies not in taking action over a great cause,
But in nobly taking action in a trivial matter
When one's honor is at risk. How do I stand, then?
I have a father murdered, a mother defiled,
Causes for moving mind and passion,   60
Yet I have done nothing. To my shame,
I see the imminent death of twenty thousand men,
Who for a fantasy and illusion of fame,
Go to their graves like beds, fight for ground
That is not big enough to hold their numbers   65
Nor to contain the bodies of those
Who are slain. Oh, from this time on
My thoughts be bloody, or let them be gone.
                                                    Exits

Scene 5 *Enter* HORATIO, GERTRUDE, *and a* GENTLEMAN
GERTRUDE I will not speak with her.

GENTLEMAN She is importunate, indeed distract;
    Her mood will needs be pitied.
GERTRUDE What would she have?
GENTLEMAN She speaks much of her father, says she hears   5
    There's tricks i' th' world, and hems, and beats her heart,
    Spurns enviously at straws, speaks things in doubt
    That carry but half sense. Her speech is nothing,
    Yet the unshaped use of it doth move
    The hearers to collection. They yawn at it,   10
    And botch the words up to fit their own thoughts,
    Which, as her winks and nods and gestures yield them,
    Indeed would make one think there might be thought,
    Though nothing sure, yet much unhappily.
HORATIO 'Twere good she were spoken with, for she may strew   15
    Dangerous conjectures in ill-breeding minds.
GERTRUDE Let her come in.

                                      Exit GENTLEMAN

    [*Aside*] To my sick soul, as sin's true nature is,
    Each toy seems prologue to some great amiss.
    So full of artless jealousy is guilt,   20
    It spills itself in fearing to be spilt.
                    Enter OPHELIA *distracted*
OPHELIA Where is the beauteous majesty of Denmark?
GERTRUDE How now, Ophelia?
OPHELIA [*She sings*]
        How should I your true love know
           From another one?   25
        By his cockle hat and staff
           And his sandal shoon.
GERTRUDE Alas, sweet lady, what imports this song?
OPHELIA Say you? Nay, pray you, mark. [*She sings*]
        He is dead and gone, lady,   30
        He is dead and gone;

GENTLEMAN She is persistent—indeed, out of her senses.
    Her state of mind must cause pity.
GERTRUDE What does she want?
GENTLEMAN She talks much about her father, says she hears   5
    There are plots in the world, goes "h'm," and beats her breast,
    Kicks out angrily at trifles, speaks in uncertain meanings
    That carry only half sense. What she says is nonsense,
    So its formless manner prompts those who listen
    To guess at what she means. They are astonished   10
    And piece the words together and draw their own conclusions.
    To judge by her winks and nods and gestures,
    One might think there was some deep thought there,
    Though one can't be sure, only that it's distressed.
HORATIO It would be a good idea to talk with her, for she may spread   15
    Dangerous rumors among scandal-mongers.
GERTRUDE Let her come in.
                                  Exit GENTLEMAN
    [*Aside*] To my sick soul—and that is sin's true nature—
    Each trifle seems a prelude to some great disaster.
    So full of awkward suspicion is guilt   20
    That it spills itself for fear of being spilt.
                          Enter OPHELIA *confused*
OPHELIA Where is the beautiful queen of Denmark?
GERTRUDE How are you, Ophelia?
OPHELIA [*She sings*]
        How could I a true love know
          From one that is not so?   25
        By his pilgrim's hat and staff
          And his sandal shoes.
GERTRUDE Alas, sweet lady, what does this song mean?
OPHELIA What's that? Now, please, listen. [*She sings*]
        He is dead and gone, lady,   30
          He is dead and gone;

At his head a grass-green turf,
  At his heels a stone.
 Oho!
GERTRUDE Nay, but Ophelia—   35
OPHELIA Pray you mark. [*She sings*]
  White his shroud as the mountain snow—
     Enter CLAUDIUS
GERTRUDE Alas, look here, my lord.
OPHELIA [*She sings*]
  Larded all with sweet flowers.
   Which bewept to the grave did not go   40
  With true-love showers.
CLAUDIUS How do you, pretty lady.
OPHELIA Well, God dild you. They say the owl was a baker's
 daughter. Lord, we know what we are, but not what we
 may be. God be at your table.   45
CLAUDIUS Conceit upon her father.
OPHELIA Pray, let's have no words of this, but when they ask you
 what it means, say you this: [*She sings*]
  Tomorrow is Saint Valentine's day,
   All in the morning betime,   50
  And I a maid at your window,
   To be your Valentine.
  Then up he rose and donned his clothes
   And dupped the chamber door;
  Let in the maid that out a maid   55
   Never departed more.
CLAUDIUS Pretty Ophelia!
OPHELIA Indeed, without an oath, I'll make an end on 't. [*She sings*]
  By Gis and by Saint Charity
   Alack and fie for shame,   60
  Young men will do 't, if they come to 't—
   By Cock, they are to blame.

At his head is grass-green turf,
    At his feet a stone.
  Ooh!
GERTRUDE No, but Ophelia—   35
OPHELIA Please listen. [*She sings*]
    White his shroud as the mountain snow—
            Enter CLAUDIUS
GERTRUDE Alas, my lord, look at her.
OPHELIA [*She sings*]
    Strewn all with sweet flowers.
      Which tearful to the grave did not go   40
    With true-love showers.
CLAUDIUS How are you, pretty lady?
OPHELIA Well, God thank you. They say the owl was a baker's
    daughter. Lord, we know what we are, but not what we may
    become. May God be at your table.   45
CLAUDIUS Thinking about her father.
OPHELIA Please, no more of this, but when they ask you what
    it means, tell them this: [*She sings*]
    Tomorrow is Saint Valentine's day,
      Early in the morning time,   50
    And I come a maid at your window
      To be your valentine.
    Then up he rose, put on his clothes,
      And opened the bedroom door;
    He let in a maid that out a maid   55
      Never departed more.
CLAUDIUS Pretty Ophelia—
OPHELIA Indeed, without cursing, I'll end the story. [*She sings*]
    By Gis and by Saint Charity
      Alas and fie for shame,   60
    Young men will do it, given the chance;
      By Cock, they are to blame.

Quoth she, "Before you tumbled me,
    You promised me to wed."
He answers: 65
    "So would I ha' done, by yonder sun
        And thou hadst not come to my bed."
CLAUDIUS How long hath she been thus?
OPHELIA I hope all will be well. We must be patient, but I cannot
  choose but weep to think they would lay him i' th' cold ground.   70
My brother shall know of it, and so I thank you for your good
counsel. Come, my coach! Good night ladies, good night
sweet ladies, good night, good night.
Exit
CLAUDIUS Follow her close; give her good watch, I pray you.
Exit HORATIO
O, this is the poison of deep grief. It springs   75
All from her father's death, and now behold!
O Gertrude, Gertrude,
When sorrows come, they come not single spies,
But in battalions. First, her father slain,
Next, your son gone, and he most violent author   80
Of his own just remove; the people muddied,
Thick, and unwholesome in their thoughts and whispers
For good Polonius' death—and we have done but greenly
In hugger-mugger to inter him; poor Ophelia
Divided from herself and her fair judgment,   85
Without the which we are pictures or mere beasts;
Last, and as much containing as all these,
Her brother is in secret come from France,
Feeds on his wonder, keeps himself in clouds,
And wants not buzzers to infect his ear   90
With pestilent speeches of his father's death,
Within necessity, of matter beggared,
Will nothing stick our person to arraign

Said she, "Before you made love to me,
    You promised me you'd wed."
He answers,   65
    "So would I have done, by yonder sun,
        If you hadn't come to my bed."
CLAUDIUS How long has she been like this?
OPHELIA I hope all will be well. We must be patient. But I cannot
    help weeping when I think how they laid him in the cold   70
    ground. My brother shall hear of this. And so I thank you for
    your good advice. Come, bring my coach! Good night ladies,
    good night sweet ladies, good night, good night.

Exits

CLAUDIUS Follow her closely. Watch over her, please!

Exit HORATIO

O, this is the poison of deep grief. It all flows   75
From her father's death, and now look!
O Gertrude, Gertrude,
When sorrows come, they don't come singly,
But as battalions. First, her father murdered,
Next, your son gone, the violent author   80
Of his own just exile; the people stirred up,
Clouded and unhealthy in their thoughts and whispers
Over the death of good Polonius—and we were foolish
To have buried him secretly. Poor Ophelia,
Divided from herself and her judgment,   85
Without which, we are shadows or mere beasts.
Lastly, as much as any of these things,
Her brother has returned secretly from France,
Astonished at what has happened, keeps himself aloof,
And does not lack for rumor mongers to infect his mind   90
With poisonous accounts of his father's death.
In this respect, with few facts to go on,
They will not stop at accusing us

In ear and ear. O, my dear Gertrude, this,
Like a murdering piece, in many places   95
Gives me superfluous death.

A noise within.

GERTRUDE Alack, what noise is this?

CLAUDIUS Attend! Where are my Switzers? Let them guard the
door.

Enter a MESSENGER

What is the matter?   100

MESSENGER Save yourself, my lord.
The ocean, overpeering of his list,
Eats not the flats with more impiteous haste
Than young Laertes, in a riotous head,
O'erbears your officers. The rabble call him "lord,"   105
And, as the world were now but to begin,
Antiquity forgot, custom not known,
The ratifiers and props of every word,
They cry "Choose we! Laertes shall be king!"
Caps, hands, and tongues applaud it to the clouds,   110
"Laertes shall be king, Laertes king!"

GERTRUDE How cheerfully on the false trail they cry!
O, this is counter, you false Danish dogs!

A noise within.

CLAUDIUS The doors are broke.

Enter Laertes *with others*

LAERTES Where is this king?—Sirs, stand you all without.   115

ALL No, let's come in.

LAERTES I pray you, give me leave.

ALL We will, we will.

LAERTES I thank you. Keep the door.

Exeunt followers

O, thou vile king,   120
Give me my father!

In every ear. Oh, my dear Gertrude, this
Is like a cannon firing scattershot, killing   95
Me over and over again.

A noise within.

GERTRUDE Did you hear that noise?

CLAUDIUS Listen! Where are my Swiss bodyguards? Have them
    guard the door.

Enter a MESSENGER

What is the matter?   100

MESSENGER Save yourself, my lord.
    Not even the ocean flooding its shores
    Eats away the flats with more pitiless haste
    Than young Laertes with a rebel force
    Sweeps aside your soldiers. The rabble call him "lord,"   105
    And, as if the world had just begun,
    Tradition forgotten and custom unknown—
    Those supports of words and promises—
    They cry "We will choose! Laertes is our king!"
    Caps, hands, tongues applaud it to heaven!   110
    "Laertes for king. Laertes king!"

GERTRUDE Like hounds they bay enthusiastically!
    Oh, but they run the wrong way, false Danish dogs.

A noise within

CLAUDIUS The doors are broken.

Enter LAERTES *with others*

LAERTES Where is this king?—Gentlemen, wait outside.   115

ALL No, let us come in.

LAERTES Please, wait for me there.

ALL We will, we will.

LAERTES I thank you. Guard the door.

Exit followers

Oh, you vile king,   120
Give me back my father!

GERTRUDE Calmly, good Laertes.

LAERTES That drop of blood that's calm proclaims me bastard,
    Cries "cuckold" to my father, brands the harlot
    Even here, between the chaste unsmirched brow   125
    Of my true mother.

CLAUDIUS What is the cause, Laertes,
    That thy rebellion looks so giant-like?—
    Let him go, Gertrude. Do not fear our person.
    There's such divinity doth hedge a king   130
    That treason can but peep to what it would,
    Acts little of his will.—Tell me, Laertes,
    Why thou art thus incensed.—Let him go, Gertrude.—
    Speak, man.

LAERTES Where is my father?   135

CLAUDIUS Dead.

GERTRUDE But not by him.

CLAUDIUS Let him demand his fill.

LAERTES How came he dead? I'll not be juggled with.
    To hell allegiance! Vows, to the blackest devil!   140
    Conscience and grace, to the profoundest pit!
    I dare damnation. To this point I stand,
    That both the worlds I give to negligence,
    Let come what comes, only I'll be revenged
    Most thoroughly for my father.   145

CLAUDIUS Who shall stay you?

LAERTES My will, not all the world.
    And for my means, I'll husband them so well,
    They shall go far with little.

CLAUDIUS Good Laertes,   150
    If you desire to know the certainty
    Of your dear father, is't writ in your revenge
    That, swoopstake, you will draw both friend and foe,
    Winner and loser?

GERTRUDE Be calm, good Laertes.

LAERTES That drop of my blood that stays calm, proclaims me a bastard,
    Says my father was betrayed, and brands as harlot
    Right here, the unstained brow   125
    Of my chaste mother.

CLAUDIUS What is the cause, Laertes,
    Of this gigantic rebellion of yours?—
    Let him go, Gertrude. Do not fear for our safety.
    There's a providence that surrounds a king,   130
    So that treason can only peep at what it would do,
    Perform only a part of its will.—Tell me, Laertes,
    Why are you so incensed?—Let him go, Gertrude.—
    Speak, man.

LAERTES Where is my father?   135

CLAUDIUS Dead.

GERTRUDE But he didn't kill him.

CLAUDIUS Let him ask anything.

LAERTES How did he die? I'll not be deceived.
    To hell with my allegiance! My vows, to the blackest devil!   140
    Conscience and grace, to the bottomless pit!
    I'll dare damnation. I am so resolved on this,
    That both this world and the next, I disregard.
    Come what may, I'll be thoroughly revenged
    For my father's death.   145

CLAUDIUS Who would stop you?

LAERTES Only my own will, no matter what the world did.
    And for means, I'll use what I have so well,
    That I shall go far with little.

CLAUDIUS Good Laertes,   150
    In wanting to know the truth
    About your dear father, is it part of your revenge
    To uncaringly draw in both friend and foe,
    Winner and loser?

LAERTES None but his enemies. 155

CLAUDIUS Will you know them, then?

LAERTES To his good friends, thus wide I'll ope my arms
    And, like the kind life-rendering pelican,
    Repast them with my blood.

CLAUDIUS Why, now you speak 160
    Like a good child and a true gentleman.
    That I am guiltless of your father's death
    And am most sensibly in grief for it,
    It shall as level to your judgment pierce
    As day does to your eye. 165

A noise within.

    Let her come in.

LAERTES How now, what noise is that?

               Enter OPHELIA

    O heat, dry up my brains; tears seven times salt
    Burn out the sense and virtue of mine eye!
    By heaven, thy madness shall be paid with weight 170
    Till our scale turn the beam. O rose of May,
    Dear maid, kind sister, sweet Ophelia—
    O heavens, is 't possible a young maid's wits
    Should be as mortal as an old man's life?
    Nature is fine in love, and, where 'tis fine, 175
    It sends some precious instance of itself
    After the thing it loves.

OPHELIA [*She sings*]
       They bore him barefaced on the bier
           Hey non nonny, nonny, hey nonny,
       And in his grave rained many a tear— 180
    Fare you well, my dove.

LAERTES Hadst thou thy wits, and didst persuade revenge,
    It could not move thus.

OPHELIA You must sing "A-down a-down," and you "Call him

LAERTES Only his enemies.   155
CLAUDIUS Do you know who they are?
LAERTES To his good friends, I'll open wide my arms,
    And like the life-giving pelican,
    Feed them with my blood.
CLAUDIUS Why, now you speak   160
    Like a good son and a true gentleman.
    That I am guiltless of your father's death,
    And am intensely grieved by it,
    It shall become as plain to your judgment
    As daylight strikes the eye.   165
A noise within.
    Let her come in.
LAERTES Look, what is that noise?
               Enter OPHELIA
LAERTES Oh, anger dry up my brain. Tears loaded with salt
    Burn out this sight from my eyes!
    By heaven, your madness shall be repaid in weight   170
    Till our scale overbalances the other. Oh, rose of May,
    Dear maid, kind sister, sweet Ophelia—
    Oh heavens, is it possible a young maid's sanity
    Is as open to attack as an old man's life?
    Our nature is refined by love, and this refined nature   175
    Sends a precious part of itself
    After the one it loves has departed.
OPHELIA [*She sings*]
    They bore him barefaced on the bier
        Hey non nonny, nonny, hey nonny,
    And in his grave rained many a tear—   180
    Farewell, my dove.
LAERTES If you were sane and argued for revenge,
    You could not be more persuasive than this.
OPHELIA You must sing "A-down a down," and you "Call him

a-down-a." O, how the wheel becomes it. It is the false 185
    steward that stole his master's daughter.
LAERTES This nothing's more than matter.
OPHELIA There's rosemary, that's for remembrance—pray you, love,
    remember—and there is pansies, that's for thoughts.
LAERTES A document in madness, thoughts and remembrance fitted. 190
OPHELIA There's fennel for you, and columbines. There's rue for
    you, and here's some for me; we may call it herb of grace a
    Sundays. O, you must wear your rue with a difference. There's
    a daisy. I would give you some violets, but they withered all
    when my father died. They say a made a good end. 195
    [*She sings*] For bonny sweet Robin is all my joy.
LAERTES Thought and affliction, passion, hell itself,
    She turns to favor and to prettiness.
OPHELIA [*She sings*]
    And will a not come again?
    And will a not come again? 200
      No, no, he is dead,
      Go to thy death-bed,
    He never will come again.
    His beard was as white as snow,
    All flaxen was his poll, 205
      He is gone, he is gone,
      And we cast away moan,
    God-a-mercy on his soul.
    And of all Christian souls, I pray God. God buy you.
                             Exit
LAERTES Do you see this, O God? 210
CLAUDIUS Laertes, I must commune with your grief,
    Or you deny me right. Go but apart,
    Make choice of whom your wisest friends you will,
    And they shall hear and judge 'twixt you and me.
    If by direct or by collateral hand 215

a-down-a." Oh, it's a clever refrain. Then the false steward   185
    stole his master's daughter.
LAERTES There's meaning in this nonsense.
OPHELIA Here's some rosemary. That's for remembrance. Please,
    love, remember. And here's some pansies. They're for thoughts.
LAERTES A lesson in madness, thoughts and remembrance connected.   190
OPHELIA There's fennel for you, and columbines. There's rue for you,
    and here's some for me. On Sundays, we call it herb of grace.
    Oh, but you must wear your rue for a different reason. Here's a
    daisy. I would give you some violets, but they all withered when
    my father died. They say he died well.   195
    [*She sings*] For bonny sweet robin is all my joy.
LAERTES Sorrow and trouble, suffering, hell itself
    She turns to beauty and to prettiness.
OPHELIA [*She sings*]
      And will he not come again?
      And will he not come again?   200
         No, no, he is dead.
         Go to your deathbed.
      He never will come again.
      His beard was as white as snow,
      All white was his head,   205
         He is gone, he is gone,
         In vain do we mourn,
      God have mercy on his soul.
    And on all Christian souls, I pray God. God be with you.
                         Exit
LAERTES Do you see this, oh God?   210
CLAUDIUS Laertes, I must share your grief,
    Or you deny me my right. Leave now,
    And choose from among the wisest friends you have,
    And they shall hear and judge between you and me.
    If they find, either directly or indirectly,   215

They find us touched, we will our kingdom give,
Our crown, our life, and all that we call ours,
To you in satisfaction. But if not,
Be you content to lend your patience to us,
And we shall jointly labor with your soul   220
To give it due content.
LAERTES Let this be so.
His means of death, his obscure funeral—
No trophy, sword, nor hatchment o'er his bones,
No noble rite, nor formal ostentation—   225
Cry to be heard, as 'twere from heaven to earth,
That I must call 't in question.
CLAUDIUS So you shall.
And where th' offense is, let the great ax fall.
I pray you, go with me.   230

Exeunt

Scene 6 *Enter* HORATIO *with an* ATTENDANT
HORATIO What are they that would speak with me?
ATTENDANT Seafaring men, sir. They say they have letters for you.
HORATIO Let them come in.

Exit ATTENDANT

I do not know from what part of the world
I should be greeted, if not from Lord Hamlet.   5

Enter SAILORS

FIRST SAILOR God bless you, sir.
HORATIO Let Him bless thee too.
FIRST SAILOR A shall, sir, an't please Him. There's a letter for you,
      sir. It came from th' ambassador that was bound for England, if
      your name be Horatio, as I am let to know it is.   10
HORATIO [*Reads the letter*] "Horatio, when thou shalt have overlooked
      this, give these fellows some means to the king. They have letters for
      him. Ere we were two days old at sea, a pirate of very warlike

That we were implicated, then I will give my kingdom,
My crown, my life, and all that I call mine
To you in satisfaction. But if they do not,
Be content and bear with us patiently,
And we shall work with you   220
To satisfy your concerns.

LAERTES Let's agree to that.
How my father died, his secret funeral—
No memorial, sword, no coat of arms over his body,
No formal rites or ceremony—   225
These cry out to be answered, as it were from heaven to earth.
I must demand an explanation.

CLAUDIUS So you shall.
And where the guilt lies, let the great ax fall.
Now, please, come with me.   230

They exit

Scene 6 *Enter* HORATIO *and an* ATTENDANT

HORATIO Who are they that want to speak with me?

SERVANT Seafaring men, sir. They say they have letters for you.

HORATIO Let them come in.

Exit SERVANT

I do not know of anyone abroad   5
Who would write to me, except Hamlet.

Enter SAILORS

FIRST SAILOR God bless you, sir.

HORATIO May He bless you too.

FIRST SAILOR He shall, sir, if it's His will. Here's a letter for you,
sir. It came from that ambassador who was bound for England—
if your name is Horatio, as I am led to believe.   10

HORATIO [*Reads the letter*] "Horatio, when you have read over this,
arrange for these fellows to meet the king. They have letters for
him. Not two days out at sea, a very well-armed pirate ship

appointment gave us chase. Finding ourselves too slow of
sail, we put on a compelled valor, and in the grapple I   15
boarded them. On the instant, they got clear of our ship; so
I alone became their prisoner. They have dealt with me like
thieves of mercy, but they knew what they did: I am to do
a good turn for them. Let the king have the letters I have
sent, and repair thou to me with as much speed as thou   20
wouldest fly death. I have words to speak in thine ear
will make thee dumb, yet are they much too light for the
bore of the matter. These good fellows will bring thee where
I am. Rosencrantz and Guildenstern hold their course for
England. Of them I have much to tell thee. Farewell.   25
           He that knowest thine,
               Hamlet"
Come, I will give you way for these your letters,
And do 't the speedier that you may direct me
To him from whom you brought them.   30

                    Exeunt

Scene 7 *Enter* CLAUDIUS *and* LAERTES
CLAUDIUS Now must your conscience my acquittance seal,
    And you must put me in your heart for friend,
    Sith you have heard, and with a knowing ear,
    That he which hath your noble father slain
    Pursued my life.   5
LAERTES It well appears. But tell me
    Why you proceeded not against these feats,
    So crimeful and so capital in nature,
    As by your safety, wisdom, and all things else,
    You mainly were stirred up.   10
CLAUDIUS O, for two special reasons,
    Which may to you perhaps seem much unsinewed,
    But yet to me they're strong. The queen his mother

pursued us. Finding ourselves too slow, we were compelled
to take a heroic course of action, and when the two ships   15
grappled, I boarded theirs. In an instant, they got clear of our
ship, and I alone became their prisoner. They have dealt with
me like merciful thieves. But they knew what they were doing:
I have to do a good turn for them. Let the king have the letters
I have sent, and make your way to me as fast as you would run   20
from death. You will be struck dumb by what I have to tell you.
Yet my words are too small for the size of the cannon. These
good fellows will bring you where I am. Roscencrantz and
Guildenstern are on their way to England. Of them, I have
much to tell you. Farewell.   25
   He that knows you,
    Hamlet"
Come, I will get you access for these letters of yours,
And do it as quickly as possible so that you may direct me
To him from whom you brought them.   30

       They exit

Scene 7 *Enter* CLAUDIUS *and* LAERTES
CLAUDIUS Now must your reason confirm my innocence,
  And you must accept me in your heart as a friend,
  Since, as you have heard and understood,
  He who killed your noble father also
  Sought my life.   5
LAERTES So it appears. But tell me,
  Why did you take no action against these deeds,
  So criminal and capital in nature,
  When for your safety, wisdom, and everything else,
  You were so provoked?   10
CLAUDIUS Oh, for two special reasons,
  Which may to you perhaps seem very weak,
  But still to me are strong. The queen, his mother,

Lives almost by his looks, and for myself,
My virtue or my plague, be it either which,   15
She's so conjunctive to my life and soul,
That as the star moves not but in his sphere,
I could not but by her. The other motive,
Why to a public count I might not go,
Is the great love the general gender bear him,   20
Who, dipping all his faults in their affection,
Work like the spring that turneth wood to stone,
Convert his gyves to graces, so that my arrows,
Too slightly timbered for so loud a wind,
Would have reverted to my bow again,   25
And not where I aimed them.
LAERTES And so have I a noble father lost,
    A sister driven into desperate terms,
    Whose worth, if praises may go back again,
    Stood challenger on mount of all the age   30
    For her perfections. But my revenge will come.
CLAUDIUS Break not your sleeps for that. You must not think
    That we are made of stuff so flat and dull
    That we can let our beard be shook with danger
    And think it pastime. You shall shortly hear more.   35
    I loved your father, and we love ourself,
    And that I hope will teach you to imagine—
              Enter a MESSENGER *with letters*
    How now? What news?
MESSENGER Letters, my lord, from Hamlet.
    These to your majesty, this to the queen.   40
CLAUDIUS From Hamlet? Who brought them?
MESSENGER Sailors, my lord, they say. I saw them not.
    They were given me by Claudio—he received them
    Of him that brought them.

Dotes on his every look. And, as for myself,
Whether to my credit or my bad luck, whichever it is,   15
She's so closely joined to my life and soul
That, like a star moving in its orbit,
I cannot move without her. The other reason
Why I cannot permit a public indictment
Is the great love the people have for him.   20
So strong is their affection, they overlook all his faults.
Like the waters of a spring that turns wood to stone,
They would convert his fetters into honors. My arrows
Of accusation, too light for so strong a wind,
Would have blown back into my face,   25
And not where I aimed them.

LAERTES And so I have lost a noble father,
My sister is driven into insanity,
She whose worth in former times
Stood like a challenger mounted above all the age   30
For her perfection. But I will have my revenge.

CLAUDIUS Lose no sleep over that. You must not think
That we are made of stuff so spiritless and dull
That we will let danger shake our beard
And treat it as a joke. You shall hear more soon.   35
I loved your father, and I love myself,
And that, I hope, will help you to see—

Enter a MESSENGER *with letters*

What's happened? What's the news?

MESSENGER Letters, my lord, from Hamlet.
This is for your majesty. This is for the queen.   40

CLAUDIUS From Hamlet? Who brought them?

MESSENGER Sailors, my lord, so they say. I did not see them.
They were given to me by Claudio—he got them
From the man who brought them.

CLAUDIUS Laertes, you shall hear them— 45
    Leave us.

                        Exit MESSENGER

    [*Reads*] "High and mighty, you shall know I am set naked on
    your kingdom. Tomorrow shall I beg leave to see your kingly
    eyes, when I shall, first asking your pardon thereunto, recount
    the occasion of my sudden and more strange return. 50

                       Hamlet"
    What should this mean? Are all the rest come back?
    Or is it some abuse and no such thing?

LAERTES Know you the hand?

CLAUDIUS 'Tis Hamlet's character. "Naked"? 55
    And in a postscript here, he says "alone."
    Can you devise me?

LAERTES I'm lost in it, my lord. But let him come—
    It warms the very sickness in my heart
    That I shall live and tell him to his teeth 60
    "Thus didest thou!"

CLAUDIUS If it be so, Laertes—
    And how should it be so?—how otherwise?—
    Will you be ruled by me?

LAERTES Ay, my lord, 65
    So you will not o'errule me to a peace.

CLAUDIUS To thine own peace. If he be now returned,
    As checking at his voyage, and that he means
    No more to undertake it, I will work him
    To an exploit, now ripe in my device, 70
    Under the which he shall not choose but fall,
    And for his death no wind of blame shall breathe,
    But even his mother shall uncharge the practice
    And call it accident.

LAERTES My lord, I will be ruled, 75
    The rather if you could devise it so

CLAUDIUS Laertes, you shall hear what's in them—   45
    Leave us.

                                  Exit MESSENGER
    [*Reads*] "High and mighty, you should know that I am back in
    your kingdom and destitute. Tomorrow shall I beg leave to
    appear in your presence when I shall, first begging your
    pardon, provide reasons for my sudden and unusual return.   50
                                    Hamlet"
    What does this mean? Have the others come back too?
    Or is this some deceit and has not happened?
LAERTES Do you recognize the handwriting?
CLAUDIUS It's Hamlet's. "Destitute"?   55
    And in a postscript here, he says "alone."
    Can you guess what it means?
LAERTES I'm lost, my lord. But let him come—
    It is good for my sick heart
    To think I shall live to tell him to his face   60
    "Take that now!"
CLAUDIUS If this is true, Laertes—
    And how can it be?—yet how otherwise?—
    Will you follow my advice?
LAERTES Yes, my lord,   65
    So long as you don't command me to be peaceful.
CLAUDIUS Only with yourself. If he has now returned,
    Diverted from his voyage and with no intention
    Of resuming it, I will steer him
    Into a scheme, now ready in my planning,   70
    That cannot help but bring about his downfall.
    And his death will be received without a whisper of blame.
    Even his mother will not connect his death to our plot,
    But call it an accident.
LAERTES My lord, I shall be guided by you,   75
    Especially if you could arrange it so

That I might be the organ.
CLAUDIUS It falls right.
    You have been talked of since your travel much,
    And that in Hamlet's hearing, for a quality   80
    Wherein they say you shine. Your sum of parts
    Did not together pluck such envy from him
    As did that one, and that in my regard,
    Of the unworthiest siege.
LAERTES What part is that, my lord?   85
CLAUDIUS A very riband in the cap of youth—
    Yet needful too, for youth no less becomes
    The light and careless livery that it wears
    Than settled age his sables and his weeds,
    Importing health and graveness. Two months since   90
    Here was a gentleman of Normandy.
    I've seen myself, and served against, the French,
    And they can well on horseback, but this gallant
    Had witchcraft in 't. He grew unto his seat,
    And to such wondrous doing brought his horse   95
    As he had been incorpsed and demi-natured
    With the brave beast. So far he topped my thought,
    That I in forgery of shapes and tricks
    Came short of what he did.
LAERTES A Norman was 't?   100
CLAUDIUS A Norman.
LAERTES Upon my life, Lamord.
CLAUDIUS The very same.
LAERTES I know him well. He is the brooch indeed
    And gem of all the nation.   105
CLAUDIUS He made confession of you
    And gave you such a masterly report
    For art and exercise in your defense,
    And for your rapier most especial,

That I am the instrument.

CLAUDIUS Exactly so.
You have been much talked of since you went abroad,
And in Hamlet's hearing, for a skill   80
At which they say you shine. All your accomplishments
Together did not provoke as much envy from him
As this one that, in my opinion,
Was least worthy.

LAERTES What skill was that, my lord?   85

CLAUDIUS A mere ribbon in the cap of youth—
But suiting it too, for in youth
Light and careless clothes are as appropriate
As furs and dark clothes in middle age,
Suggesting well-being and serious purpose. Two months ago   90
There was a gentleman here from Normandy.
I've seen the French myself and fought against them,
And they are good on horseback, but this young man
Was a wizard at it. He was rooted in his saddle
And performed such wonderful routines with his horse   95
That he might have been one body, dual-natured,
With the splendid beast. He so far surpassed my imagination
That I, imagining displays of horsemanship,
Fell short of what he did.

LAERTES A Norman, was he?   100

CLAUDIUS A Norman.

LAERTES I'll bet my life, it was Lamord.

CLAUDIUS The very same.

LAERTES I know him well. He is the chief
Jewel of his nation.   105

CLAUDIUS He told us all about you.
And gave you such a marvelous report
Of your skillful practice of swordsmanship,
And especially for your use of the rapier,

That he cried out 'twould be a slight indeed 110
If one could match you. Th' escrimers of their nation
He swore had neither motion, guard, nor eye,
If you opposed them. Sir, this report of his
Did Hamlet so envenom with his envy
That he could nothing do but wish and beg 115
Your sudden coming o'er to play with you.
Now out of this—

LAERTES What out of this, my lord?

CLAUDIUS Laertes, was your father dear to you?
Or are you like the painting of a sorrow, 120
A face without a heart?

LAERTES Why ask you this?

CLAUDIUS Not that I think you did not love your father,
But that I know love is begun by time,
And that I see, in passages of proof, 125
Time qualifies the spark and fire of it.
There lives within the very flame of love
A kind of wick or snuff that will abate it,
And nothing is at a like goodness still,
For goodness, growing to a pleurisy, 130
Dies in his own too-much. That we would do,
We should do when we would, for this "would" changes,
And hath abatements and delays as many
As there are tongues, are hands, are accidents;
And then this "should" is like a spendthrift sigh, 135
That hurts by easing. But to the quick of th' ulcer—
Hamlet comes back; what would you undertake
To show yourself in deed your father's son
More than in words?

LAERTES To cut his throat i' th' church. 140

CLAUDIUS No place indeed should murder sanctuarize;
Revenge should have no bounds. But, good Laertes,

That he declared it would be a surprise indeed 110
To find one to match you. The fencers of their nation,
He swore, had neither the strokes, the guard, nor accuracy
To match you. Sir, this report of his
Did so embitter Hamlet with envy
That he could do nothing but wish and beg 115
For your swift return so that he could fence with you.
Now, out of this—

LAERTES What can come of this, my lord?

CLAUDIUS Laertes, was your father dear to you?
Or are you like a painting of sorrow, 120
A face without a heart?

LAERTES Why do you ask?

CLAUDIUS Not that I think you didn't love your father.
But I know that love is a creature of time,
And what I see, in incidents that prove me right, 125
Is that time weakens the spark and fire of it.
There lives within the very flame of love
A kind of wick, a charred part, that will lower it.
Nothing stays good all the time,
For goodness, swelling to excess, 130
Dies in its own too-much. What we would do,
We should do when we can, for this "would" changes
And has qualifications and delays that are as numerous
As there are words and deeds and chance events.
And then this "should" is like a wasteful sigh 135
That does more harm than good. But, to the heart of the matter—
Hamlet has come back; what will you do
To show yourself your father's son in deeds
Rather than words?

LAERTES I would cut his throat in church. 140

CLAUDIUS Indeed, no place should be a sanctuary against murder;
Revenge should know no bounds. But, good Laertes,

Will you do this? Keep close within your chamber.
Hamlet, returned, shall know you are come home.
We'll put on those shall praise your excellence,   145
And set a double varnish on the fame
The Frenchman gave you; bring you, in fine, together,
And wager on your heads. He, being remiss,
Most generous, and free from all contriving
Will not peruse the foils, so that with ease,   150
Or with a little shuffling, you may choose
A sword unbated, and in a pass of practice
Requite him for your father.
LAERTES I will do 't,
And for that purpose I'll anoint my sword.   155
I bought an unction of a mountebank,
So mortal that, but dip a knife in it,
Where it draws blood no cataplasm so rare,
Collected from all simples that have virtue
Under the moon, can save the thing from death   160
That is but scratched withal. I'll touch my point
With this contagion, that, if I gall him slightly,
It may be death.
CLAUDIUS Let's further think of this,
Weigh what convenience both of time and means   165
May fit us to our shape. If this should fail,
And that our drift look through our bad performance,
'Twere better not assayed. Therefore this project
Should have a back or second, that might hold
If this did blast in proof. Soft, let me see.   170
We'll make a solemn wager on your cunnings—
I ha't!
When in your motion you are hot and dry,
As make your bouts more violent to that end,
And that he calls for drink, I'll have preferred him   175

If you are to do this, you must keep to your room.
Hamlet, now returned, shall be told you have come home.
We'll arrange for those who will praise your skill   145
And set a double luster on the fame
The Frenchman gave you; in sum, bring you together,
With wagers on each man. He, being trusting,
High-spirited, and free from all plotting,
Will not inspect the foils, so that with ease   150
And with a little deception, you may choose
A sword not blunted, and in a malicious thrust,
You may settle with him for your father.
LAERTES I will do it.
    And to that end, I'll smear my sword with   155
An ointment I bought from a quack doctor.
It's so lethal that you have only to dip a knife in it,
And where it draws blood, there's no medicine so good,
Collected from all the strongest remedies available
Anywhere that can save the thing from death   160
That is only scratched by it. I'll put this poison
On the tip of my sword so that, if I nick him slightly,
It will be his death.
CLAUDIUS Let's think more about this
    And decide what is the best time and means   165
For us to act the parts we'll play. If this should fail
And our real purpose show through our bad performance,
It were better not attempted. Therefore this project
Should have a secondary backup that would work
If it explodes in being tested. Wait, let me see.   170
We'll make a solemn wager on your skills—
I have it!
When, in your exertion, you are hot and dry—
So make your bouts more violent with that in mind—
And he calls for drink, I'll have offered to him   175

A chalice for the nonce, whereon but sipping,
If he by chance escape your venomed stuck,
Our purpose may hold there. But stay, what noise?
Enter GERTRUDE
How, sweet queen!
GERTRUDE One woe doth tread upon another's heel,   180
So fast they follow. Your sister's drowned, Laertes.
LAERTES Drowned! O, where?
GERTRUDE There is a willow grows askant the brook
That shows his hoar leaves in the glassy stream.
Therewith fantastic garlands did she make,   185
Of crowflowers, nettles, daisies, and long purples,
That liberal shepherds give a grosser name,
But our cold maids do "dead men's fingers" call them.
There on the pendant boughs her coronet weeds
Clamb'ring to hang, an envious sliver broke,   190
When down her weedy trophies and herself
Fell in the weeping brook. Her clothes spread wide,
And mermaid-like awhile they bore her up,
Which time she chanted snatches of old lauds,
As one incapable of her own distress   195
Or like a creature native and endued
Unto that element. But long it could not be
Till that her garments, heavy with their drink,
Pulled the poor wretch from her melodious lay
To muddy death.   200
LAERTES Alas, then she is drowned?
GERTRUDE Drowned, drowned.
LAERTES Too much of water hast thou, poor Ophelia,
And therefore I forbid my tears. But yet
It is our trick; nature her custom holds,   205
Let shame say what it will. When these are gone,
The woman will be out. Adieu, my lord,

A goblet for the occasion. He has only to sip,
And if by chance he escapes your poisoned thrust,
We'll achieve our goal that way. Wait, what's that noise?

Enter GERTRUDE

Greetings, sweet queen!
GERTRUDE One sorrow follows on the heels of another,   180
    They happen so quickly. Your sister's drowned, Laertes.
LAERTES Drowned! Oh, where?
GERTRUDE There is a willow that overhangs the brook
    And reflects its silver leaves in the glass-like stream.
    From the willow, she made garlands plaited   185
    With buttercups, nettles, daisies, and orchids
    That our plainspoken shepherds give a coarser name
    But our chaste maids call "dead men's fingers."
    There, while climbing on the leaning boughs to hang
    Her crown of flowers, a malicious branch broke.   190
    Then down she fell with her garlands
    Into the weeping brook. Her clothes spread wide
    And bore her up for awhile, like a mermaid.
    All the time she sang snatches of old hymns,
    Like one unaware of his own distress   195
    Or like a creature native and brought up
    In that element. But it could not be long
    Before her garments, heavy with water,
    Pulled the poor wretch from her melodious song
    To a muddy death.   200
LAERTES Alas, then she is drowned?
GERTRUDE Drowned, drowned.
LAERTES Too much water have you had, poor Ophelia,
    And so I will restrain my tears. But yet
    It is a way we have; nature must be obeyed,   205
    No matter how shameful it seems. When these tears are gone,
    It will be the last of the woman in me. Farewell, my lord,

I have a speech of fire that fain would blaze,
But that this folly douts it.

Exit

CLAUDIUS Let's follow, Gertrude.   210
How much I had to do to calm his rage!
Now fear I this will give it start again.
Therefore, let's follow.

Exeunt

I have a speech of fire that would gladly blaze out,
But this folly of tears douses it.

Exits

CLAUDIUS Let's follow him, Gertrude.   210
    How hard I had to work to calm his rage!
    Now I fear this will start it up again.
    Therefore, let's follow him.

They exit

Act Five

Scene 1 [*A graveyard. Enter a* GRAVEDIGGER *and* ANOTHER]

GRAVEDIGGER Is she to be buried in Christian burial, when she
    wilfully seek her own salvation?

OTHER I tell thee she is, therefore make her grave straight. The
    crowner hath sat on her, and finds it Christian burial.

GRAVEDIGGER How can that be, unless she drowned herself in her   5
    own defense?

OTHER Why, 'tis found so.

GRAVEDIGGER It must be *se offendendo*, it cannot be else. For here
    lies the point: if I drown myself wittingly, it argues an act, and
    an act hath three branches—it is to act, to do, to perform.   10
    Argal, she drowned herself wittingly.

OTHER Nay, but hear you, goodman delver—

GRAVEDIGGER Give me leave. Here lies the water—good. Here
    stands the man—good. If the man go to this water and drown
    himself,
    it is will he, nill he, he goes—mark you that. But if the water   15
    come to him, and drown him, he drowns not himself. Argal, he that
    is not guilty of his own death shortens not his own life.

OTHER But is this law?

GRAVEDIGGER Ay, marry is 't, crowner's 'quest law.

OTHER Will you ha' the truth on 't? If this had not been a   20
    gentlewoman, she should have been buried out o' Christian burial.

Act Five

Scene 1 [*A graveyard. Enter a* GRAVEDIGGER *and* ANOTHER]

GRAVEDIGGER Is she to have a Christian burial, when she willfully
sought her own salvation?

OTHER I tell you she is, so start digging. The coroner has heard her
case and decided on a Christian burial.

GRAVEDIGGER How can that be, unless she drowned herself in   5
self-defense?

OTHER Well, that's what he decided.

GRAVEDIGGER It must be *se offendendo.* It could not be anything else.
For here's the point: if I drown myself intentionally, it is an act,
and an act has three parts—to act, to do, to perform.   10
Therefore, she drowned herself intentionally.

OTHER No, just listen, master digger—

GRAVEDIGGER Let me continue. Here lies the water—good. Here stands
the man—good. If the man goes to the water and drowns himself,
like it or not, that's the end of him—note that. But if the water   15
comes to him and drown him, he doesn't drown himself. Therefore,
he who is not guilty of his own death does not shorten his own life.

OTHER But is this the law?

GRAVEDIGGER Yes, certainly, coroner's inquest law.

OTHER Do you want the real truth of it? If this had not been a   20
gentlewoman, she would not have been given a Christian burial.

GRAVEDIGGER Why, there thou sayst—and the more pity that great
    folk should have countenance in this world to drown or hang
    themselves more than their even-Christen. Come, my spade.
    There is no ancient gentlemen but gardeners, ditchers, and   25
    grave-makers; they hold up Adam's profession.
OTHER Was he a gentleman?
GRAVEDIGGER A was the first that ever bore arms.
OTHER Why, he had none.
GRAVEDIGGER What, art a heathen? How dost thou understand the   30
    scripture? The scripture says Adam digged. Could he dig without
    arms? I'll put another question to thee. If thou answerest me not
    to the purpose, confess thyself—
OTHER Go to!
GRAVEDIGGER What is he that builds stronger than either the   35
    mason, the shipwright, or the carpenter?
OTHER The gallows-maker, for that frame outlives a thousand tenants.
GRAVEDIGGER I like thy wit well, in good faith. The gallows does
    well, but how does it well? It does well to those that do ill. Now,
    thou dost ill to say the gallows is built stronger than the   40
    church. Argal, the gallows may do well to thee. To 't again, come.
OTHER "Who builds stronger than a mason, a shipwright, or a carpenter?"
GRAVEDIGGER Ay, tell me that, and unyoke.
OTHER Marry, now I can tell.
GRAVEDIGGER To 't.   45
OTHER Mass, I cannot tell.
                Enter HAMLET *and* HORATIO *afar off*
GRAVEDIGGER Cudgel thy brains no more about it, for your dull
    ass will not mend his pace with beating. And, when you are
    asked this question next, say "a grave-maker." The houses he
    makes last till doomsday. Go, get thee to Yaughan; fetch   50
    me a stoup of liquor. [*He sings*]

                        The OTHER MAN *exits*

GRAVEDIGGER You've said it right. And the more's the pity
    that great folk should have approval in this world to drown or
    hang themselves more than their fellow Christians. Give me
    my spade. There were no gentlemen in ancient times but gardeners,   25
    ditch diggers, and grave-makers. They followed Adam's profession.
OTHER Was he a gentleman?
GRAVEDIGGER He was the first who ever bore arms.
OTHER Why, he had none.
GRAVEDIGGER What, are you a heathen? How do you understand   30
    the scripture? The scripture says, "Adam digged." Could he dig
    without arms? I'll put another question to you. If you don't
    answer me right, confess your sins and be hanged.
OTHER Go to the devil!
GRAVEDIGGER Who is it that builds stronger than either the mason,   35
    the shipwright, or the carpenter?
OTHER The gallows-maker, for his structure outlives a thousand tenants.
GRAVEDIGGER I like that, really I do. The gallows is a good answer,
    but how good is it? It is good for those who are evil-doers. Now,
    you are wrong to say the gallows is built stronger than the   40
    church. So the gallows might do you some good. Try again, come on.
OTHER "Who builds stronger than a mason, a shipwright, or a carpenter?"
GRAVEDIGGER Yes, tell me that and relax.
OTHER Oh, now I know.
GRAVEDIGGER Go on.   45
OTHER By heaven, I cannot tell.
          Enter HAMLET *and* HORATIO *afar off*
GRAVEDIGGER Beat your brains no more. You can't make a stupid
    ass go more quickly by beating it. And, when you are next asked
    this question, say "a grave-maker." The houses he makes last
    till doomsday. Now go on. Go to Yaughan's and get me a   50
    pitcher of whiskey. [*He sings*]

                    The OTHER MAN *exits*

> In youth when I did love, did love,
>> Methought it was very sweet
> To contract—O—the time for—a—my behove,
>> O, methought there—a—was nothing—a—meet.   55

HAMLET Has this fellow no feeling of his business? A sings in
    grave-making.

HORATIO Custom hath made it in him a property of easiness.

HAMLET 'Tis e'en so, the hand of little employment hath the
    daintier sense.   60

GRAVEDIGGER [*He sings*]

> But age with his stealing steps
>> Hath clawed me in his clutch,
> And hath shipped me into the land,
>> As if I had never been such.

[*Throws up a skull*]

HAMLET That skull had a tongue in it and could sing once. How   65
    the knave jowls it to the ground, as if 'twere Cain's jawbone
    that did the first murder. This might be the pate of a politician
    which this ass now o'erreaches, one that would circumvent God,
    might it not?

HORATIO It might, my lord.   70

HAMLET Or of a courtier, which could say "Good morrow, sweet
    lord! How dost thou, sweet lord?" This might be my Lord Such-
    a-one that praised my Lord Such-a-one's horse when a meant to
    beg it, might it not?

HORATIO Ay, my lord.   75

HAMLET Why, e'en so, and now my Lady Worm's, chapless and
    knocked about the mazard with a sexton's spade. Here's fine
    revolution, an we had the trick to see 't. Did these bones cost
    no more the breeding but to play at loggets with 'em? Mine
    ache to think on 't.   80

GRAVEDIGGER [*He sings*]

> A pickax and a spade, a spade,

In youth when I did love, did love,
    I thought it was very sweet
To pass away—oh—the time for—ah—my delight,
    Oh, I thought there—ah—was no—greater—ah—treat.   55

HAMLET Has this fellow no feeling for his work? He sings while
    digging a grave.

HORATIO He's so used to his work he doesn't give it a thought.

HAMLET You're right, the idle hand has a more fastidious sense
    of touch.   60

GRAVEDIGGER [*He sings*]
    But age creeps up on me
        And has grabbed me in his clutch
    And has taken me back to earth
        As if I had never been such.

[*Throws up a skull*]

HAMLET That skull had a tongue in it and could sing once. How   65
    the rascal bangs it on the ground, as if it were the jawbone of
    Cain, who committed the first murder. This might be the head
    of a cunning schemer, whom this ass now manipulates, one who
    would try to outsmart God, might it not?

HORATIO It might, my lord.   70

HAMLET Or of a courtier, who would say, "Good morning, dear
    lord! How are you, dear lord?" This might be my Lord Such-
    and-such who praised Lord Such-and-such's horse when he
    meant to borrow it, might it not?

HORATIO Yes, my lord.   75

HAMLET Why, even so, and he's now with my Lady Worm,
    jawless and knocked about his top with a sexton's spade. Here's
    a fine turnabout, if one had the knack to see it. Were these bones
    bred for no better purpose than to play games with? My own
    ache to think about.   80

GRAVEDIGGER [*He sings*]
    A pickax and a spade, a spade,

> For and a shrouding sheet,
> O, a pit of clay for to be made,
> For such a guest is meet.
> [*Throws up another skull*]

HAMLET There's another. Why, may not that be the skull of a lawyer?   85
Where be his quiddities now, his quillets, his cases, his tenures,
and his tricks? Why does he suffer this rude knave to knock him
about the sconce with a dirty shovel, and will not tell him of his
action of battery? Hum, this fellow might be in 's time a great
buyer of land, with his statutes, his recognizances, his fines,   90
his double vouchers, his recoveries. Is this the fine of his fines
and the recovery of his recoveries, to have his pate full of fine
dirt? Will his vouchers vouch him no more of his purchases,
and double ones too, than the length and breadth of a pair of
indentures? The very conveyances of his lands will scarcely   95
lie in this box, and must th' inheritor himself have no more, ha?

HORATIO Not a jot more, my lord.

HAMLET Is not parchment made of sheepskins?

HORATIO Ay, my lord, and of calves' skins too.

HAMLET They are sheep and calves which seek out assurance in   100
that. I will speak to this fellow. Whose grave's this, sirrah?

GRAVEDIGGER Mine, sir. [*He sings*]

> O, a pit of clay for to be made
> For such a guest is meet.

HAMLET I think it be thine indeed, for thou liest in 't.   105

GRAVEDIGGER You lie out on 't, sir, and therefore 'tis not yours.
For my part, I do not lie in 't, yet it is mine.

HAMLET Thou dost lie in 't, to be in 't and say 'tis thine. 'Tis for the
dead, not for the quick, therefore thou liest.

GRAVEDIGGER 'Tis a quick lie, sir, 'twill away again from me to you.   110

HAMLET What man dost thou dig it for?

GRAVEDIGGER For no man, sir.

HAMLET What woman then?

Then a shroud that is a sheet,
O, a pit of clay that is to be made,
For such a guest is neat.
[*Throws up another skull*]

HAMLET There's another. Why, might this not be the skull of a lawyer?   85
Where are his subtle distinctions now, his quibbles, his law suits, his
title deeds, and his tricks? Why does he allow this coarse rascal to
knock him about the noggin with a dirty shovel and not threaten him
with an action of battery? Hm, this fellow might have been in his great
time a buyer of land, with his mortgages, his bonds, his transfers,   90
his double guarantors, his court orders. Is this the conclusion of his
conclusions and the court order of his court orders—to have his head
full of fine dirt? Will his guarantors guarantee no more of his purchases,
and double ones at that, than the length and breadth of a
pair of documents? The very deeds to his lands would hardly fit   95
this space. Must the buyer himself have no more, eh?

HORATIO Not the least bit more, my lord.

HAMLET Is not parchment made of sheepskin?

HORATIO Yes, my lord, and of calfskin, too.

HAMLET People are sheep and calves, then, to put their trust in a legal   100
document. I'll speak to this fellow. Whose grave is this, sir?

GRAVEDIGGER Mine, sir. [*He sings*]
Oh, a pit of clay that is to be made
For such a guest is neat.

HAMLET I think it is yours, indeed, because you are lying in it.   105

GRAVEDIGGER You lie out of it, sir, and therefore, it's not yours.
As for me, I do not lie in it, yet it is mine.

HAMLET You are lying in it, and you say it's yours. It's for the dead,
not the living. Therefore, you are lying.

GRAVEDIGGER That's a living lie, sir. If I'm lying, so are you.   110

HAMLET What man do you dig for?

GRAVEDIGGER For no man, sir.

HAMLET What woman then?

GRAVEDIGGER For none, neither.

HAMLET Who is to be buried in 't?   115

GRAVEDIGGER One that was a woman, sir, but rest her soul,
    she's dead.

HAMLET How absolute the knave is! We must speak by the card, or
    equivocation will undo us. By the Lord, Horatio, this three years
    I have took note of it: the age has grown so picked that the toe   120
    of the peasant comes so near the heel of the courtier, he galls
    his kibe. How long hast thou been a grave-maker?

GRAVEDIGGER Of all the days i' th' year, I came to 't that day that
    our last King Hamlet o'ercame Fortinbras.

HAMLET How long is that since?   125

GRAVEDIGGER Cannot you tell that? Every fool can tell that. It was
    the very day young Hamlet was born, he that is mad and sent
    into England.

HAMLET Ay, marry, why was he sent into England?

GRAVEDIGGER Why, because he was mad. A shall recover his   130
    wits there, or if a do not, 'tis no great matter there.

HAMLET Why?

GRAVEDIGGER 'Twill not be seen in him there. There the men are
    as mad as he.

HAMLET How came he mad?   135

GRAVEDIGGER Very strangely, they say.

HAMLET How "strangely"?

GRAVEDIGGER Faith, e'en with losing his wits.

HAMLET Upon what ground?

GRAVEDIGGER Why, here in Denmark. I have been sexton here,   140
    man and boy, thirty years.

HAMLET How long will a man lie i' th' earth ere he rot?

GRAVEDIGGER Faith, if a be not rotten before a die, as we have
    many pocky corses nowadays that will scarce hold the laying
    in, a will last you some eight year or nine year. A tanner   145
    will last you nine year.

GRAVEDIGGER No woman either.

HAMLET Who is to be buried in it?   115

GRAVEDIGGER Someone who was a woman, sir, but, rest her soul,
 she's dead.

HAMLET How literal the rascal is! We must navigate by his compass
 or double-meanings will wreck us. By heavens, Horatio, these
 last three years I've noticed that our times are so refined that   120
 the toe of the peasant comes so close to the heel of the courtier,
 he rubs sore his heel. How long have you been a grave-maker?

GRAVEDIGGER Of all the days of the year, I started on the day that
 our last king, Hamlet, defeated Fortinbras.

HAMLET How long ago is that?   125

GRAVEDIGGER Can't you count? Every fool knows that. It was the
 very day that young Hamlet was born—the one who's gone
 mad and was sent to England.

HAMLET Yes, indeed. Why was he sent to England?

GRAVEDIGGER Why, because he was mad. He shall recover his   130
 wits there, or if he doesn't, it won't matter much there.

HAMLET Why?

GRAVEDIGGER They will not notice it there. There the men are as
 mad as he.

HAMLET How did he become mad?   135

GRAVEDIGGER Very strangely, they say.

HAMLET What do you mean "strangely"?

GRAVEDIGGER Truly, by losing his wits.

HAMLET What were the grounds for that?

GRAVEDIGGER Why, the ground here in Denmark. I have been   140
 a sexton here, man and boy, for thirty years.

HAMLET How long will a man lie in the earth before he rots?

GRAVEDIGGER Truly, if he is not rotten before he dies—and we have
 many rotten corpses nowadays that will scarcely hold together
 before they're buried—he will last some eight or nine years.   145
 A tanner will last you nine years.

HAMLET Why he more than another?

GRAVEDIGGER Why, sir, his hide is so tanned with his trade that a
will keep out water a great while, and your water is a sore
decayer of your whoreson dead body. Here's a skull now; 150
this skull hath lien you i' th' earth three-and-twenty years.

HAMLET Whose was it?

GRAVEDIGGER A whoreson mad fellow's it was. Whose do you think
it was?

HAMLET Nay, I know not. 155

GRAVEDIGGER A pestilence on him for a mad rogue! A poured a
flagon of Rhenish on my head once. This same skull, sir, was
Yorick's skull, the king's jester.

HAMLET This?

GRAVEDIGGER E'en that. 160

HAMLET Let me see. [*Takes the skull*] Alas, poor Yorick! I knew him,
Horatio, a fellow of infinite jest, of most excellent fancy. He hath
borne me on his back a thousand times—and now how abhorred
in my imagination it is! My gorge rises at it. Here hung those lips
that I have kissed I know not how oft. Where be your gibes now? 165
your gambols? your songs? your flashes of merriment that were
wont to set the table on a roar? Not one now to mock your own
grinning? Quite chap-fallen? Now, get you to my lady's chamber
and tell her, let her paint an inch thick, to this favor she must come
Make her laugh at that.—Prithee, Horatio, tell me one thing. 170

HORATIO What's that, my lord?

HAMLET Dost thou think Alexander looked o' this fashion i' th' earth?

HORATIO E'en so.

HAMLET And smelt so? Pah! [*Puts down the skull*]

HORATIO E'en so, my lord. 175

HAMLET To what base uses we may return, Horatio! Why may not
imagination trace the noble dust of Alexander, till a find it
stopping a bunghole?

HORATIO 'Twere to consider too curiously to consider so.

HAMLET Why he more than another?

GRAVEDIGGER Because, sir, his hide is so tanned by his work that
 he will keep out water a long time; and your water is a great
 destroyer of your vile dead body. Here's a skull now; this   150
 skull has been lying in the earth three-and-twenty years.

HAMLET Whose was it?

GRAVEDIGGER A rascally mad fellow he was. Who do you think
 it was?

HAMLET No, I don't know.   155

GRAVEDIGGER A plague on him, for the mad rogue he was. Once
 he poured a pitcher of Rhine wine on my head. This same skull,
 sir, was Yorick's skull, the king's jester.

HAMLET This?

GRAVEDIGGER The very one.   160

HAMLET Let me see. [*Takes the skull*] Alas, poor Yorick! I knew
 him, Horatio. He was a fellow of irrepressible humor, of
 delightful imagination. He carried me on his back a thousand
 times—and now hateful it is to think about it! I retch at the idea.
 Here hung those lips I have kissed I don't know how often. Where   165
 are your witty remarks now? your practical jokes? your songs? your
 flashes of merriment that set the table roaring? Not one left to mock
 your own grins? Quite down-in-the mouth? Now, go to my lady's
 room and tell her no matter how thick she paints her face, she will
 come to this. Make her laugh at that.—Please, Horatio, tell me this. 170

HORATIO What's that, my lord?

HAMLET Do you think Alexander the Great looked like this in the earth?

HORATIO Just the same.

HAMLET And smelled so? Ugh! [*Puts down the skull*]

HORATIO Just the same, my lord.   175

HAMLET To what mean tasks we may be used, Horatio! Cannot
 imagination trace the noble dust of Alexander to find it used
 as a stopper for a beer barrel?

HORATIO That's too far-fetched.

HAMLET No, faith, not a jot; but to follow him thither, with modesty   180
    enough and likelihood to lead it, as thus: Alexander died,
    Alexander was buried, Alexander returneth to dust, the dust
    is earth, of earth we make loam, and why of that loam
    whereto he was converted might they not stop a beer barrel?
    Imperious Caesar, dead and turned to clay,   185
    Might stop a hole, to keep the wind away.
    O, that that earth which kept the world in awe
    Should patch a wall t' expel the winter's flaw!
    But soft, but soft awhile! Here comes the king,
    The queen, the courtiers.   190
Enter CLAUDIUS, GERTRUDE, LAERTES, *and a coffin, with* PRIEST
        and LORDS *attendant*
    Who is this they follow?
    And with such maimed rites? This doth betoken
    The corse they follow did with desperate hand
    Fordo its own life. 'Twas of some estate.
    Couch we awhile and mark. [*They step aside*]   195
LAERTES What ceremony else?
HAMLET That is Laertes, a very noble youth. Mark.
LAERTES What ceremony else?
PRIEST Her obsequies have been as far enlarged
    As we have warranty. Her death was doubtful,   200
    And but that great command o'ersways the order,
    She should in ground unsanctified have lodged
    Till the last trumpet. For charitable prayers,
    Shards, flints, and pebbles should be thrown on her.
    Yet here she is allowed her virgin crants,   205
    Her maiden strewments, and the bringing home
    Of bell and burial.
LAERTES Must there no more be done?
PRIEST No more be done.
    We should profane the service of the dead   210

HAMLET No, by heaven, not a jot. It's a question of following him   180
    closely enough, guided by what's probable. Thus: Alexander
    died, Alexander was buried, Alexander returned to dust, dust
    is earth, from earth we make mortar, and why, from that mortar
    to which he was converted, should they not stop up a beer
    barrel?
    Imperious Caesar, dead and turned to clay,   185
    Might stop a hole to keep the wind away.
    Oh, that the earth that kept the world in thrall
    Should patch a wall to keep out winter's squall!
    But enough, enough for now! Here comes the king,
    The queen, the courtiers.   190

Enter CLAUDIUS, GERTRUDE, LAERTES, *and a coffin, with* PRIEST
                and LORDS *attendant*

    Who is it they mourn?
    And with such a shortened ceremony? This implies
    The person they mourn did with a desperate hand
    Take his own life. It was someone of high rank.
    Let us conceal ourselves and watch. [*They step aside*]   195
LAERTES What other ceremonies?
HAMLET That is Laertes, a very noble youth. Listen.
LAERTES What other ceremonies?
PRIEST Her funeral rites have been extended
    As far as we have grounds. Her death raises questions,   200
    And, except that higher authority overruled normal practice,
    She should have been buried in unsanctified ground
    Till the trumpet of doomsday. In place of sympathetic prayers,
    Broken pottery, flints, and pebbles should be thrown on her.
    Here she is allowed her virgin garlands,   205
    Her maiden flowers, and being brought to her last home
    With bell ringing and proper burial.
LAERTES Can no more be done?
PRIEST No more can be done.
    We would profane the Service for the Dead   210

To sing sage requiem and such rest to her
As to peace-parted souls.

LAERTES Lay her i' th' earth,
And from her fair and unpolluted flesh
May violets spring. I tell thee, churlish priest,   215
A ministering angel shall my sister be
When thou liest howling.

HAMLET What, the fair Ophelia!

GERTRUDE [*Scattering flowers*] Sweets to the sweet, farewell.
I had hoped thou shouldst have been my Hamlet's wife.   220
I thought thy bride-bed to have decked, sweet maid,
And not t' have strewed thy grave.

LAERTES O, treble woe
Fall ten times treble on that cursed head
Whose wicked deed thy most ingenious sense   225
Deprived thee of. Hold off the earth awhile,
Till I have caught her once more in mine arms.

[*Leaps into the grave*]
Now pile your dust upon the quick and the dead,
Till of this flat a mountain you have made
T' o'ertop old Pelion or the skyish head   230
Of blue Olympus.

HAMLET [*Advancing*] What is he whose grief
Bears such an emphasis, whose phrase of sorrow
Conjures the wandering stars, and makes them stand
Like wonder-wounded hearers? This is I,   235
Hamlet the Dane.

LAERTES [*Climbs out of the grave*] The devil take thy soul.

HAMLET Thou pray'st not well. [*Grappling with him*]
I prithee take thy fingers from my throat,
For though I am not splenitive and rash,   240
Yet I have in me something dangerous,
Which let thy wisdom fear. Hold off thy hand.

To sing solemn requiem and pray for such rest
Like those souls who parted this life in peace.

LAERTES Lay her in the earth,
And from her fair and virginal flesh
May violets grow. I tell you, uncharitable priest,   215
A ministering angel shall my sister be
When you lie howling in hell.

HAMLET What, the beautiful Ophelia!

GERTRUDE [*Scattering flowers*] Sweets to the sweet. Farewell.
I hoped you would have been my Hamlet's wife.   220
I hoped to have adorned your bridal bed, sweet maid,
Not strewn flowers on your grave.

LAERTES Oh, triple woe
Fall ten times three on that cursed head
Whose wicked deed deprived you   225
Of your reason. Hold off the earth awhile,
Till I have held her once more in my arms.

[*Leaps into the grave*]
Now pile your earth upon the living and the dead,
Till on this flat ground you have made a mountain
Higher than Mount Pelion or the skies   230
Of blue above Olympus.

HAMLET [*Advancing*] Who is this that makes such a noise
Of his grief, whose sorrowful words
Charm the wandering stars and make them stand
Struck with wonder? This is I,   235
Hamlet the Dane.

LAERTES [*Climbs out of grave*] The devil take your soul!

HAMLET Not a good prayer. [*Grappling with him*]
Please, take your fingers from my throat.
Though I am not easily angered or hasty,   240
There is a dangerous streak in me
Which you would be wise to fear. Take your hand away.

CLAUDIUS Pluck them asunder.

GERTRUDE Hamlet, Hamlet!

ALL Gentlemen!   245

HORATIO Good my lord, be quiet.

    [*Attendants part them*]

HAMLET Why, I will fight with him upon this theme

    Until my eyelids will no longer wag.

GERTRUDE O my son, what theme?

HAMLET I have loved Ophelia. Forty thousand brothers   250

    Could not with all their quantity of love

    Make up my sum. What wilt thou do for her?

CLAUDIUS O, he is mad, Laertes.

GERTRUDE For the love of God, forbear him.

HAMLET 'Swounds, show me what thou't do.   255

    Woo't weep, woo't fight, woo't fast, woo't tear thyself?

    Woo't drink up eisel, eat a crocodile?

    I'll do 't. Dost thou come here to whine?

    To outface me with leaping in her grave?

    Be buried quick with her, and so will I.   260

    And if thou prate of mountains, let them throw

    Millions of acres on us, till our ground,

    Singeing his pate against the burning zone,

    Make Ossa like a wart. Nay, and thou'lt mouth,

    I'll rant as well as thou.   265

GERTRUDE This is mere madness,

    And thus awhile the fit will work on him.

    Anon, as patient as the female dove

    When that her golden couplets are disclosed,

    His silence will sit drooping.   270

HAMLET Hear you, sir,

    What is the reason that you use me thus?

    I loved you ever—but it is no matter.

CLAUDIUS Pull them apart.
GERTRUDE Hamlet, Hamlet!
ALL Gentlemen!   245
HORATIO My good lord, compose yourself.
    [*Attendants part them*]
HAMLET Why, I will fight him on this issue
    Until my eyes will no longer open.
GERTRUDE Oh, my son, what issue?
HAMLET I loved Ophelia. Forty thousand brothers   250
    Could not with all their love added together
    Equal the sum of mine. What will you do for her?
CLAUDIUS Oh, he is mad, Laertes.
GERTRUDE For the love of God, leave him alone.
HAMLET By God, show me what you would do.   255
    Will you weep, fight, fast, will you wound yourself?
    Will you drink vinegar, eat a crocodile?
    I'll do it. Did you come here to whine?
    To outdo me by leaping in her grave?
    Be buried alive with her, and so will I.   260
    And if you prattle about mountains, let them throw
    Millions of acres on us, till the ground
    Singes its head against the sun's burning zone,
    Making Mount Ossa look like a wart. No, if you bluster,
    I'll rant as loud as you.   265
GERTRUDE This is simply madness.
    He will be in this fit for awhile.
    Soon, he will be as meek as the mother dove
    When her golden chicks have hatched,
    Sitting in silence, drooping.   270
HAMLET Listen, sir,
    What is the reason that you treat me like this?
    I have always liked you—but it doesn't matter.

233

Let Hercules himself do what he may,
The cat will mew, and dog will have his day.   275
                                  Exit
CLAUDIUS I pray thee, good Horatio, wait upon him.
                            Exit HORATIO
[*To* LAERTES] Strengthen your patience in our last
    night's speech;
We'll put the matter to the present push.—
Good Gertrude, set some watch over your son.—   280
This grave shall have a living monument.
An hour of quiet shortly shall we see,
Till then in patience our proceeding be.
                          Exeunt

Scene 2 [*In the hall of the castle*]
                Enter HAMLET *and* HORATIO
HAMLET So much for this, sir. Now shall you see the other.
    You do remember all the circumstance?
HORATIO Remember it, my lord!
HAMLET Sir, in my heart there was a kind of fighting
    That would not let me sleep. Methought I lay   5
    Worse than the mutines in the bilboes. Rashly—
    And praised be rashness for it—let us know,
    Our indiscretion sometime serves us well
    When our deep plots do pall, and that should learn us
    There's a divinity that shapes our ends,   10
    Rough-hew them how we will—
HORATIO That is most certain.
HAMLET Up from my cabin,
    My sea-gown scarfed about me, in the dark
    Groped I to find out them, had my desire,   15
    Fingered their packet, and in fine withdrew
    To mine own room again, making so bold,

Even Hercules himself does what he may,
The cat will mew, the dog will have his day.   275
Exits

CLAUDIUS Please, good Horatio, look after him.
Exit HORATIO

[*To* LAERTES] Be patient, remember our conversation
    of last night;
We'll bring the matter to a head shortly.—
Good Gertrude, have someone guard your son.—   280
This grave shall have an enduring monument.
An hour of quiet we surely need,
Till then in patience we shall proceed.
They exit

Scene 2 [*In the hall of the castle*]
Enter HAMLET *and* HORATIO

HAMLET So much for that, sir. Now for the rest.
    Do you remember all the circumstances?
HORATIO I remember, my lord!
HAMLET Sir, in my heart there was a kind of turmoil
    That would not let me sleep. I felt I lay there   5
    Worse than mutineers in their shackles. Rashly—
    And praised be the rashness of it—let us admit
    Our imprudence sometimes serves us well
    When our careful plots fail, which should teach us
    There's a divinity that gives our ends a final form,   10
    No matter how crudely we botch them—
HORATIO That is most certain.
HAMLET Up from my cabin,
    My sailor's coat wrapped around me, in the dark
    I groped my way to find them, which I did.   15
    I stole their documents and, in sum, withdrew
    To my own cabin again. I made so bold,

My fears forgetting manners, to unseal
Their grand commission; where I found, Horatio—
O royal knavery!—an exact command,   20
Larded with many several sorts of reasons
Importing Denmark's health, and England's too,
With ho! such bugs and goblins in my life,
That on the supervise, no leisure bated,
No, not to stay the grinding of the ax,   25
My head should be struck off.
HORATIO Is 't possible?
HAMLET Here's the commission, read it at more leisure.
    But wilt thou hear how I did proceed?
HORATIO I beseech you.   30
HAMLET Being thus benetted round with villainies,
    Ere I could make a prologue to my brains,
    They had begun the play. I sat me down,
    Devised a new commission, wrote it fair.
    I once did hold it, as our statists do,   35
    A baseness to write fair, and labored much
    How to forget that learning; but, sir, now
    It did me yeoman's service. Wilt thou know
    Th' effect of what I wrote?
HORATIO Ay, good my lord.   40
HAMLET An earnest conjuration from the king,
    As England was his faithful tributary,
    As love between them like the palm might flourish,
    As peace should still her wheaten garland wear
    And stand a comma 'tween their amities,   45
    And many such like *as'*s of great charge,
    That on the view and knowing of these contents,
    Without debatement further, more or less,
    He should those bearers put to sudden death,
    Not shriving time allowed.   50

My fears getting the better of my manners, as to unseal
Their grand commission, where I found, Horatio—
Oh, royal trickery!—a precise command,   20
Larded with a variety of reasons
Concerning Denmark's welfare, and that of England too,
With, oh, such monstrosities to be feared from me,
That on viewing the letter, no time to be wasted,
No, not even to sharpening of the ax,   25
My head should be struck off.
HORATIO Is that possible?
HAMLET Here's the commission. Read it at your leisure.
    But do you want to know how I dealt with it?
HORATIO Please, go on.   30
HAMLET Being thus ensnared with villainies,
    Before I could write a part for my brains to act,
    They had begun the play. I sat down,
    Made up a new commission, wrote it out clearly.
    I once believed, as our statesmen do,   35
    That it is improper to write clearly and worked hard
    To unlearn what I had learned. But, sir, now
    It did me a yeoman's service. Do you want to know
    What I wrote?
HORATIO Yes, my good lord.   40
HAMLET I wrote a solemn appeal from the king.
    As England was one who paid tribute,
    As love between them should flourish like the palm tree,
    As peace should still a garland of wheat wear
    And stand like a comma joining their friendship,   45
    And as many such like *as*'s of great weight,
    That on seeing and digesting these contents,
    Without further debate, more or less,
    He should put the bearers of these letters to death,
    Giving them no time for absolution.   50

HORATIO How was this sealed?
HAMLET Why, even in that was heaven ordinant.
    I had my father's signet in my purse,
    Which was the model of the Danish seal;
    Folded the writ up in the form of th' other,   55
    Subscribed it, gave 't th' impression, placed it safely,
    The changeling never known. Now, the next day
    Was our sea-fight, and what to this was sequent
    Thou know'st already.
HORATIO So Guildenstern and Rosencrantz go to 't.   60
HAMLET Why man, they did make love to this employment.
    They are not near my conscience. Their defeat
    Does by their own insinuation grow.
    'Tis dangerous when the baser nature comes
    Between the pass and fell incensed points   65
    Of mighty opposites.
HORATIO Why, what a king is this!
HAMLET Does it not, think thee, stand me now upon—
    He that hath killed my king and whored my mother,
    Popped in between th' election and my hopes,   70
    Thrown out his angle for my proper life,
    And with such cozenage—is 't not perfect conscience
    To quit him with this arm? And is 't not to be damned
    To let the canker of our nature come
    In further evil?   75
HORATIO It must be shortly known to him from England
    What is the issue of the business there.
HAMLET It will be short. The interim's mine,
    And a man's life's no more than to say "one."
    But I am very sorry, good Horatio,   80
    That to Laertes I forgot myself,
    For by the image of my cause, I see
    The portraiture of his. I'll court his favors.

HORATIO How did you seal it?
HAMLET Why, even there heaven was in control.
    I had my father's seal in my bag,
    Which was a copy of the king's own seal.
    I folded my letter up like the real one,   55
    Signed it, marked it with the seal, and replaced it safely,
    The switch going undetected. Now, the next day
    Was our sea-battle, and what happened after,
    You already know.
HORATIO So Guildenstern and Rosencrantz went to their deaths.   60
HAMLET Why man, they were eager to act for the king.
    They are not close to touching my conscience. Their downfall
    Was the result of their own attempt to creep into favor.
    It's dangerous for lesser natures to come
    Between the thrust and angry strokes   65
    Of mighty opponents.
HORATIO Why, what kind of king is this!
HAMLET Is it not, don't you think, up to me now—
    He killed the king my father and whored my mother,
    Pushed in between the election and my succession,   70
    Cast his line and hook for my own life,
    And with such cheating—can I not in perfect conscience
    Kill him with this hand? Would it not be damnable
    To let this cancer of our nature grow
    To further evil?   75
HORATIO He will shortly know from the English king
    What happened there.
HAMLET Very shortly. But the time in between is mine,
    And in any case, a man's life is short.
    But I am very sorry, good Horatio,   80
    That I forgot myself with Laertes.
    By the mirror-image of my cause, I see
    The portrait of his. I'll make it up to him.

But sure the bravery of his grief did put me
Into a towering passion.   85

HORATIO Peace, who comes here?

Enter OSRIC, *a courtier*

OSRIC Your lordship is right welcome back to Denmark.

HAMLET I humbly thank you, sir. [*Aside to* HORATIO] Dost know
this water-fly?

HORATIO No, my good lord.   90

HAMLET Thy state is the more gracious, for 'tis a vice to know him.
He hath much land, and fertile. Let a beast be lord of beasts, and
his crib hall stand at the king's mess. 'Tis a chough, but, as I say,
spacious in the possession of dirt.

OSRIC Sweet lord, if your lordship were at leisure, I should impart a   95
thing to you from his majesty.

HAMLET I will receive it, sir, with all diligence of spirit. Put your
bonnet to his right use, 'tis for the head.

OSRIC I thank your lordship; it is very hot.

HAMLET No, believe me, 'tis very cold. The wind is northerly.   100

OSRIC It is indifferent cold, my lord, indeed.

HAMLET But yet methinks, it is very sultry and hot for my complexion.

OSRIC Exceedingly, my lord, it is very sultry, as 'twere—I cannot tell
how. But, my lord, his majesty bade me signify to you that a has
laid a great wager on your head. Sir, this is the matter—   105

HAMLET I beseech you, remember.

OSRIC Nay, good my lord, for my ease in good faith. Sir, here is
newly come to court Laertes; believe me, an absolute gentleman,
full of most excellent differences, of very soft society and great
showing. Indeed, to speak feelingly of him, he is the card or   110
calendar of gentry, for you shall find in him the continent of what
part a gentleman would see.

HAMLET Sir, his definement suffers no perdition in you, though I know
to divide him inventorially would dozy th' arithmetic of memory,
and yet but yaw neither, in respect of his quick sail. But in the   115

But his boastful display of grief put me
    In a towering rage.   85

HORATIO Wait, who's coming?

Enter OSRIC, *a courtier*

OSRIC Your lordship is most welcome back to Denmark.

HAMLET I humbly thank you, sir. [*Aside to* HORATIO] Do you
    know this pretty insect?

HORATIO No, my good lord.   90

HAMLET Your position is blessed; it's a vice to know him. He owns
    much fertile land. Let one dumb animal own a lot of other dumb
    animals, and the king will invite him to eat at his table. He's a
    country bumpkin, but, as I say, spacious in the possession of dirt.

OSRIC Sweet lord, if your lordship has the time, I should impart to you   95
    a message from his majesty.

HAMLET I will receive it, sir, with all the attention of my being. Put
    your hat to its proper use; it's for the head.

OSRIC I thank your lordship. It's very hot.

HAMLET No, believe me, it's very cold. The wind is from the north.   100

OSRIC It is rather cold, my lord, indeed.

HAMLET Still, I think it is very sultry and hot for my temperament.

OSRIC Exceeding, my lord, it is very sultry, as it were—I cannot say
    how. But, my lord, his majesty has told me to signify to you that
    he has laid a great wager on your head. Sir, it is like this—   105

HAMLET I ask you, remember the hat.

OSRIC No, my good lord, for my ease in showing respect. Sir, Laertes
    has just come to court; believe me, he's an absolute gentleman, full
    of different excellences, very sociable, and of pleasing appearance.
    Indeed, to speak personally of him, he is the map or guide to   110
    gentility. You shall find in him the sum of those qualities of what
    one would look for in a gentleman.

HAMLET Sir, his description suffers no loss by you, though I know
    his category of qualities would make the mind dizzy and steer us
    off course compared to his quick sailing. But to do him full   115

verity of extolment, I take him to be a soul of great article,
and his infusion of such dearth and rareness as, to make true
diction of him, his semblable is his mirror, and who else would
trace him, his umbrage, nothing more.

OSRIC Your lordship speaks most infallibly of him.   120

HAMLET The concernancy, sir? Why do we wrap the gentleman in
our more rawer breath?

OSRIC Sir?

HORATIO [*Aside to* HAMLET] Is 't not possible to understand in
another tongue? You will to 't sir, really.   125

HAMLET What imports the nomination of this gentleman?

OSRIC Of Laertes?

HORATIO His purse is empty already, all 's golden words are spent.

HAMLET Of him, sir.

OSRIC I know you are not ignorant—   130

HAMLET I would you did, sir. Yet, in faith, if you did, it would
not much approve me. Well, sir?

OSRIC You are not ignorant of what excellence Laertes is—

HAMLET I dare not confess that, lest I should compare with him
in excellence. But to know a man well were to know himself.   135

OSRIC I mean, sir, for his weapon; but in the imputation laid on
him by them, in his meed he's unfellowed.

HAMLET What's his weapon?

OSRIC Rapier and dagger.

HAMLET That's two of his weapons, but well—   140

OSRIC The king, sir, has wagered with him six Barbary horses,
against the which he has impawned, as I take it, six French
rapiers and poniards, with their assigns, as girdle, hangers, and
so. Three of the carriages in faith are very dear to fancy, very
responsive to the hilts, most delicate carriages, and of very   145
liberal conceit.

HAMLET What call you the "carriages"?

HORATIO [*Aside to* HAMLET] I knew you must be edified by the

justice, I take him to be a soul of great importance,
and his nature of such splendor and rareness, that to give a true
account of him only the reflection in his mirror would do.
Those who would match him are shadows, nothing more.

OSRIC Your lordship speaks most flawlessly of him.   120

HAMLET The relevancy, sir? Why do we attempt to clothe the
gentleman in our crude speech?

OSRIC Sir?

HORATIO [*Aside to* HAMLET] Is it possible he doesn't understand his
own tongue when another speaks it? You'll get there, finally.   125

HAMLET What is the point in naming this gentleman?

OSRIC Laertes?

HORATIO His purse is empty. All his golden words are spent.

HAMLET Yes, of him, sir.

OSRIC I know you are not ignorant—   130

HAMLET I wish you did, sir, yet even if you did, your testimony
would be little to my credit. Well, sir?

OSRIC You are not ignorant of Laertes' excellence—

HAMLET I dare not admit that, lest I compare myself with him in
excellence. To know a man well one has to know oneself.   135

OSRIC I mean, sir, excellence with his weapon. In the reputation
given him, he has no equal.

HAMLET What's his weapon?

OSRIC Rapier and dagger.

HAMLET That's two of his weapons, but never mind—   140

OSRIC The king, sir, has wagered with him six Arab horses, against
which Laertes has staked, as I understand, six French rapiers
and poniards with their equipment such as belts, straps, and so
on. Three of the carriages indeed are very tasteful, very well
matched at the hilts, most finely constructed, and very elegantly   145
designed.

HAMLET What are these "carriages"?

HORATIO [*Aside to* HAMLET] I knew you would need a footnote margent ere you had done.

OSRIC The carriages, sir, are the hangers.   150

HAMLET The phrase would be more germane to the matter if we
carry a cannon by our sides; I would it might be "hangers" till
then. But on. Six Barbary horses against six French swords, their
assigns, and three liberal-conceited carriages—that's the French
bet against the Danish. Why is this "impawned," as you call it?   155

OSRIC The king, sir, hath laid, sir, that in a dozen passes between
yourself and him, he shall not exceed you three hits. He hath laid
on twelve for nine. And it would come to immediate trial, if your
lordship would vouchsafe the answer.

HAMLET How if I answer no?   160

OSRIC I mean, my lord, the opposition of your person in trial.

HAMLET Sir, I will walk here in the hall. If it please his majesty, it is
the breathing time of day with me. Let the foils be brought, the
gentleman willing, and the king hold his purpose, I will win for
him, an I can. If not, I will gain nothing but my shame and the   165
odd hits.

OSRIC Shall I redeliver you e'en so?

HAMLET To this effect, sir, after what flourish your nature will.

OSRIC I commend my duty to your lordship.

HAMLET Yours, yours.   170

Exit OSRIC

He does well to commend it himself; there are not tongues else
for 's turn.

HORATIO This lapwing runs away with the shell on his head.

HAMLET A did comply with his dug before a sucked it. Thus has he,
and many more of the same bevy that I know the drossy age   175
dotes on, only got the tune of the time and outward habit of
encounter, a kind of yeasty collection, which carries them through
and through the most fanned and winnowed opinions: and do but
blow them to their trial, the bubbles are out.

Enter a LORD

before you had finished.

OSRIC The carriages, sir, are the straps.   150

HAMLET That word would be more appropriate if we carried cannons
　　　　at our sides; till then I prefer to call them "straps." But go on.
　　　　Six Arabian horses against six French swords, their equipment,
　　　　and three imaginatively named "carriages"—that's the French bet
　　　　against the Danish. What is this "staked," as you call it?   155

OSRIC The king, sir, has wagered, sir, that in a dozen bouts between
　　　　you and Laertes, he will not win three more than you. He has bet
　　　　nine hits for twelve bouts. And it could be settled immediately if
　　　　your lordship would grant an answer.

HAMLET Even if I were to answer "No"?   160

OSRIC I mean, my lord, if you accept the challenge.

HAMLET Sir, I will walk here in the hall. If it please his majesty, that's
　　　　my time for exercise. If the foils are brought, the gentleman is
　　　　willing, and the king has not changed his mind, I will win for him,
　　　　if I can. If not, I will gain nothing but my own shame and the   165
　　　　odd hits.

OSRIC Shall I report back what you say?

HAMLET To that effect, sir, with whatever flourish is natural to you.

OSRIC I commend my service to your lordship.

HAMLET Yours, yours.   170

Exit OSRIC

He does well to commend himself, for there are no others who
do it for him.

HORATIO This baby bird runs off with the shell still stuck on his head.

HAMLET He did bow before his mother's nipple before he sucked it. Like
　　　　many more of his sort that I know this rubbishy age dotes upon, he   175
　　　　is only in tune with the time and the outward fashion of society.
　　　　These people are like a frothy mass, working its way through the
　　　　refined brew, to the top, where they appear as mere bubbles which
　　　　can be blown away. Put to the test, they are hollow.

Enter a LORD

LORD My lord, his majesty commended him to you by young Osric, 180
    who brings back to him that you attend him in the hall. He
    sends to know if your pleasure hold to play with Laertes, or
    that you will take longer time.

HAMLET I am constant to my purposes, they follow the king's
    pleasure. If his fitness speaks, mine is ready now or provided 185
    whensoever, I be so able as now.

LORD The king and the queen and all are coming down.

HAMLET In happy time.

LORD The queen desires you to use some gentle entertainment to
    Laertes, before you fall to play. 190

HAMLET She well instructs me.

Exit LORD

HORATIO You will lose, my lord.

HAMLET I do not think so. Since he went into France, I have been in
    continual practice. I shall win at the odds; but thou wouldst not
    think how ill all's here about my heart—but it is no matter. 195

HORATIO Nay, good my lord—

HAMLET It is but foolery, but it is such a kind of gaingiving as would
    perhaps trouble a woman.

HORATIO If your mind dislike anything, obey it. I will forestall their
    repair hither, and say you are not fit. 200

HAMLET Not a whit. We defy augury. There is a special providence
    in the fall of a sparrow. If it be now, 'tis not to come. If it be
    not to come, it will be now. If it be not now, yet it will come—
    the readiness is all. Since no man of aught he leaves knows,
    what is 't to leave betimes? Let be. 205

*A table with flagons of wine on it is prepared by attendants. Trumpets,
drums, and officers with cushions. Enter* CLAUDIUS, GERTRUDE,
LAERTES, *and* LORDS *and other attendants with foils, daggers, and
gauntlets*

CLAUDIUS Come Hamlet, come and take this hand from me.

[*He puts* LAERTES' *hand in* HAMLET'S]

HAMLET [*To* LAERTES] Give me your pardon, sir, I've done you wrong.

LORD My lord, his majesty sent greetings to you by way of young   180
    Osric, who returned with the message that you await him in
    the hall. He would like to know if you still wish to compete
    with Laertes or would rather wait till later.
HAMLET I am faithful to my cause. It waits upon the king's desire.
    If he says he is ready, so am I—now or whenever, provided I am   185
    as prepared as now.
LORD The king and the queen and the court are on their way down.
HAMLET At the right moment.
LORD The queen would like you to give Laertes a courteous
    reception before you begin the contest.   190
HAMLET I accept her advice.

Exit LORD

HORATIO You will lose, my lord.
HAMLET I do not think so. Since he went to France, I have been in
    continual practice. I shall win, as the odds stand. But you won't
    believe how uneasy I feel—but it doesn't matter.   195
HORATIO Yes, my good lord—
HAMLET It's foolish. It is the kind of foreboding that would perhaps
    trouble a woman.
HORATIO If your mind tells you something's wrong, obey it. I will
    stop them coming here and say you are not well.   200
HAMLET Not at all. We defy omens. There is a special providence,
    even in the death of a sparrow. If death comes now, it will not
    come later. If not later, then now. If not now, yet it will
    come—readiness is everything. Since no man knows what he
    will miss, what does it matter if he dies early? Enough of that.   205
A table with jugs of wine on it is prepared by attendants. Trumpets and
drums sound. Officers come with cushions. Enter CLAUDIUS, GERTRUDE,
LAERTES, and LORDS *and other attendants with foils, daggers, and*
gloves
CLAUDIUS Come Hamlet, come and take Laertes' hand.
[*He puts* LAERTES' *hand in* HAMLET'S]
HAMLET [*To* LAERTES] Give me your pardon, sir. I have done you wrong.

But pardon 't as you are a gentleman.
This presence knows,
And you must needs have heard, how I am punished   210
With sore distraction. What I have done
That might your nature, honor, and exception
Roughly awake, I here proclaim was madness.
Was 't Hamlet wronged Laertes? Never Hamlet.
If Hamlet from himself be tane away,   215
And when he's not himself does wrong Laertes,
Then Hamlet does it not, Hamlet denies it.
Who does it then? His madness. If 't be so,
Hamlet is of the faction that is wronged;
His madness is poor Hamlet's enemy.   220
Sir, in this audience,
Let my disclaiming from a purposed evil
Free me so far in your most generous thoughts,
That I have shot my arrow o'er the house
And hurt my brother.   225
LAERTES I am satisfied in nature,
Whose motive in this case should stir me most
To my revenge; but in terms of honor
I stand aloof, and will no reconcilement
Till by some elder masters of known honor   230
I have a voice and precedent of peace
To keep my name ungored. But till that time
I do receive your offered love like love,
And will not wrong it.
HAMLET I embrace it freely,   235
And will this brother's wager frankly play.
Give us the foils, come on.
LAERTES Come on, one for me.
HAMLET I'll be your foil, Laertes. In mine ignorance
Your skill shall like a star i' th' darkest night   240

But pardon me, as you are a gentleman.
This gathering knows,
And you must surely have heard, how I have suffered   210
From severe confusion. Whatever I have done
That might your nature, honor, and sense of grievance
Provoke, I here proclaim was madness.
Was it Hamlet that wronged Laertes? No, never Hamlet.
If Hamlet be divided from himself,   215
And when he's not himself he wrongs Laertes,
Then Hamlet doesn't do it; Hamlet denies it.
Who does it then? His madness. If that is so,
Hamlet is the party that is wronged,
His madness is poor Hamlet's enemy.   220
Sir, before this audience,
Let me deny any intended evil
And free me that far in your generosity.
I have shot an arrow into the air
And hurt my brother.   225
LAERTES I am satisfied so far as personal feelings go,
 Whose cause in this case should move me most
 To my revenge; but so far as honor is concerned,
 I reserve judgment and will not reconcile
 Till by some older experts on the subject   230
 I have approval and precedent for reconciliation
 That will keep my reputation undamaged. Till then
 I accept your peace offer at face value
 And will not reject it.
HAMLET I welcome this wholeheartedly   235
 And will play this brother's wager with an unburdened mind.
 Give us the foils, come on.
LAERTES Come, one for me.
HAMLET I'll be your foil, Laertes. In my clumsiness,
 Your skill shall, like a star in the darkest night,   240

Stick fiery off indeed.

LAERTES You mock me, sir.

HAMLET No, by this hand.

CLAUDIUS Give them the foils, young Osric. Cousin Hamlet,
    You know the wager? 245

HAMLET Very well, my lord.
    Your grace has laid the odds o' th' weaker side.

CLAUDIUS I do not fear it, I have seen you both.
    But, since he is bettered, we have therefore odds.

LAERTES This is too heavy. Let me see another. 250

HAMLET This likes me well. These foils have all a length?

OSRIC Ay, my good lord.

[*They prepare to play*]

CLAUDIUS Set me the stoups of wine upon that table.
    If Hamlet give the first or second hit
    Or quit in answer of the third exchange, 255
    Let all the battlements their ordnance fire.
    The king shall drink to Hamlet's better breath,
    And in the cup an union shall he throw,
    Richer than that which four successive kings
    In Denmark's crown have worn. Give me the cups, 260
    And let the kettle to the trumpet speak,
    The trumpet to the cannoneer without,
    The cannons to the heavens, the heaven to earth,
    "Now the king drinks to Hamlet!" Come, begin,
    And you judges bear a wary eye. 265

Trumpets the while.

HAMLET Come on, sir.

LAERTES Come, my lord.

[*They play*]

HAMLET One!

LAERTES No!

HAMLET Judgment. 270

    Stand out brilliantly in contrast.

LAERTES You mock me, sir.

HAMLET No, I swear it.

CLAUDIUS Give them the foils, young Osric. Nephew Hamlet,
    You know the wager?   245

HAMLET Very well, my lord.
    Your grace has bet on the weaker side.

CLAUDIUS I am not worried, I have seen you both.
    But since he has improved, we have the odds.

LAERTES This one's too heavy. Let me see another.   250

HAMLET This one pleases me. These foils are all the same length?

OSRIC Yes, my good lord.

[*They prepare to fence*]

CLAUDIUS Put the jugs of wine on that table.
    If Hamlet scores the first or second hit
    Or is even in the third bout,   255
    Let all the battlements fire their cannons.
    The king shall drink to Hamlet's better life,
    And in the goblet he shall throw a pearl,
    More precious than any worn by four successive kings
    Of Denmark in their crown. Give me the goblets,   260
    And let the kettle drum sound to the trumpets,
    And the trumpets to the artillery outside,
    The cannons to the heavens, the heaven to earth,
    "Now the king drinks to Hamlet!" Come, begin,
    And you judges keep a watchful eye.   265

Trumpets sound.

HAMLET Come on, sir.

LAERTES Come, my lord.

[*They fence*]

HAMLET One!

LAERTES No!

HAMLET Ruling.   270

OSRIC A hit, a very palpable hit.

LAERTES Well, again.

CLAUDIUS Stay, give me drink. Hamlet, this pearl is thine.
      Here's to thy health.

Drum, trumpets sound, and shot goes off.
      Give him the cup.   275

HAMLET I'll play this bout first. Set it by awhile.
      Come.

[*They play*]
      Another hit. What say you?

LAERTES A touch, a touch, I do confess 't.

CLAUDIUS Our son shall win.   280

GERTRUDE He's fat and scant of breath.
      Here Hamlet, take my napkin, rub thy brows.
      The queen carouses to thy fortune, Hamlet.

[*She lifts the cup*]

HAMLET Good madam.

CLAUDIUS Gertrude, do not drink.   285

GERTRUDE I will, my lord, I pray you pardon me.

[*Drinks*]

CLAUDIUS [*Aside*] It is the poisoned cup. It is too late.

HAMLET I dare not drink yet, madam—by and by.

GERTRUDE Come, let me wipe thy face.

LAERTES [*Aside to* CLAUDIUS] My lord, I'll hit him now.   290

CLAUDIUS I do not think 't.

LAERTES [*Aside*] And yet it is almost against my conscience.

HAMLET Come, for the third, Laertes. You do but dally.
      I pray you pass with your best violence.
      I am afeard you make a wanton of me.   295

LAERTES Say you so? Come on.

[*They play*]

OSRIC Nothing neither way.

LAERTES Have at you now! [*Wounds* HAMLET]

OSRIC A hit, a very clear hit.

HAMLET Well, again.

CLAUDIUS Wait. Give me a drink. Hamlet, this pearl is yours.
>   Here's to your health.

Drums, trumpets, and cannons sound.
>   Give him the cup.   275

HAMLET I'll play this bout first. Set it aside for awhile.
>   Come.

[*They fence*]
>   Another hit. What do you say?

LAERTES A touch, a touch. I admit it.

CLAUDIUS Our son will win!   280

GERTRUDE He's soft and short of breath.
>   Here Hamlet, take my handkerchief and wipe your brow.
>   The queen drinks to your good fortune, Hamlet.

[*She picks up the poisoned cup*]

HAMLET Good madam.

CLAUDIUS Gertrude, do not drink.   285

GERTRUDE I will, my lord, if you will excuse me.

[*Drinks*]

CLAUDIUS [*Aside*] It is the poisoned cup. It is too late.

HAMLET I dare not drink yet, madam—by and by.

GERTRUDE Come, let me wipe your face.

LAERTES [*Aside to* CLAUDIUS] My lord, I'll hit him now.   290

CLAUDIUS I do not think so.

LAERTES [*Aside*] And yet it is almost against my conscience.

HAMLET Come, the third bout, Laertes. You waste time.
>   Please, thrust with your most forceful skill.
>   I am afraid you treat me as a child.   295

LAERTES Is that what you think? Come on.

[*They fence*]

OSRIC Nothing either way.

LAERTES Take that now! [*Wounds* HAMLET]

[*They lose self-control, drop their weapons, and scuffle. They change weapons.*]

CLAUDIUS Part them. They are incensed.

HAMLET Nay, come again. [*Wounds* LAERTES]   300

[GERTRUDE *falls*]

OSRIC Look to the queen there, ho!

HORATIO They bleed on both sides. How is it, my lord?

OSRIC How is it, Laertes?

LAERTES Why, as a woodcock to mine own springe, Osric.

    [*He falls*] I am justly killed with mine own treachery.   305

HAMLET How does the queen?

CLAUDIUS She sounds to see them bleed.

GERTRUDE No, no, the drink—O, my dear Hamlet—

    The drink, the drink—I am poisoned. [*She dies*]

HAMLET O villainy! Ho! Let the door be locked!   310

    Treachery! Seek it out!

LAERTES [*He falls*] It is here, Hamlet. Hamlet, thou art slain,

    No medicine in the world can do thee good,

    In thee there is not half an hour of life—

    The treacherous instrument is in thy hand,   315

    Unbated and envenomed. The foul practice

    Hath turned itself on me. Lo, here I lie,

    Never to rise again. Thy mother's poisoned—

    I can no more—the king, the king's to blame.

HAMLET The point envenomed too! Then, venom, to thy work!   320

[*Hurts* CLAUDIUS]

ALL Treason, treason!

CLAUDIUS O, yet defend me, friends. I am but hurt.

HAMLET Here, thou incestuous, murderous, damned Dane,

    Drink off this potion. Is thy union here?

    Follow my mother.   325

[CLAUDIUS *dies*]

[*They lose self-control, drop their weapons, and scuffle. They change weapons.*]

CLAUDIUS Part them. They are enraged.

HAMLET No, come again. [*Wounds* LAERTES]   300

[GERTRUDE *falls to the ground*]

OSRIC Look after the queen, now!

HORATIO They both bleed. How are you, my lord?

OSRIC How are you, Laertes?

LAERTES Like a decoy caught in my own trap, Osric.

    [*He falls*] I am justly killed by my own treachery.   305

HAMLET How is the queen?

CLAUDIUS She faints at the sight of their blood.

GERTRUDE No, no, the drink—Oh, my dear Hamlet—

    The drink, the drink—I am poisoned. [*She dies*]

HAMLET Oh, villainy! Stop! Lock the door!   310

    Treachery! Seek it out!

LAERTES [*He falls*] It is here, Hamlet. Hamlet, you are doomed.

    No medicine in the world can help you.

    You have less than half an hour to live—

    In your hand, you hold the treacherous weapon,   315

    Not blunted but poisoned. This foul plot

    Has turned itself on me. Look, here I lie,

    Never to rise again. Your mother's poisoned—

    I can say no more—the king, the king's to blame.

HAMLET The tip poisoned too! Then, venom, do your work.   320

[*He wounds* CLAUDIUS]

ALL Treason, treason!

CLAUDIUS Oh, defend me, my friends. I'm only wounded.

HAMLET Here, you incestuous, murderous, damned Dane,

    Finish this drink. Is your pearl in here?

    Follow my mother.   325

[CLAUDIUS *dies*]

LAERTES He is justly served,
    It is a poison tempered by himself.
    Exchange forgiveness with me, noble Hamlet.
    Mine and my father's death come not upon thee,
    Nor thine on me.   330
[*He dies*]
HAMLET Heaven make thee free of it! I follow thee.
    I am dead, Horatio. Wretched queen, adieu.
    You that look pale and tremble at this chance,
    That are but mutes or audience to this act,
    Had I but time, as this fell sergeant death   335
    Is strict in his arrest, O, I could tell you—
    But let it be. Horatio, I am dead,
    Thou livest. Report me and my cause aright
    To the unsatisfied.
HORATIO Never believe it.   340
    I am more an antique Roman than a Dane.
    Here's yet some liquor left.
HAMLET As th'art a man,
    Give me the cup. Let go! By heaven I'll ha 't.
    O God, Horatio, what a wounded name,   345
    Things standing thus unknown, shall live behind me!
    If thou didst ever hold me in thy heart,
    Absent thee from felicity awhile,
    And in this harsh world draw thy breath in pain
    To tell my story.   350
[*March far off, and shot within*]
    What warlike noise is this?
OSRIC Young Fortinbras, with conquest come from Poland,
    To the ambassadors of England gives
    This warlike volley.
HAMLET O, I die, Horatio!   355
    The potent poison quite o'ercrows my spirit.

LAERTES He is justly served.
    It is a poison he himself prepared.
    Exchange forgiveness with me, noble Hamlet.
    Let not my and my father's death weigh upon you,
    Nor yours on me.   330
[*He dies*]
HAMLET May heaven absolve you of it. I follow you.
    I am a dead man, Horatio. Unhappy queen, adieu.
    You who look pale and tremble at these events,
    Who have no parts or are only an audience,
    Had I the time, since death's fierce officer   335
    Is making his arrests, oh, I could tell you—
    But let it be. Horatio, I am dying,
    You are alive. Report me and my motives justly
    To those who need to be satisfied.
HORATIO Never believe it.   340
    I am more like an ancient Roman than a Dane.
    There's still some drink left.
HAMLET As you are a man,
    Give me the cup. Let go! By heaven, I'll have it.
    Oh God, Horatio, what a bad reputation,   345
    As things stand now, I shall leave behind me!
    If you ever held me in your heart,
    Suffer a while yet,
    And in this harsh world draw your breath in pain
    To tell my story.   350
[*Sounds of far-off marching and the firing of cannons*]
    What warlike noise is that?
OSRIC Young Fortinbras, returning from conquests in Poland,
    Salutes the ambassadors of England
    With this warlike volley.
HAMLET Oh, I am dying, Horatio!   355
    The potent poison overcomes my spirit.

I cannot live to hear the news from England.
But I do prophesy th' election lights
On Fortinbras; he has my dying voice.
So tell him, with th' occurrents, more and less,   360
Which have solicited—the rest is silence.

[*He dies*]

HORATIO Now cracks a noble heart. Good night, sweet prince,
And flights of angels sing thee to thy rest.—
Why does the drum come hither?

Enter FORTINBRAS *and* ENGLISH AMBASSADORS,
with drum, colors, and Attendants

FORTINBRAS Where is this sight?   365

HORATIO What is it you would see?
If aught of woe or wonder, cease your search.

FORTINBRAS This quarry cries on havoc. O proud death,
What feast is toward in thine eternal cell
That thou so many princes at a shot   370
So bloodily hast struck?

FIRST AMBASSADOR The sight is dismal,
And our affairs from England come too late.
The ears are senseless that should give us hearing
To tell him his commandment is fulfilled,   375
That Rosencrantz and Guildenstern are dead.
Where should we have our thanks?

HORATIO Not from this mouth,
Had it th' ability of life to thank you.
He never gave commandment for their death.   380
But since, so jump upon this bloody question,
You from the Polack wars, and you from England,
Are here arrived, give order that these bodies
High on a stage be placed to the view,
And let me speak to th' yet unknowing world   385
How these things came about. So shall you hear

258

I cannot stay alive to hear the news from England.
But I now predict the election of the next king—
Fortinbras. He has my dying voice.
Tell him so, with what has happened, more or less,   360
Which have prompted—the rest is silence.
[*He dies*]
HORATIO Now cracks a noble heart. Good night, sweet prince,
　　And flights of angels sing you to your rest.—
　　Why are the drums coming here?
　　　　　Enter FORTINBRAS *and* ENGLISH AMBASSADORS,
　　　　　　with drum, colors, and Attendants
FORTINBRAS Where is this spectacle?   365
HORATIO What is it you wish to see?
　　If it is grief and destruction, look no further.
FORTINBRAS This heap of dead proclaims no mercy given. O, proud death,
　　What feast are you preparing in your infernal room
　　That so many nobles at a shot you have   370
　　So bloodily struck?
FIRST AMBASSADOR The sight is dismal,
　　And our news from England comes too late.
　　Those ears are stopped that should give us a hearing
　　And tell him that his command has been fulfilled—   375
　　That Rosencrantz and Guildenstern are dead.
　　From whom should we receive thanks?
HORATIO Not from this mouth,
　　Even if it were able to thank you.
　　He never gave the command for their death.   380
　　But since you come immediately after this bloody quarrel,
　　You from the Polish wars and you from England,
　　Give the order that these bodies
　　Be placed high on a platform to the public view.
　　And let me speak to the uninformed world   385
　　How these things came about. Then shall you hear

Of carnal, bloody, and unnatural acts,
Of accidental judgments, casual slaughters,
Of deaths put on by cunning and forced cause,
And in this upshot, purposes mistook   390
Fallen on th' inventors' heads. All this can I
Truly deliver.
FORTINBRAS Let us haste to hear it,
And call the noblest to the audience.
For me, with sorrow I embrace my fortune.   395
I have some rights of memory in this kingdom,
Which now to claim my vantage doth invite me.
HORATIO Of that I shall have also cause to speak,
And from his mouth whose voice will draw on more.
But let this same be presently performed,   400
Even while men's minds are wild, lest more mischance
On plots and errors happen.
FORTINBRAS Let four captains
Bear Hamlet like a soldier to the stage,
For he was likely, had he been put on,   405
To have proved most royal; and for his passage,
The soldier's music and the rite of war
Speak loudly for him.
Take up the bodies. Such a sight as this
Becomes the field, but here shows much amiss.   410
Go, bid the soldiers shoot.

Exeunt marching, after the which a peal
of ordinance are shot off

Of lustful, bloody, and unnatural acts,
Of false decisions, random slaughter,
Of deaths inflicted by cunning and compelling reason,
And, as a final result, plans gone wrong   390
That fell on the plotters' heads. All this I can
Report truly.
FORTINBRAS Let us move quickly to hear it,
And call the nobility for an audience.
As for me, it is with sorrow that I embrace my opportunity.   395
I have some ancient rights in this kingdom,
Which, now, chance invites me to claim.
HORATIO Of that I shall also have cause to speak,
From the mouth of him whose voice will lead on,
But let this be immediately performed,   400
Even while everyone is anxious, to avoid
More bungled plots and errors.
FORTINBRAS Have four captains
Bear Hamlet like a soldier to the platform.
Had he lived to be crowned, he would surely   405
Have proved most royal. And for his passing,
Martial music and the rituals of war
Shall sound his praises loudly.
Take up the bodies. Such a sight as this
Suits the battlefield, but is out of place here.   410
Go, have the soldiers fire a volley.

Everyone leaves to a slow march, after which
a salute of cannons is fired

Glossary

The following terms are taken from the translation of *The Tragedy of Hamlet, Prince of Denmark*. The scene and line numbers are given in parentheses after the terms, which are listed in the order they first occur.

Act One

Caesar (scene 1, line 128): Julius Caesar (100-44 B.C.), general and statesman of Rome, whose assassination was preceded by disturbances in nature

University of Wittenberg (scene 2, line 115): German university founded in 1502, famous as the university of Dr. Faustus and Martin Luther

Niobe (scene 2, line 151): the mythical mother whose children were slain by the gods after she boasted of them. At her request, Zeus turned her into a rock from which tears flowed forever. Weeping women are sometimes likened to "Niobe, all tears"

Hercules (scene 2, line 155): a mythical Greek hero of fabulous strength

Nemean lion (scene 4, line 91): the lion, thought to be invulnerable, killed by Hercules as one of his twelve tasks

Lethe (scene 5, line 38): a mythical river of the underworld, from which the dead drink so that they may forget everything they said and did when they were alive

St. Patrick (scene 5, line 150): in addition to being the patron saint of Ireland, Patrick is also the patron saint of Purgatory, where the spirit of Hamlet's father resides

Act Two

figure of speech (scene 2, line 104): a form of expression used to heighten an effect; here, chiasmus, an inversion of parallel phrases

nest of child actors (scene 2, line 331): these were boys' acting companies, revived about 1600 and, for a brief time, serious rivals to the adult companies. Shakespeare is referring, of course, to the theatrical situation in the London of his own time, not to something taking place in Denmark

Globe (scene 2, line 349): the Globe was the name of the theatre where Shakespeare's company performed. A flag, flown from the top of the theatre on days when a performance was given, showed Hercules carrying the globe of earth on his shoulders. Shakespeare is saying that the rival companies of boy actors cut into the business of his company

Roscius (scene 2, line 373): a great Roman comic actor of the first century B.C., and a teacher of Cicero

Jephthah (scene 2, line 385): one of the Judges of Israel who vowed to sacrifice the first person he met if he returned successfully from war. That person turned out to be his daughter

voice not broken (scene 2, lines 406-407): the parts of women in Shakespeare's time were played by boys, and when their voices changed, they could no longer take these roles

Aeneas...Dido...Priam (scene 2, lines 421-422): characters in the *Aeneid,* an epic poem by Virgil, first century B.C., about, among other things, the Greek siege and destruction of the city of Troy. Aeneas tells the story of the fall of Troy to Dido, queen of Carthage. Priam was the king of Troy. Other Elizabethan dramatists, Marlowe and Nashe, also used this subject

Pyrrhus (scene 2, line 424): the son of Achilles sent to the Trojan War to avenge the death of his father

Hyrcanian tiger (scene 2, line 424): a tiger from the region near the Caspian Sea

Trojan horse (scene 2, line 428): the wooden horse in which the Greeks hid to gain entry to the fortified city of Troy

Ilium (scene 2, line 448): the citadel of Troy, famous for its towers

Cyclops (scene 2, line 463): a race of one-eyed giants who worked at the forge of Vulcan, metal worker to the gods

Mars (scene 2, line 464): Roman god of war

Hecuba (scene 2, line 475): wife of Priam, king of Troy

Act Three

groundlings (scene 2, line 9): spectators who paid the cheapest admissions and stood in the pit of an Elizabethan theatre during a performance

Herod (scene 2, line 12): king of Judea, who was portrayed in medieval drama as a raging tyrant

Vulcan (scene 2, line 78): Roman god of fire and metalworking

chameleon (scene 2, line 88): a lizard that changes color to match its surroundings and was believed to live on air

Jove (scene 2, line 269): in Roman myth the ruler of the gods

recorders (scene 2, line 278): musical instruments like flutes

Nero (scene 2, line 369): Roman emperor who arranged for his mother to be murdered

Cain (scene 3, line 40): having murdered his brother Abel, Cain was cursed by God and excluded from human society (Genesis 4: 10-12)

Act Four

baker's daughter (scene 5, lines 43-44): a folktale in which a baker's daughter denies bread to a beggar. The beggar turns out to be Jesus, and He turns her into an owl

Gis...Cock (scene 5, lines 59, 62): substitutes for the words *Jesus* and *God,* used to avoid blasphemy; the latter term is also a sexual pun

life-giving pelican (scene 5, line 158): the pelican was thought to pierce its breast with its bill and feed its young by allowing them to drink its blood

Norman (scene 7, line 100): someone from the historical region of northwest France, Normandy, bounded on the west by the English Channel

Act Five

se offendendo (scene 1, line 8): in self-offense; the gravedigger mistakes this phrase for *se defendendo*, in self-defense

jawbone of Cain (scene 1, line 66): Cain was supposed to have used the jawbone of an ass to kill his brother Abel

Alexander the Great (scene 1, line 172): king of Macedon (356-323 B.C.) who conquered all the then known world and was a symbol of imperial power during the Elizabethan Age

Mount Pelion (scene 1, line 230): in Greek myth there was an attempt to reach heaven by putting Mount Pelion on top of Mount Ossa

Olympus (scene 1, line 231): in Greek myth the home of the gods whose ruler was Zeus